Scratch For Kids

FOR DUMMIES®
A Wiley Brand

by Derek Breen

Scratch For Kids For Dummies®

Published by: **John Wiley & Sons, Inc.,** 111 River Street, Hoboken, NJ 07030-5774, www.wiley.com

Copyright © 2015 by John Wiley & Sons, Inc., Hoboken, New Jersey

Published simultaneously in Canada

For general information on our other products and services, please contact our Customer Care Department within the U.S. at 877-762-2974, outside the U.S. at 317-572-3993, or fax 317-572-4002. For technical support, please visit www.wiley.com/techsupport.

Wiley publishes in a variety of print and electronic formats and by print-on-demand. Some material included with standard print versions of this book may not be included in e-books or in print-on-demand. If this book refers to media such as a CD or DVD that is not included in the version you purchased, you may download this material at http://booksupport.wiley.com. For more information about Wiley products, visit www.wiley.com.

Library of Congress Control Number: 2014958472

ISBN 978-1-119-01487-4 (pbk); ISBN 978-1-119-01476-8 (ebk); ISBN 978-1-119-01457-7 (ebk)

Manufactured in the United States of America

10 9 8 7 6 5 4 3 2

Dedication

To my niece and nephew, Katelyn and Ryan.

To my fairy-god-children Jonah, Gwendolyn, and Henry.

And to nieces, nephews, and fairy-god-children throughout the world.

Contents at a Glance

Introduction 1

Part 1: Become a Scratch Designer 9
Chapter 1: Getting Started with Scratch....................................11
Chapter 2: Create Your Own Comics 35
Chapter 3: Design Scratch Animals..60
Chapter 4: Build Vector Robots..79
Chapter 5: Digital Collages 99

Part 2: Become a Scratch Animator 127
Chapter 6: Animation Essentials 129
Chapter 7: Animate Great Characters 152
Chapter 8: Location, Location, Location 176
Chapter 9: Sounds Good to Me 197
Chapter 10: Lights, Camera, ACTION!.....................................217

Part 3: Become a Scratch Game Developer 241
Chapter 11: Design a Classic Videogame 243
Chapter 12: Super Snake...266
Chapter 13: A-Maze-ing Game 289
Chapter 14: Attacking the Clones 319
Chapter 15: Game Not Over! 354

Index.. 362

Table of Contents

Introduction 1

    About Scratch 2
    About This Book 3
    Icons Used in This Book 4
    Beyond the Book 5
    Where to Go from Here 6
    Oh Yeah 7

Part 1: Become a Scratch Designer 9

    Chapter 1: Getting Started with Scratch 11

        Access Scratch on Your Computer 12
        Create a New Project 13
        Bring Game to Life with Code 19
        Add Collision to Your Game 26
        Adjust Pipe Size and Location 29
        Wrapping Up the Flapping 33

    Chapter 2: Create Your Own Comics 35

        Modify Sprites from the Library 36
        Modify Scratch Characters 39
        Tell Your Super Story 50
        Wrapping Up 57

    Chapter 3: Design Scratch Animals 60

        Create a Great Turtle 61
        Add Code to Animate the Turtle 67
        I Want a Wild Hippogriff! 71
        Add Code for the Hippogriff's Whinny 75
        Moving On 76

    Chapter 4: Build Vector Robots 79

        Diving into Vector Design 80
        Sculpting Robot Shapes 82
        Start Your Robot Design 86
        What's a Robot Without Code? 95
        Finishing Your Project 96

Chapter 5: Digital Collages **99**

Create a New Project..100
Start Composing Elements 101
Transform Your Sprites 105
Adding Vector Graphics 106
Designing Advanced Collages 107
Getting into a Great Collage 108
Erase Part of an Image 110
Modify Sprites with Visual Effects....................................117
Use Vector Text for Title 121
Finish Up Your Collage 123

Part 2: Become a Scratch Animator.................. 127

Chapter 6: Animation Essentials **129**

Draw Your First Character 130
Animate the Stick Figure...133
Animate with Code Blocks...137
Bring Humor to Your Animation.......................................140
Add Stick Man's Best Friend 141
Walk Like a Man 144
Animate the Dog 146

Chapter 7: Animate Great Characters **152**

Keep It Simple, Stupid...153
Getting a Head Start 155
A Little Body Work 159
Apply Finishing Touches 162
It's Okay to Clone Scratch People 163
From Dead Skin to Furry Beast 163
Fangs Make the Beast..165
Undress the Beast...166
Strike a Pose..167
Add Finishing Touches 167
Create a Third Character 169
Assembling Your Cast 174

Chapter 8: Location, Location, Location **176**

Planning Animation Scenes 177
Design an Interior Scene...177
Make Scenes More Immersive...181
Design an Exterior Scene 188

Chapter 9: Sounds Good to Me **197**

That's What He Said 198
Record Dialogue in Scratch..199
Edit Audio Clips 203
Trim Beginning of Sound 204
Play Sound with Code Blocks...206
Animate Character Speech 207

Chapter 10: Lights, Camera, ACTION! **217**

(Not) Starting from Scratch...218
Camera (or What Do I Focus On?)...225
Action! (or Let's Get the Story Moving)................................231
Broadcast Animation Messages..233
Switch between Animation Scenes..236
And CUT!..239

Part 3: Become a Scratch Game Developer 241

Chapter 11: Design a Classic Videogame **243**

This Game Looks LAME! 244
Create a New Project..244
Change the Background Color 245
Add a Bouncing Ball 245
Add the Paddles 251
Make the Ball Bounce Off the Paddle...................................254
Add a Second Player 255
Keep Track of Player Scores 258
Check for the Winning Score..262
Add Sound Effects..264

Chapter 12: Super Snake. **266**

Create a New Project..267
Use Gradient for Background..267
Construct Your Snake 268
Set the Snake in Motion 271
Add Body to the Snake..272
Add Food for the Snake...276
Set Up Game Collisions 278
Code Snake Growth 283
Track Player Score 286

Chapter 13: A-Maze-ing Game 289

Create a New Project...290
Choose Game Characters 290
Design Maze Background 293
Add Player Keyboard Controls 303
The Mouse Eats the Cheese 306
Program Enemy Patrol...310
Track Player Lives 313
Give Player a Chance to Win 315

Chapter 14: Attacking the Clones. 319

Create a New Project...320
Choose a Game Background 320
Create Player and Enemy Sprites 321
Clone a Bunch of Aliens 323
Add Laser Blaster to Spaceship..333
Enable Spaceship Movement 337
Use Collision to Destroy Aliens 337
Program Enemies to Drop Bombs 340
Add Sound to Your Game 344
Give the Player Three Lives 346
Destroy a Player on Impact 347
Keeping Score 350

Chapter 15: Game Not Over! 354

Index... 362

Introduction

Do not read this book! Who bought it for you? Was it your mom? An uncle? A friend? Oh, please do not tell me you bought it for yourself!?!

Let me guess, you were at your local bookstore, scanning the shelves for a REALLY great Newbury Award winning novel like *Holes* or *The Giver* or *Bridge to Terabithia.* If you have never heard of *A Wrinkle in Time,* you should throw this book across the room and go look the other one up under the author, Madeleine L'Engle, because it is AMAZING!

Maybe you were searching on Amazon.com for the *Minecraft Red Stone* book or a book about training dogs or learning street magic tricks and you mistyped a word or accidentally clicked something or . . . Please, oh please, tell me you were not looking for a book about Scratch! Seriously, I am a Scratch MASTER who literally wrote the book you are holding in your hands, and still reading, even though I told you to STOP READING!!! Do you think I became a Scratch Master by reading some stupid old book? No WAY!

Do you honestly believe the people at MIT who built Scratch thought, "Oh, we should make it really hard to learn so kids will need to buy books by old bald guys who like to use a lot of exclamation points in their introductions!"?

Well, if you ARE stuck with the book, if whoever bought it threw away the receipt or you are a compassionate person who wants to make sure I get paid for the hard (but fun) work I put into this, then maybe I should make sure you are getting a REALLY USEFUL book.

And who am I kidding — of COURSE I want you to buy my book, because every time somebody buys this book, I get a little bit richer (ka-ching!). Instead of trying to talk you out of reading *Scratch For Kids For Dummies,* I should be thanking you and encouraging you to tell everybody you know about the book, right?

About Scratch

Scratch was created for YOU and the designers at the MIT Media Lab had several goals:

1. Give you powerful software for free.

2. Make it easy for you to learn.

3. Allow many different ways for you to use the software.

4. Enable you to browse/play/remix other projects.

5. Enable you to share your projects.

6. Create an online community where you can learn from one another.

Now review that list of six goals. Where does it say, "Force parents/teachers/coaches/kids to buy a big, fat Scratch book"? NOWHERE! So why are you still reading? Don't you know you can go to `scratch.mit.edu` right now and start SCRATCHING?!?

About This Book

Can I tell you a secret? You know what is more valuable than money? Time! I am being completely honest. Even if you are a young woman in fifth grade or a seventh grade guy, you can spend your time *all kinds* of ways, and once you "spend" it, just like when you spend ten dollars, you never get it back. Guess what? That goes for me, too. If I am going to spend several months writing about Scratch, then I want to make sure I am producing a book that is genuinely going to help you learn some REALLY cool stuff!

I did not choose the title of this book. If the publisher let me choose my own title, you would now be reading, *Delete the Cat,* by Scratch Master Derek Breen. Why would I call it *Delete the Cat?* No matter where I am or whom I'm teaching — my nephew's fifth grade computer class, my niece's eighth videogame-making birthday party (wouldn't that be an AWESOME way to celebrate YOUR special day?), or a room full of teachers — the first instruction is always the same: "Okay Scratchers, delete that cat!"

Why do the Scratch makers insist on representing one of the most powerful applications in the history of computer software with a cuddly, smiling, cartoon cat?!? That cat makes Scratch look like it is just for little kids, even though it is now being taught in high school, and even college classes all around the world.

Okay, maybe I should admit here that I'm not much of a cat person, but I SERIOUSLY LOVE SCRATCH! (*AND* I put the Scratch cat on my own business card, so whom am I kidding?)

Now let me make a deal with you; if you are willing to invest your time by reading even a few chapters in this book, I will do my very best to get you *creating* a cool design, a hilarious animation, an addictive video game ASAP. You will hardly even need to *read*. Seriously, you can follow along as little or as much as you want and still end up with a KILLER project!

This is one of those books where you can start with any chapter; if you are most interested in making your own videogame, feel free to skip ahead to Part 3 (though you *may* want to check out Chapter 1. . . I'm just sayin'). If you have been using Scratch for a long time and want to learn some new animation tricks, you might want to go right to Chapter 10 (which covers a bunch of special effects techniques).

Icons Used in This Book

The Tip icon marks tips and shortcuts that you can use to make coding easier.

The Technical Stuff icon is for more of the nitty-gritty stuff and details that are good to know.

The Coding Connections icon describes how a coding concept you're working on connects to the big picture of coding.

The Math Connections icon shows you ways math is used in coding. Finally, from computation and algebra to geometry and logic, you might see how that stuff really is used!

The Warning icon tells you to watch out! It marks important information that may save you from scratching your head a ton.

Beyond the Book

I've got WAY more to share than could fit between the covers of this book. Good thing we are in the 21st century, right? Since you probably are online using Scratch, you can open these great resources in another tab and push your mad Scratch skills even farther:

🖊 **Web Extras:** www.dummies.com/extras/scratchforkids

Web Extras are online articles that expand on some concept I've discussed in that particular section. I think we should be charging you EXTRA for all these great online things, but the publisher told me to stop being greedy and just give it all away. . . .

🖊 **Online projects:** www.scratch4kids.com/projects

I almost don't want to tell you this until you finish the very last project, but since Scratch is online, and since I had to create every single project in this book, it would be pretty selfish of me NOT to share those projects with you. I still think you should try to create each project from *scratch (get it?),* but if you are stuck, or you are in a super rush, head to the book's companion website and steal — I mean *remix* — any project you wish.

🖊 **Cheat Sheet:** www.dummies.com/cheatsheet/scratchforkids

I crammed as much as I possibly could into one page, an overview of the drawing and paint tools, keyboard shortcuts, and a list of all the blocks by category. It is formatted so you can print it, stick it next to your screen, and think about this great author all day long!

✓ **Updates:** www.scratch4kids.com/updates

This could be important if the Scratch team makes a major change, like replacing the Scratch cat with a hippogriff, in which case I will have to change the first step of every project in this book . . . Man, that Scratch cat is looking a little better to me now.

Where to Go from Here

There is no one right way to start using Scratch, so you could begin with any project in any section of this book. If you have never used Scratch before, I suggest starting with Chapter 1 (which is far less lame than you might think).

My editors and I did our best to refer back to certain techniques covered in previous chapters in case you skipped over them or need a refresher because you began the book like three years ago and suddenly decided Scratch is not as lame as you thought because you saw this amazing project created by another kid in your class and thought, "Yah, that's pretty cool, but I learned all these tricks reading *Scratch For Kids For Dummies,* so I bet I can remix their project and make it even MORE AMAZING!"

Oh Yeah . . .

I forgot to mention that my 9-year-old niece, Katelyn, and my just-turned-11-years-old nephew, Ryan, gave not only moral support during the six months it took to write this book, but also contributed several awesome images, some in Scratch, some more old-school. You'll be able to tell when it's their artwork because they are BOTH better artists than their over-the-hill uncle.

I also snuck in a few shots from my favorite kids from Virginia, Jonah and Gwendolyn, who started using Scratch before I did! Thanks, guys!

Part 1

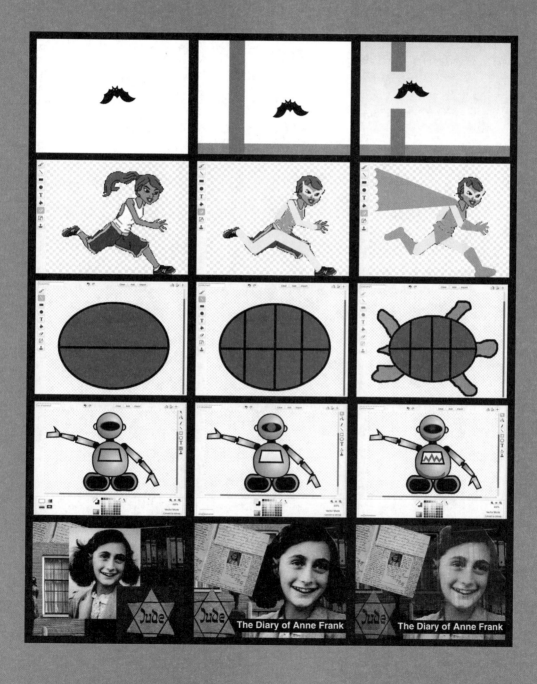

Become a Scratch Designer . . .

Getting Started with Scratch 11

Create Your Own Comics..................................... 35

Design Scratch Animals 60

Build Vector Robots 79

Digital Collages 99

For Dummies can help you get started with lots of cool stuff! Check out www.dummies.com to learn more and do more with *For Dummies!*

Getting Started with Scratch

I don't know if you have ever read one of these "How-to-do-something-with-your-computer-other-than-watching-funny-cat-videos-on-YouTube" books before, but I read a BUNCH. The first chapter usually describes all the parts of the screen with labels to tell you what each thing does or means or whatever. Totally BORING!

Maybe it's because I am a dummy, but I want to flip the typical "how to" book on its head. Instead of learning all the parts of Scratch and starting with basic stuff, let's build a REALLY cool game RIGHT NOW!

Access Scratch on Your Computer

The easiest way to start using Scratch is to visit `www.scratch.mit.edu`, create an online account, and start Scratching. To use Scratch without creating an account, you will have to download and install the offline version of Scratch (see the upcoming "Use Scratch offline" section).

Technically, you can use the Scratch website without an account, but you will have to save projects to your computer and then upload them each time you visit the Scratch website to continue working on them. With an account, you can save files online and share projects with other Scratch users.

Create online account

Go ahead and start up Scratch! Turn on your computer, open a web browser, and visit `scratch.mit.edu`. If you already have a Scratch account, click the Sign In button in the top-right corner of the page. If you do not have an account, click the Join Scratch button and fill in the brief online form. If you are under 13 or do not have an email account, please ask an adult to help you create an account (or skip ahead to the upcoming "Use Scratch offline" section).

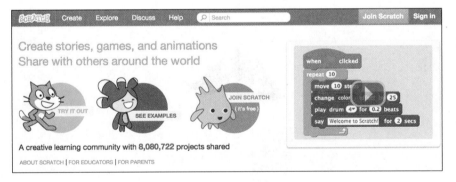

 To run Scratch online, you need a relatively recent web browser (Chrome 35 or later, Firefox 31 or later, or Internet Explorer 8 or later) with Adobe Flash Player version 10.2 or later installed. Scratch 2 is designed to support screen sizes 1024 x 768 or larger.

Use Scratch offline

You can install the Scratch 2 Offline Editor to work on projects without requiring a Scratch user account. After Scratch 2 is installed you will not need an Internet connection to work on projects. This version will work on Mac, Windows, and some versions of Linux (32 bit). Visit `www.scratch.mit.edu/scratch2download` to download and install Adobe Air (required to run Scratch offline) and the Scratch 2 Offline Editor.

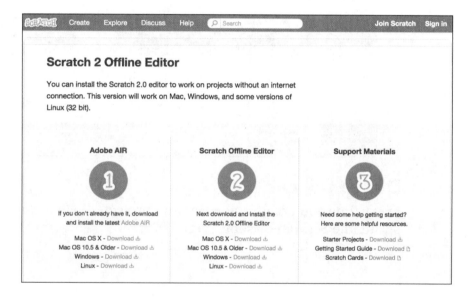

Create a New Project

Have you played *Flappy Bird?* You are going to make a game that works quite a bit like *Flappy Bird* but is NOT *Flappy Bird.* Why NOT? Because if you make a game that looks and works like *Flappy Bird* and you CALL it *Flappy Bird,* then the guy who CREATED *Flappy Bird* would be displeased. Plus, it is actually AGAINST THE LAW! So I will be teaching you how to make a game called *Flapping Bat,* instead.

Create online project

1. Go to `scratch.mit.edu` and click the Create button.

2. Change the name from *Untitled* to *Flapping Bat*.

While logged in, Scratch will automatically save your project while you work.

Create offline project

1. Open the Scratch 2 Offline Editor on your computer.

2. Select File ⇨ Save As and type **Flapping Bat**.

Delete the cat

Every time you create a new Scratch project, it will include one sprite, the Scratch mascot: Scratch Cat.

I am so not a fan of that smiling cat that most chapters in this book begin with two instructions:

1. Create a new project.

2. Delete the cat.

You can delete the cat (or any other sprite) by holding the Shift key on your keyboard while clicking it directly. A small menu will appear with the option to delete whatever you Shift-clicked. You will be doing a lot of Shift-clicking to save you time while working on Scratch projects.

So go ahead . . . Delete that smiling Scratch cat!

 If you are used to right-clicking with a mouse or trackpad, you may use that technique as an alternative to Shift-clicking.

Choose Player sprite

A *sprite* is any graphic element in a Scratch project other than the *Stage,* which represents the background. For our game, we will create three sprites: Player, Ground, and Pipe.

1. Look for the New Sprite area beneath the Stage and click the first icon: Choose Sprite from Library.

2. Select the sprite named *Bat2* and then click OK.

 3. Shift-click the *Bat2* sprite and choose *Info*.

4. Change the name from *Bat2* to *Player* because, in your game, the player will control the bat sprite.

5. Click the Back button (white triangle on blue circle) to close the Info window.

Paint Ground sprite

 1. In the New Sprite area, click the second icon: Paint New Sprite.

2. Shift-click the new sprite, choose *Info,* and change the name to *Ground.*

3. Click the Costumes tab.

4. Click the Rectangle tool on the Paint Editor canvas beneath the Costumes tab.

5. Click the Solid rectangle option.

6. Click a green color swatch.

7. Click near the bottom-left corner of the Paint Editor canvas and then drag up and to the right side until you have a rectangle all the way across the bottom.

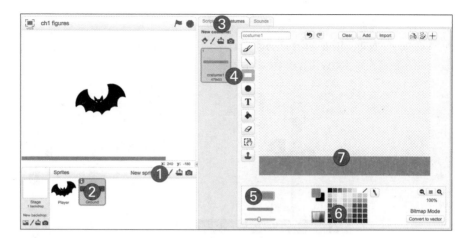

If the ground sprite appears off-center on the Stage, click and drag it into place. (I'll also drag mine down a bit to give the bat more room to fly.)

Paint Pipe sprite

The goal of your game is to flap the bat's wings and fly through holes between two pipes. You will use a cool programming trick so that you only need one Pipe sprite.

1. Click the Paint New Sprite icon.

2. Shift-click the sprite, choose *Info,* and change the name to *Pipe.*

3. Click the Costumes tab.

4. Click the Rectangle tool on the Paint Editor canvas beneath the Costumes tab.

5. Click the Solid rectangle option.

6. Click a gray color swatch.

7. Click and drag across the middle of the Paint Editor canvas to draw a vertical pipe.

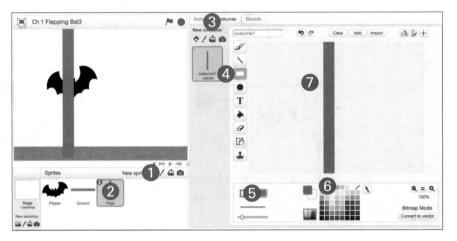

 To make a hole for the bat to fly through, click the Select tool, click and drag across the middle of the pipe, and press the Delete or Backspace key on your keyboard. (Don't worry if your bat is too big; you will fix that soon.)

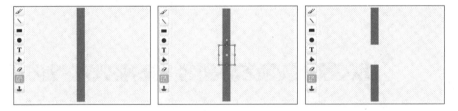

Good work! Now you have all three sprites you need to make your game. What comes next? That white background is a bit plain. Here's a quick way to make a realistic sky.

Paint sky gradient on the Stage

The term *gradient* may be new to you. Scratch includes three types of gradients, which allow you to fade between two colors. Part of what makes a sky look realistic is when it appears brighter toward the horizon and darker at the top of your game screen.

1. Click the Stage button.

2. Click the Backdrops tab.

3. Select the Fill with Color tool.

4. Click the Horizontal Gradient button.

5. Select the white color swatch.

6. Click the Swap Colors button.

7. Select a light blue color swatch.

8. Click anywhere to fill the Paint Editor canvas with the color gradient.

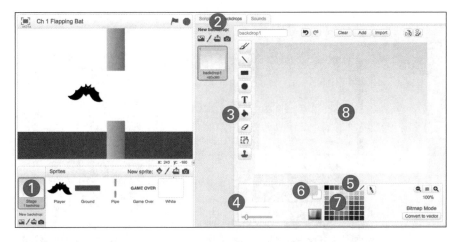

Doesn't the sky look more realistic now? Gradients can be used for all sorts of effects (like making something look metallic), so you will be using gradients quite a bit in the coming chapters. (Did somebody say, "Vector Robots"?)

Bring Game to Life with Code

I just HAD to sneak a bit of coding into this first chapter! Before Scratch, to program a videogame, you had to learn a bunch of commands, type them out, and make sure everything was in the right place. Well, no more, my Scratch Friend! Now, you just drag a few blocks into the Scripts Area of your selected sprite and you can have that bat moving around, responding to keys being pressed, slamming into pipes, and causing endless frustration . . . I mean FUN!

Add flapping wings animation

If you click the Player sprite and then click the Costumes tab, you should see two costumes: one with wings up and one with wings down. If you click each costume, you will see the Player bat flapping its wings on the Stage. If you want the bat to keep flapping its wings, you need to add some code blocks.

Click the Scripts tab and you see ten categories listed: Motion, Events, and so on. Notice how all the blocks in each category are the same color.

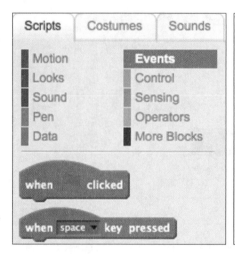 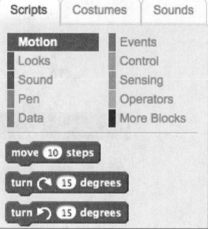

As you follow the steps below, use the color of each block shown in the image to guide you toward the category where you will find it on the Scripts tab.

1. Select the Player sprite by clicking once on its icon beneath the Stage.

2. Click the Scripts tab.

3. Drag the following blocks into the Scripts Area and snap each one into place:

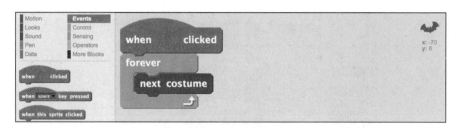

 4. Click the Green Flag button on the top of the Stage to test your code.

Your bat should be flapping awfully fast. How do you slow it down?

Adjust flapping speed

 Click the Stop button (beside the Green Flag button) to stop the code from running. See how the NEXT COSTUME block is inside a FOREVER block? You need to add another block inside that FOREVER block to slow it down. Can you find the right block in the Control category (same color as the FOREVER block)?

Drag and snap a WAIT block inside the FOREVER block, then click the Green Flag button again to test your code.

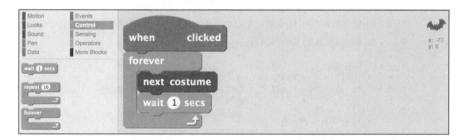

Now the bat is flapping too slowly, right? (This is beginning to feel like Goldilocks and the Three Bears!) What can you change if you want the wings to flap faster than 1 time every 1 second?

By default, the WAIT block has a value of 1. The white background means you can click and type to change the value. Try changing the value from 1 secs (seconds) to .2 secs, then click the Green Flag button again to test the change in your code.

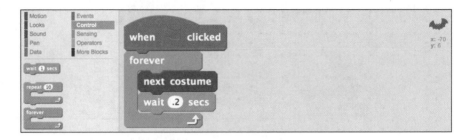

How does it look? I'm going to stick with .2 seconds, but you can adjust the WAIT SECS to whatever value works best for you because YOU are the GAME DESIGNER!

Add keyboard controls

Here comes one of my favorite moments in game design! So far, your flappy project just seems like a simple animation, but these next steps will transform your static project into an interactive game. Let's start by allowing the player to control the bat. Like that other flappy game, you will tap one key to make the bat move up a bit; let's use the spacebar because it is the largest key and can easily be tapped by *righties* or *lefties*.

1. Click the Player sprite and then click the Scripts tab.

2. Drag the following new blocks to the right of the other blocks already in the Scripts Area:

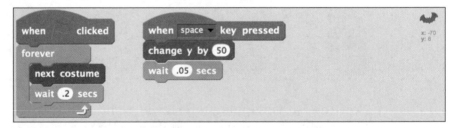

3. Click the Green Flag button to test your code.

Each time you tap the spacebar, the bat should move a bit higher, so the CHANGE Y block must have something to do with vertical movement. In Scratch, the vertical position of a sprite is represented by the Y value and the horizontal position is represented by the X value. (I cover this more in later chapters.)

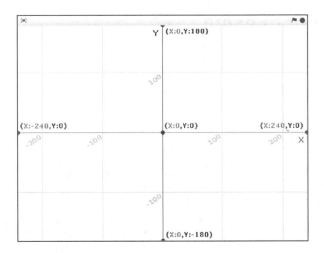

 See how the shape of the WHEN KEY PRESSED block is the same as the WHEN GREEN FLAG CLICKED block? Each hat-shaped block represents an action, such as clicking the Green Flag button or pressing the spacebar. When the action occurs, the code snapped beneath its related hat-shaped block runs. If you want to use a different key to control the flapping, click *Spacebar* and drag down to a new keyboard key inside WHEN KEY PRESSED.

Why does the bat keep flying up until it reaches the top of the Stage?

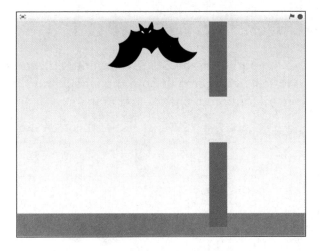

What do we call that mysterious force that pulls objects toward the ground? Gravity! Can you think of a good way to simulate gravity in your game using the blocks you have learned so far?

Add gravity to game

The following steps show one of the simplest ways to simulate gravity in your game.

1. Click the Player sprite and then click the Scripts tab.

2. Drag a third set of blocks into the Scripts Area to make the bat fall toward the ground.

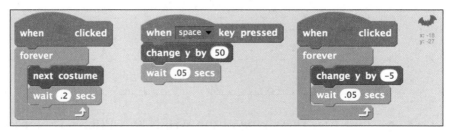

3. Click the Green Flag button to test your code.

The player has to keep flapping or he or she will take a nosedive. Notice how there are now two sets of blocks that begin with WHEN GREEN FLAG CLICKED; part of Scratch's power comes from being able to run several sets of code blocks all at the same time.

Full-screen Stage mode

Use the button in the top-left corner of the Stage to go into Full-screen Stage mode. It is useful to test your game at both the smaller and larger size because players have the option to change the Stage size at any time.

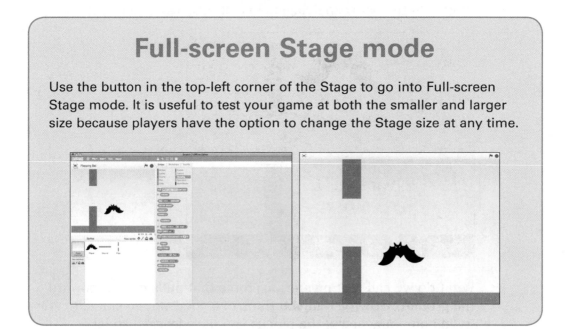

While you are still on the Scripts tab, you should add a GO TO block with X and Y values each set to *0* to reset the position of the Bat sprite to the center of the screen when the game begins.

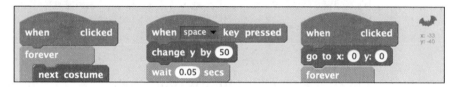

Make pipe move

In the original game, pipes keep moving from right to left, while the player moves up and down. To further distinguish your game from that *other Flappy,* you will add code which moves the pipe from left to right.

1. On the Stage, click and drag the pipe all the way to the left edge.

2. Click the Scripts tab.

3. Drag the following blocks into the Scripts Area to make the pipes move left to right:

```
when    clicked
go to x: -200 y: 0
forever
    change x by 10
```

4. Click the Green Flag to test your code.

The pipe should zoom right past the bat. The blocks should look familiar now. Can you figure out how to slow down the pipe? Click the Player sprite icon if you need to refresh your Scratch-block memory.

You could add a WAIT block to slow down the Pipe sprite movement. The more elegant solution would be to try a lower X value in CHANGE X BY. Click the default value of 10, change it to 4, and click the Green Flag button. If the pipe is still too slow, reduce X value a bit. If it's too fast, increase it a bit.

```
when    clicked
go to x: -200 y: 0
forever
    change x by 4
```

This should give you an idea about how to change the difficulty of your game, right? The game won't be very difficult if the pipe passes right over the player as if the bat were not even there.

Add Collision to Your Game

Collision is at the heart of most videogames. Whether it's Pac-Man colliding with a pink ghost, Mario jumping onto a platform, or your character picking up a new tool in Minecraft, a game designer decides what will happen when each collision occurs.

What collisions does your game need to detect? Does the bat touch the pipe? Does the bat touch the ground? If either collision happens, what should occur? The game must end.

Detect collision with the Ground sprite

1. Click the Ground sprite and then click the Scripts tab.

2. Drag the following blocks into the Scripts Area and select *Player* in the TOUCHING block.

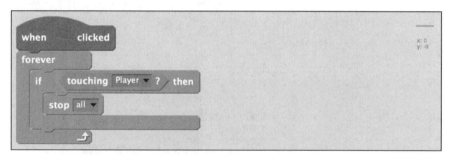

3. Click the Green Flag button.

If the player floats to the ground, the game should end as soon as they collide.

 You will usually put an IF THEN block inside a FOREVER block so the program will keep checking whether the condition is true or false and act accordingly (like a parent who keeps watching you to make sure you finish your homework before allowing you to fire up the Xbox or PlayStation). Now your program keeps checking to see whether the Player sprite is touching the Ground sprite from the instant the Green Flag button is pressed until the collision causes the STOP ALL block to end the game.

Since you will need the same code on the Pipe sprite, you can save time by copying the code blocks.

Copy blocks from Ground to Pipe

Click the top block (WHEN GREEN FLAG CLICKED) and drag the blocks from the Scripts Area directly onto the Pipe sprite icon beneath the Stage.

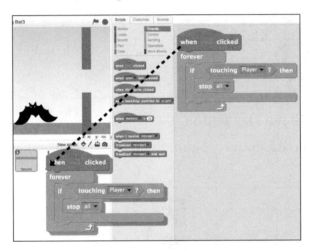

Once you release the mouse/trackpad button, you should see the original code snap back into place on the Scripts tab. If you click the Pipe sprite icon beneath the Stage, you should find the code has been copied there.

If the new blocks are overlapping the previous code, click and drag the top block to the right or beneath the other code.

Dragging the top block moves all the connected blocks. If you drag a middle block, only the blocks snapped beneath it stay connected.

Click the Green Flag button, and you should find that the game ends when the Player sprite touches the Pipe sprite or the Ground sprite.

Unless you got lucky, the size of the hole in your Pipe sprite is either too small for the bat to fly through or too large to make the game challenging.

Adjust Pipe Size and Location

Before increasing the hole size, consider one other thing the pipe should do. Part of the challenge from the original game comes from not knowing where the hole will be when each new pipe appears. So far, the Pipe sprite is always in the same vertical position, so the hole remains in the same spot.

Randomize vertical position

In Scratch, you can use a PICK RANDOM block inside the GO TO block so the pipe (and its hole) will appear in a different vertical position (Y) each time you run the game.

1. Click the Pipe sprite and then click the Scripts tab.

2. Drag a PICK RANDOM block into the Y value of the GO TO X Y block. (Notice how the round blocks can fit inside the round sockets of other blocks.)

3. Change the values in the PICK RANDOM block to –75 and 75.

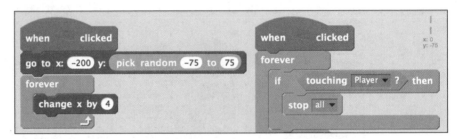

Click the Green Flag button several times and you should see the hole appear in a different position each time. You will also see the pipe is too short to span the entire Stage when shifted vertically.

Increase sprite size on the Stage

To increase the size of sprites on the Stage, you can use the Grow tool.

1. Click the Grow tool (above the Scripts, Costumes, and Sounds tab).

2. Click ten times on the Pipe sprite on the Stage.

3. Click the Green Flag button to test your game.

The Pipe sprite should span the entire Stage no matter where it is positioned vertically. But I still cannot flap my bat safely through the hole. If you try to click any more with the Grow tool, you will find the sprite will no longer increase in size because you reached the limit. Instead, why don't you try shrinking the bat?

Decrease sprite size on the Stage

To decrease the size of sprites on the Stage, you can use the Shrink tool.

1. Click the Shrink tool (above the Scripts, Costumes, and Sounds tab).

2. Click five times on the Bat sprite on the Stage.

3. Click the Green Flag button to test your game.

It took me a few tries, but I was FINALLY able to flap my bat through the pipe hole successfully!

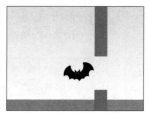

You may need to use the Shrink and Grow tools to adjust the size until it's possible to fly through the pipe, but not too easy. Then you will be ready to add more pipes.

Include additional pipes

Since you only need to have one pipe appear on the Stage, you do not need to create additional Pipe sprites. Instead, once the player successfully flies through the hole and the first pipe reaches the other side, you can reset the position of the Pipe sprite back to the left side of the screen.

1. Click the Pipe sprite icon beneath the Stage.

2. Click the Scripts tab.

3. Snap the following code blocks inside the first FOREVER block and change the values of your blocks to match the values shown.

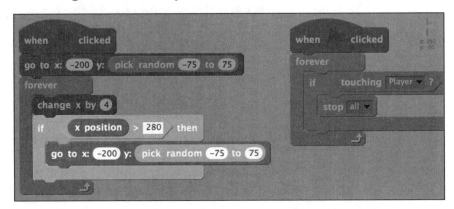

The additional GO TO X Y block should look familiar. It has exactly the same values as the GO TO X Y block above it (right under the WHEN GREEN FLAG CLICKED block). So if the X position of the Pipe sprite is greater than *280,* it resets the horizontal position to *–200* and chooses another random Y position so the hole appears in a new location.

You may need to adjust the X and Y values as you resize sprites on the Stage. Testing your game over and over will help you refine the sprite positions and sizes until you have just the right blend of *hard* and *fun* that will keep your players coming back for more.

The following remix is by my dear friend Gwendolyn (who bears a striking resemblance to the flying hippo). Notice how she added a high score. Cool, right?

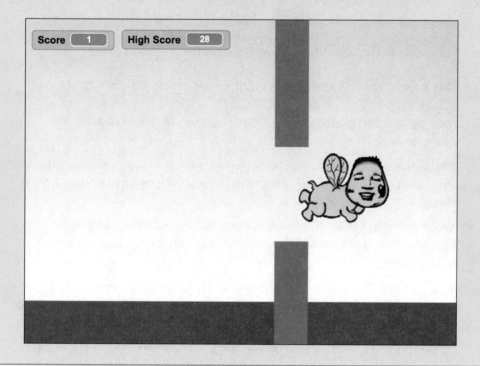

Wrapping Up the Flapping

If we had a bit more time (and my cheapo publishers would let me add JUST A FEW more pages), I could show you how to keep score and display a *Game Over* message. But we are just getting started, so hold your horses! OF COURSE I will be covering keeping score and all sorts of other game design techniques, tips, secrets, and UNBELIEVABLY COOL Scratch features in Part 3. You can skip ahead to those right now, or learn how to design better graphics and create more complex animation in the coming chapters. Totally up to you, my Scratch Friend!

Enhance your game

A videogame, like all digital projects, can (almost) always be better. Here are a few ways you might improve your game:

- **Keep score:** I know, I know, you wanna keep track of how many pipes you successfully flew through. Me, too, but you'll just have to keep reading to learn about variables and numerical displays and all sorts of other fantastic Scratch stuff.

- **New obstacles:** After you figure out how to have more than one pipe in your game, you could also add clouds, fireballs, or some other obstacles the player has to dodge.

- **Add sound:** You could add background music and a flapping bat sound, as well as trigger another sound when the player crashes into the pipe or the ground.

- **Increase difficulty:** You could give players the option to choose Easy, Hard, or NEARLY IMPOSSIBLE levels and just vary the size of the holes in the pipe or the size of your bat depending on the difficulty they choose.

Create Your Own Comics

When I was a kid, my favorite comics were *The Uncanny X-Men* and *The Avengers* because each had a large cast of super-heroes. I think I spent more time trying to draw Wolverine and the Scarlet Witch and Captain America and Dark Phoenix than I did reading the colorful pages. But my favorite things to draw were ideas for entirely new heroes and villains.

Scratch offers many ways to design your own superheroes and villains, and provides many different backdrops to set your comic stories in a bunch of different locales, from the realistic to the fantastic.

Modify Sprites from the Library

Can I let you in on a secret? Many of the sprites and backgrounds in my Scratch animations and games are *not* completely original. WHAT?! The author of *Scratch For Kids For Dummies* cannot even create his own sprites? I *could* create all my own sprites. I really do enjoy designing my own characters and animals and vehicles and backgrounds. (I even show you how I design some of them throughout this book.) But sometimes, I'm in a rush to create a quick comic strip or produce a new animation or develop a new game.

Fortunately, the Scratch development team has created a huge variety of sprites to work with. They don't provide any super-heroes, but you can modify the graphics any way you choose. Your first task is selecting a person from the built-in Sprite Library and giving the character a super-heroic makeover!

Create a new project

If you have not used Scratch before, please refer to the beginning of Chapter 1 to find out how to create an online account or install Scratch for offline use.

1. Go to scratch.mit.edu or open the Scratch 2 Offline Editor.

2. If you are online, click Create. If offline, select File⇨New.

3. Name your project. (Online, type **Comics** into the Untitled text box. Offline, select File⇨Save As and type **Comics**.)

 4. Delete that Scratch cat by selecting the Scissors and clicking the Cat sprite on the Stage.

Choose a character

Your first disguise is an ordinary looking person from the Sprite Library.

 1. Click the Choose Sprite from Library icon (beneath the Stage).

The different categories, themes, and image types running down the left side of the Sprite Library act as filters to reduce the number of sprites you see.

2. Click People so that you only see humans.

3. Click Bitmap to show only bitmap graphics (more about that later).

4. Use the scroll bar on the right side to review all the sprites available.

5. Select the sprite you want to start with and then click OK. (I am going to choose *Girl3* because I like her athletic pose.)

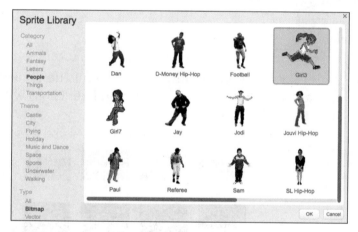

6. Shift-click the sprite and choose *Info*.

7. Change the name to your superhero's new name. I'm not sure about a superhero name yet, so I'll call her *Catalina* for now (after one of my favorite islands).

8. Click the Back button (white triangle on blue circle) to close the Info window.

Before starting to design your hero's new costume, it might be a good idea to pick a backdrop. You wouldn't want your hero blending into the setting (unless *invisibility* is one of his or her superpowers).

Choose a cool backdrop

The backdrop for your superhero should be an urban setting, somewhere outdoors, and something dramatic.

1. Click the Choose Backdrop from Library icon.

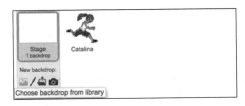

2. Under Category, click Outdoors (to limit the choices to outside scenes) and then select a scene you like. I'll go with one of my favorites, *Night City*.

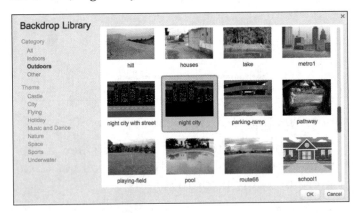

Sometimes, I browse through the Backdrop Library to see which image setting sparks my imagination. Picturing *Catalina* in her running pose against the dark city skyline helps me start imagining her costume.

Modify Scratch Characters

You can use the *bitmap* painting tools to modify your character. Bitmap graphics are made of small squares called *pixels*. Be aware that if you enlarge your bitmap sprites too much, they will become *pixelated,* or kind of blurry.

Although you will be zooming in on the Paint Editor canvas to paint details, zooming in does not affect the quality of your sprite on the Stage.

1. Select your character by clicking its sprite icon beneath the Stage.

2. Click the Costumes tab.

3. If there is more than one costume, click the one you wish to use.

4. Change the costume name to something more descriptive. (I'll choose *running*).

 5. Click the Zoom In button twice for 400% scale. (This makes working on your character easier.)

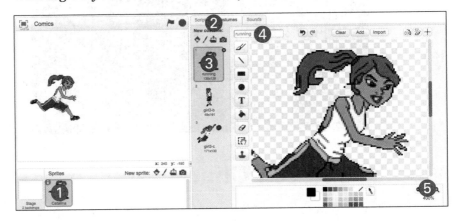

Take a few minutes to study the shape of your character's face, hairstyle, and clothes. Scratch gives you the power to change any of these features with just a few steps.

Paint a mask on a hero

Nothing says "superhero" like a colorful mask to hide an identity from the public. I'm going to paint a classic over-the-eyes mask for my new hero.

1. Make sure you selected the costume you wish to edit and zoomed in to 400% view.

 2. Click the Brush tool.

3. Click the color swatch you wish to use. (I'll start with bright yellow.)

 4. Click and drag the Line Width slider (to the left of the color swatches) to adjust the thickness of the line.

5. Click and drag around the eyes to start painting a mask.

 6. Click the Undo button to correct mistakes.

Your character sprite remains the same size on the Stage no matter how zoomed in you are in the Paint Editor. Even though the mask may appear quite blocky when zoomed in, it should look better on the Stage.

Now that you've added something to your sprite, how about taking something away?

Erase part of your sprite

Is there anything you want to remove from your character? I want my superhero to have short hair, so I will use the Erase tool to remove her ponytail.

 1. Zoomed in to 400%, click the Erase tool.

2. Use the slider in the Paint Editor to change the eraser size. Start with a larger size and then gradually reduce the size of the eraser to remove smaller and more-detailed graphics.

3. Click and drag over the area of your character that you wish to erase.

   You can also click just a spot one time to erase an individual area or create a hole.

  4. Use the Undo button if you make a mistake and the Redo button if Undo was a mistake!

After you finish erasing, be sure to check how your character looks on the Stage. I like *Catalina*'s short hair and her mask, but I don't think I've ever seen a superhero who fights crime in baggy shorts and a t-shirt. She looks like she's late for basketball practice.

Another tool makes adding long sleeves and pants easy.

Draw straight lines

Beneath the Brush tool is the Line tool. You ask, "Scratch Master, if I can draw lines with the Brush tool, why do I need a Line tool?" I find it hard to draw straight lines with the Brush tool. The Line tool allows you to draw straight lines at any angle and gives smoother edges on diagonal lines.

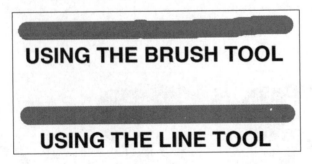

USING THE BRUSH TOOL

USING THE LINE TOOL

Here's how I quickly draw sleeves and pant legs on my superhero:

1. Zoom to 400% (or higher for a more-detailed view).

2. Click the Line tool.

3. Select a color swatch.

4. Use the Line Width slider (to the left of the color swatches) to adjust the thickness of the line.

5. Click where you want the line to start.

6. Drag your cursor to where you want the line to end and then release the mouse or trackpad button.

7. Click the Undo button and repeat Steps 1–5 if you wish to redraw your line.

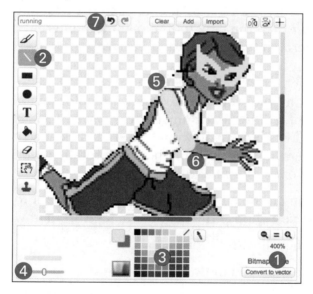

I had to try a few different line thicknesses before I found the right match for the width of her arms, so that Undo button came in handy.

If you want to select a specific color from somewhere on your costume, use the Pick Up Color tool, which is the eyedropper icon located just to the right of the color swatches).

As you use the Line tool to add sleeves and pant legs, you may need to adjust the thickness for different parts of the costume.

 Holding the Shift button on your keyboard while you use the Line tool will draw a perfect horizontal or vertical line (depending on which way you drag your cursor).

My hero's shirt is an irregular shape, so the Brush tool would work better than the Line tool to paint it a different color. Yet, another Scratch tool can make it easier to make the change.

Fill areas with new color

The Fill with Color tool fills an area with color, but changes only one color at a time. So, if somebody was wearing a really awful shirt with five colors, you would need to click each color to change them all. This is your chance to totally redesign your character, one color at a time.

1. Zoom in on the part of the character you want to change. (I'll let you choose the best Zoom level from now on).

 2. Click the Fill with Color tool.

3. Choose the Solid option.

4. Click the color swatch you wish to start with.

5. Click the area you want to change. (I'll start with my hero's lower legs.)

6. Keep clicking until you have filled all the areas you want that color.

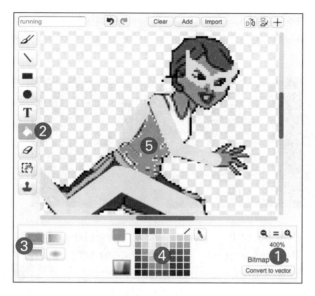

After using the Fill with Color tool, your character may need some cleaning up with the Erase tool or Brush tool. I'll use the Brush tool to paint over the bits of white that still appear around the areas I filled with orange. I'll zoom in even further (to 800%) and adjust the line width to make it easier to paint over the small details. When zoomed in, it might be easier to just click each spot rather than clicking and dragging across several spots.

I will alternate between the Line tool and the Brush tool to add more orange costume parts, including orange gloves and boots.

Use the Erase tool to remove any remaining clothing from the old sprite, such as *Catalina*'s baggy shorts and the bottom of her boots. Then check out your superhero on the Stage.

Is anything missing from your super's costume? Are there any other details that would make your character stand out? I've been thinking about *Catalina*'s possible superpowers while working on her costume. I know I want her to fly, so I think a long, flowing cape would be the perfect addition. I'll use the Line, Fill with Color, and Erase tools to whip one up for her.

Add costume outlines

My superhero looks pretty good against the dark background I chose for the first scene, but what if the next scene has a lighter backdrop or one that mixes dark and light elements? I sometimes find it useful to swap the stage backdrop back to the default white to see how a character might look against a lighter background.

You do not want to fill the background with color in the Paint Editor because it would block your backdrop on the Stage.

1. Click the Stage button.

2. Click the Backdrops tab.

3. Click the original white backdrop *(Backdrop1)*.

4. If you replaced or deleted the original backdrop, then click the Paint New Backdrop icon and use the Fill with Color tool to make it solid white.

5. Review your character's costume against the solid color on the Stage.

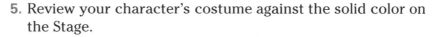
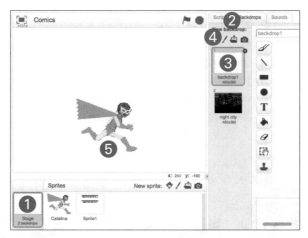

The yellow parts of *Catalina*'s costume are very light against the white backdrop; how about yours? If you look at a typical comic book or cartoon, you will notice a thin, black outline around all the parts of a character. Adding an outline will make your character look sharper.

Select your character sprite and use the Line tool and Brush tool to add thin, black outlines. Use the Line tool as much as possible to get smooth edges. Then use the Brush tool for curves and hard to reach areas.

When preparing to make several changes to a costume, I duplicate the costume by Shift-clicking the costume icon and choosing *Duplicate*. This way, if I go too far with my changes, I can just reselect the previous costume and start over.

I was able to add outlines to the entire costume except for the hands. Since the figures are too slim to add outlines, I will cheat a bit by having *Catalina* make a fist instead. Using a new tool will give her a smoother fist.

Draw ovals and circles

The Line tool gives you smoother edges than the Brush tool. If you want to draw smooth ovals and perfect circles, then you gotta try the Ellipse tool. It works like the Line tool: You click and then drag until you have the size you want, then release your mouse or trackpad button. To draw a perfect circle, hold the Shift key on your keyboard.

To draw *Catalina*'s fist, I will erase her current hand, draw a black oval for the outline, and then draw an orange oval inside it.

The fist looks a bit weird until I use the Line tool to fix the gap and the Brush tool to paint through the wrist. Now, I can zoom out to see how it looks at normal size.

While using the Ellipse tool, after you click and drag to draw your circle and release the mouse or trackpad button, you can click the oval again and drag it to a new or better position. You can resize the oval by clicking and dragging the control points that appear around it. However, as soon as you click another tool or click outside the ellipse, you will no longer be able to move or resize the shape as easily.

When you're happy with your costume design, change the backdrop back to the one you chose earlier and make sure it still looks good to you.

I could spend a bit more time tweaking parts, but I am generally happy with how *Catalina*'s costume turned out. Since the yellow and orange colors remind me of flames, I think I will give her another superpower in addition to flight: the power to shoot fire from her hands! (I know it's not the most original superpower, but there are SO MANY superheroes these days! All the great powers have been taken!)

Once you've chosen a superpower or two for your hero, move on to adding text to your comic. It might help to take a break from the computer, give your story a bit of thought, grab a snack, and return to your Scratch project refreshed. This would also be a good time to save your work if you are using the Offline Editor (choose File ⇨ Save). If you are online, your projects save while you work.

You will learn how to design smoother, more professional-looking characters using the vector painting tools in Chapter 4 and throughout the chapters in Part 2.

Tell Your Super Story

You have a hero and a setting. How did the hero get there? Some comics tell the entire story visually, but most use text to move the story along. To continue, it's really important to give *Catalina* her superhero name, so I've decided to call her *COMBUSTA* (as in *combustible*)! I won't bother to rename her sprite because her friends and family still call her *Catalina*.

The three primary uses of text in comics are description, speech, and thought. You will start with a brief description and then add both a speech and thought bubble to your scene.

Add description box

I prefer to create a new sprite for each text area so that I can move the sprite separately from my characters and backdrops.

1. Click the Paint New Sprite icon.

2. Click the Costumes tab (or go to the Paint Editor canvas).

3. Click the Rectangle tool.

4. Choose the Solid option.

5. Select a yellow color swatch (or another color that will contrast the background behind where you place your description box).

6. Zoom to 100% so you can draw a rectangle nearly as wide as the stage. You will trim it later.

7. Click where you want the rectangle to begin.

8. Drag your cursor to where you want the rectangle to end and then release the mouse or trackpad button.

9. Click and drag the rectangle into position on the Stage.

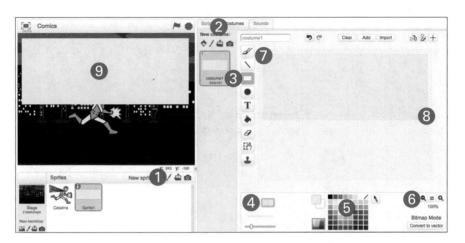

 Like the Ellipse tool, you can resize and position your rectangle until it has been deselected (by clicking another tool or clicking outside the rectangle). You can also draw perfect squares by holding the Shift key on your keyboard.

You may be thinking, "Why did we make the rectangle so large?" Because you are not sure how much text you will have yet, and it's easier to cut off the extra part of the rectangle than to add more after text has been put into place.

Type scene description

Perhaps the most familiar looking tool on the Paint Editor canvas is the Text tool. You will type your description right inside the rectangle you just drew.

1. Click the Text tool.

2. Choose a color that contrasts your rectangle. (I'll choose black.)

3. Choose a font. (I'll choose Marker, which looks like comic book text.)

4. Click inside the top-left corner of your rectangle.

5. Type the first line of your scene description.

6. Click the Return or Enter button on your keyboard to start a new line.

7. Click outside the text area when you are finished typing.

8. Click and drag your text into a better position.

9. Click outside the text window again or select a new tool to finish.

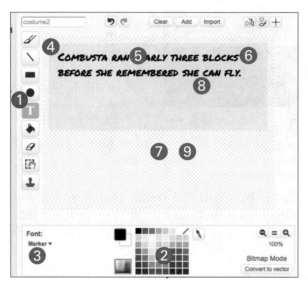

See why I suggested drawing a large rectangle before typing your text? You could use the Erase tool, but I prefer to use the Select tool to remove large areas.

After you set your text, you can't make any changes or corrections. To modify your sentence, you will need to click Undo, retype everything, and then reposition it. If you need to make changes later, you may need to redraw the rectangle and use the Text tool again.

Trim your graphics

The Select tool is more versatile than the name suggests. Although you can use it to select, move, resize, and rotate parts of your costume, you use it here to delete parts of the rectangle.

1. Click the Select tool.

2. Zoom to 100% so that you can see the entire rectangle.

3. Click and drag across the first part of the rectangle you want to erase.

4. Release the mouse or trackpad button to finish the selection.

5. Click the Delete or Backspace key on your keyboard.

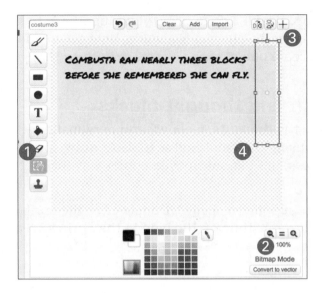

Use the same steps to trim the other sides of the rectangle until the margins around your text look right.

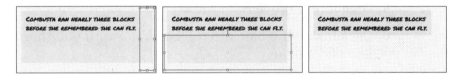

You can go to the Stage and click and drag your description sprite into a better position. Description boxes usually appear at the top or bottom of the comic panel.

Descriptions are useful, but to bring your superhero to life, you really need to give the character a voice. How do you do that? You have to create one of those classic speech or thought bubbles!

Use speech and thought blocks

You can share the thoughts, feelings, and personality of your superhero by using the Paint Editor tools to draw speech and thought bubbles, but I know an even cooler way: using programming blocks!

1. Select your superhero sprite. (Double-click the sprite on the Stage or click one time on the icon in the Sprites area beneath the stage.)

2. Click the Scripts tab.

3. Click the Looks category.

4. Locate the SAY block.

5. Drag it into the Scripts Area.

6. Click inside the block to replace *Hello* with your hero's first line of dialogue.

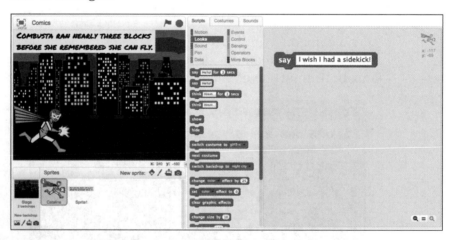

To show the speech bubble on the Stage, click the SAY block one time. Mine worked, but the speech bubble is not where it should be.

The speech bubble might be in the right place for your character, but Scratch lost track of where *Catalina*'s (I mean *COMBUSTA*'s) head is. Since I'm a bit of a control freak, I've come up with a fix that lets me position speech and thought bubbles exactly where I want them.

 You click the SAY or THINK block to make the text show up on the Stage. To make it go away, click the Stop button in the top-right corner of the Stage.

Precisely position speech bubbles

To move a speech (or thought) bubble where you want on the Stage, you can create a special *say/think* sprite. Check it out:

1. Click the Paint New Sprite icon.

2. Click the Costumes tab.

3. Click the Ellipse tool.

4. Choose the Solid option.

5. Select a bright red color swatch.

6. Zoom to 100% to see how large the shape will be on the Stage.

7. Hold the Shift key on your keyboard and then click and drag to draw a small circle.

8. On the Stage, drag the circle to cover your character's head.

9. If you do not see the circle on the Stage, you might need to click outside the circle.

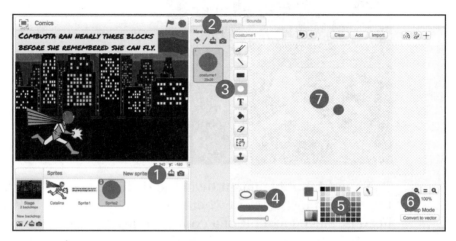

Rather than putting the SAY block on your superhero, you put the SAY (or THINK) block on the new sprite. Wherever you drag that sprite to on the Stage, the speech or thought bubble will follow.

The only problem is you probably do not want a bright red circle to cover your hero's face, am I right? There's an easy fix to that, which is a bit like Scratch magic. On the Stage, just click your superhero and hold the button down for a few seconds. Voila!

Every time you add a sprite to the Stage, it creates a new layer. When you click on a sprite for a few seconds, the sprite comes forward to the top layer on the Stage.

 You can also change a sprite's layer position by using the GO TO FRONT and GO BACK LAYERS blocks near the bottom of the Looks category (the same category the SAY and THINK blocks are in). You don't even need to drag them onto your sprite; just select the sprite and click the block right in the category to apply it. For the GO BACK LAYERS block, you can either click it several times (depending on how many sprites have been added to the stage) or increase the value inside the block before clicking it.

Wrapping Up

 During this project, you have used virtually all the bitmap painting tools and features. The only major tool that I left out is the Duplicate tool. It wasn't necessary for this project, but you should try it for yourself (it's especially fun to use on photographs).

In the next few chapters, you explore more painting tools and techniques and dive into vector graphics. If you want to bring your comic character(s) to life, you can skip ahead to Chapter 11, which walks you through the process of creating a short animation.

Load photos, drawings, or yourself into Scratch

Why should those Scratch characters have all the fun? In addition to adding new sprites from the library, you can create a new sprite by uploading a drawing or photograph. To upload an image from your computer, click the Upload Sprite from File icon. (This works for costumes and backdrops, too.)

Here is a superhero my nephew, Ryan, drew on paper. He scanned it into the computer, imported it into Scratch, used the Erase tool to remove the background, and then used the same Scratch code blocks from this chapter to make the hero speak.

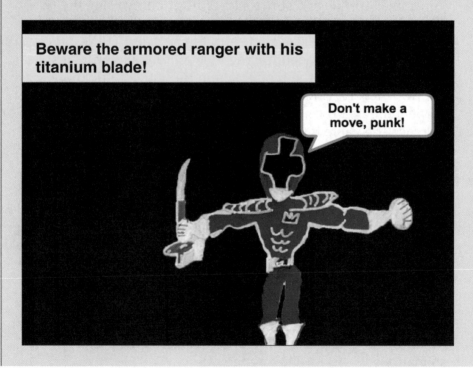

If you have a webcam, you can create a new sprite by taking a picture and clicking the New Sprite from Camera icon. The first time you use your webcam, you may have to follow these instructions to enable it to work with Scratch.

Step 1: If an Adobe Flash Player Settings window appears, click *Allow*.

Step 2: If a message appears at the top of your web page, click *Allow* there, too.

Step 3: Adjust your camera height until you are happy with the preview image and then click *Save*.

Now you can modify the image just like any other sprite costume in Scratch.

CHAPTER
3

Design Scratch Animals

Thanks to Scratch, you can have as many pets as you want, from a hamster to a hippopotamus to a hippogriff. In fact, a hippogriff would be the perfect logo for Scratch, don't you think? You can look at a hippogriff as a mix of an eagle and a horse — way more Scratchy than a plain orange cat!

Most of you can draw a horse, a lion, or a dragon, but with Scratch, you can easily populate the savannah with dozens of lions or fill the sky with 300 dragons.

In those other how-to books, a digital paint lesson would begin with a simple creature like an ant, but not this book. A true dummy would start with a rather complicated animal like a ferocious turtle! What, you think that's a joke? Not in my backyard, where I have seen a snapping turtle as large as a trash can lid and as fearless as a math teacher!

Create a Great Turtle

It's up to you whether to work in the Offline Scratch Editor or to work online. If this is your first time using Scratch, check out Chapter 1 for guidance.

1. Go to `scratch.mit.edu` or open the Scratch 2 Offline Editor.

2. If you are online, click Create in the blue toolbar. If offline, select File ⇨ New.

3. Name your project. (Online, type **Turtle** into the Untitled text box; offline, select File ⇨ Save As and type **Turtle**.)

Let's start this Scratch safari by shooing away an animal. As soon as you create a new project, delete that cat! Hold the Shift key on your keyboard, click the cat (this is called Shift-clicking), and choose *Delete*.

Draw a turtle shell outline

A good place to begin drawing a turtle is with the shell. Since Scratch lets you rotate your animal later, a common practice is to begin with your animal facing right. Be sure to leave room around the shell for the head, legs, and tail!

1. Click the Paint New Sprite icon.

2. Click the Info button (on the sprite icon beneath the Stage), change the name from *Sprite1* to *Turtle,* and then click the Back button (white triangle on blue circle).

   The more sprites you have in your project, the more important it is to name them. This will REALLY help when you get to animation and game design.

3. Go to the Paint canvas and click the Ellipse tool.

4. Click Outline mode.

5. Drag the Line Width slider right to adjust the thickness of the line.

6. Click the black color swatch.

7. Click where you want to start your oval.

8. Drag the cursor to where you want to end the ellipse and then release the mouse or trackpad button.

While the ellipse is still selected, you can drag the small dots on each side to resize it. Hold the Shift key and drag a corner to resize it evenly. If you click inside the selected ellipse, you can drag it to a new position on the canvas. When you are happy with the size and position, click outside the ellipse or click another tool to finish the shape.

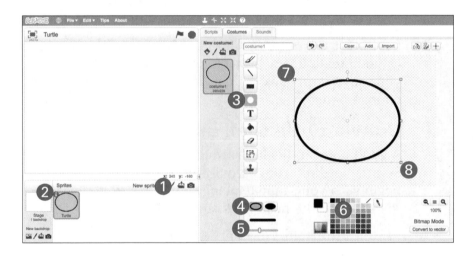

Feel free to use the Undo or Clear buttons and redraw your shell shape as often as you want. Professional designers might draw dozens, even hundreds of shapes before they find the one they're happy with.

Fill in your shell

Congratulations, you now have a hollow, black oval! Why didn't you draw a solid shell? Something about a black outline makes a digital illustration look more professional. And filling a shape is easier than adding an outline later. Scratch makes it easy to fill in shapes and begin to add details.

1. Click the Fill with Color tool.

2. Choose the Solid style this time.

3. Choose a color for your shell. (I'll choose greenish brown; or is it brownish green?)

4. Click inside your shell oval to fill it.

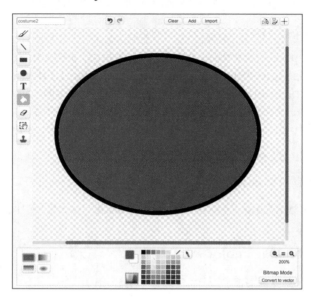

Draw shell segments

 1. Click the Zoom In button once to zoom to 200%. (Larger images are generally easier to work with on the Paint canvas.)

 2. Click the Line tool.

 3. Use the Line Width slider to adjust the line thickness.

4. Choose the black color swatch.

5. Click and drag to draw each line. (Hold the Shift key to draw perfect horizontal or vertical lines.)

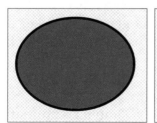 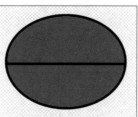 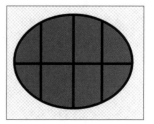

If you need more room to draw, you can expand the Paint canvas by selecting Edit➪Small Stage Layout or by clicking the small triangle on the border between the Paint canvas and the Stage. Click the same button or menu to go back to the original view.

Add head, legs, and a tail

You could just draw the turtle's head, legs, and tail right onto your current costume, but it might be a good idea to duplicate the first costume and then add the new parts to the second costume. Why? What if you want to use the turtle in an animation or game project and need to show the turtle pull its body back into its shell?

1. Shift-click *Costume1* and choose *Duplicate*.

2. Click the Brush tool.

3. Adjust the Line Width slider to about the same thickness as the oval.

4. Click the black color swatch.

5. Draw the outline of the head, legs, and tail.

6. Click the Fill with Color tool.

7. Choose the color swatch you want.

8. Click inside each shape to fill it with color.

Designing your creatures pretty large at first makes adding details easier. You can resize them later using the SIZE block or the Shrink and Grow tools.

Add body details

Here is where you can transform a simple creature design into a slicker, more realistic illustration. The details are really up to you, but I will share a few of my favorites.

1. Shift-click *Costume2* and select *Duplicate*.

2. Click the new costume *(Costume3)* to select it.

 3. Click the Ellipse tool, choose Solid, and then choose a light green or yellow swatch.

4. Add several ellipses of varying sizes to the head.

5. Here's a shortcut for adding spots to the legs:

   a. Draw several small circles off the turtle's body.

    b. Click the Duplicate tool.

   c. Click and drag over the group of spots.

   d. Click and drag the selected spots to a new position on a leg. (Click and drag corners to fit inside the leg outlines.)

   e. Click and drag the small circle attached to the box to rotate spots.

   f. Repeat several times until the legs are full of spots.

Add shell details

Adding highlights (lighter color parts) is another professional design technique that will help bring your creature to life.

 1. Click the Line tool.

 2. Adjust the Line Width slider to a thinner size than the black shell lines.

3. Choose a light color swatch. (I'll keep the same light green I used for the spots.)

4. Hold the Shift key to draw parallel horizontal lines inside each shell section.

5. Hold the Shift key to draw parallel vertical lines inside the sections.

   I find it easier to start my line at the end of the horizontal lines I've just drawn and draw each line away from the center.

6. Use the Line tool to connect the lines and finish the sections.

   I chose straight lines all the way around because I had trouble drawing a curve. (In Chapter 4, you draw curves more accurately using vector painting tools.)

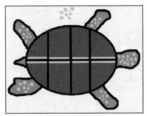  

MATH CONNECTIONS

$$\begin{array}{r} 1 \\ +1 \\ \hline 2 \end{array}$$

Forgive me for sneaking a bit of geometry into your artwork, but illustrators and designers also need to know about parallel lines. In math, *parallel* simply means lines that run along each other and never intersect.

If you look back at the turtle from the beginning of the chapter, you might notice there is no gap between the shell outline and the green fill inside. A quick way to close the gap is to draw another hollow black ellipse over the entire shell outline. (You can adjust the size while it is still selected to get it just right). While you're at it, you can also erase those extra dots if they are still to the side of your turtle.

If you zoom to 100%, your illustration should look a bit more impressive.

You don't get into animation until Chapter 6, but I can't resist sharing a few more steps that will bring your turtle to life.

Add Code to Animate the Turtle

If you completed the Flapping Bat project from Chapter 1 (or skipped ahead to one of the other projects that involves code), then this task will be super easy. In case this is your first experience coding, I won't skip over anything.

If you have trouble locating one of the code blocks, try looking for the category that matches the color of the block.

Make the turtle crawl

1. Click the Turtle sprite and then click the the Scripts tab.

2. Drag the following blocks into the Scripts Area so they snap together:

 Click the Green Flag button on the top-right side of the Stage to test your code. What happens? Fastest turtle you ever saw, right? He scoots right off the side of the stage.

Slow down the turtle

You can bring the turtle back to the center and slow him down by adding a GO TO block and a WAIT block.

```
when       clicked
go to x: 0 y: 0
forever
    move 10 steps
    wait 1 secs
```
x: 50
y: 0

I changed the values in the GO TO block so X is *0* and Y is *0*. X is the horizontal position and Y is the vertical position. When X and Y equal 0, the block should move a sprite to the center of the screen.

Now when you click the Green Flag button, the turtle should jump back to the center of the screen and then start moving, VERY slowly. Can you figure out how to speed the turtle up a little?

Speed up the turtle

 Click the Stop button on the Stage. You can either have the turtle move more than ten steps at a time or reduce the WAIT time. Try changing the MOVE value to *5* and the WAIT value to *.25*. Also, I want to add a block that tells the turtle what to do when it reaches the edge of the stage.

```
when       clicked
go to x: 0 y: 0
forever
    move 5 steps
    wait .25 secs
    if on edge, bounce
```
x: -33
y: 0

Now when the Green Flag button is clicked, the turtle should move a bit faster and, when it gets to the edge of the stage, flip around and start crawling in the opposite direction. The turtle will crawl back and forth, back and forth, for as long as you can stand to watch it!

Not too exciting, right? What if we shrink the turtle to give it more room to move around, and have it turn occasionally?

I added another WHEN GREEN FLAG CLICKED block and then snapped new blocks under it. One set of blocks moves the turtle to the center and then makes the turtle move forward, while another set of blocks makes the turtle smaller and then makes the turtle turn a bit every second.

Animate the turtle legs

What if there were an easy way to make it look like the legs are moving? I know, I know, this isn't the animation section. But I have to share this cheap trick to make the movement more realistic.

1. Click the Costumes tab.

2. Rename the current costume *Right.*

3. Shift-click that costume and select *Duplicate.*

4. Click to select the copy and rename it *Left.*

5. Click the Flip Up-Down button.

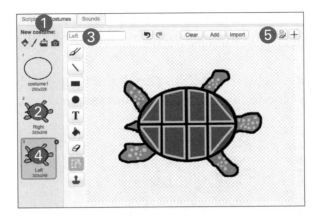

Now click the Scripts tab and add this third set of blocks. Be sure to change the costume names to *Right* and *Left* and the value of the WAIT blocks to *.25*.

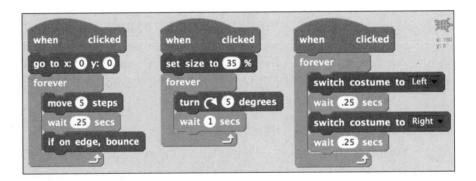

Did you click the Green Flag button yet? What are you waiting for?!?

If all your blocks are in the right place, you should have a pretty realistic little turtle waddling around the stage. Cool, right?!? But enough with turtles, let's move on to a far more dangerous beast.

"Easily offended, hippogriffs are. Don't never insult one, 'cause it might be the last thing yeh do."

—Rubeus Hagrid discussing hippogriffs with his Hogwarts class

I Want a Wild Hippogriff!

Can you guess why I might want you to design your own hippogriff? The average kid (and most adults) would be more confident about their ability to draw a turtle than to draw a hippogriff. Fortunately, in Scratch, you do not always need to start with a blank page (or blank Stage).

You can work in the same project as your turtle (Scratch projects can have as many sprites as you want), but I prefer to create a new project.

1. Go to scratch.mit.edu or open the Scratch 2 Offline Editor.

2. If you are online, click Create in the blue toolbar. If offline, select File ⇨ New.

3. Name your project. (Online, type **Hippogriff** into the Untitled text box; offline, select File ⇨ Save As and type **Hippogriff**.)

4. Delete that cat by selecting the Scissors and clicking the cat or by right-clicking the cat and choosing *Delete*.

Look in the Sprite Library

You need to start with a good sprite from the Sprite Library and then gradually modify the sprite until you have a spot-on hippogriff. The horse in the Sprite Library is a bit too cartoony, so begin with the unicorn instead.

1. Click the Choose Sprite from Library icon beneath the Stage.

2. Find and double-click the *Unicorn* sprite. (Click the Fantasy category to reduce the number of choices.)

3. Click the Info button (on the sprite icon beneath the Stage) and change the name to *Hippogriff.*

4. Click the Back button (white triangle on blue circle).

5. Click the Costumes tab.

6. Click the Grow tool (above the Scripts, Costumes, and Sounds tab).

7. Click the unicorn (soon to be a hippogriff) 12 times.

Convert to bitmap   8. Click the Convert to Bitmap button.

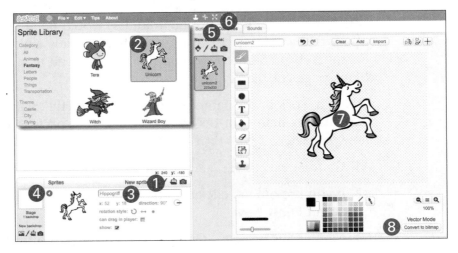

What was that all about!? The *Unicorn* sprite is a *vector graphic,* which means you can zoom in as much as you want and it will still look smooth. But you did not zoom; you used Grow to make the unicorn bigger before converting it to a bitmap graphic. So why did you have to convert it? Because I say so! Kidding. Actually, we are sticking to the bitmap painting tools in this chapter because they are a bit easier to work with. Vector painting tools are coming up in the next chapter.

How can you tell if your sprite is a bitmap or a vector graphic? Look at the bottom-right corner of the Paint Editor. Also if the painting tools are on the left, then you are in Bitmap mode. (And, if the painting tools are on the right? Yes, Vector mode, baby!) Don't worry, you'll get the hang of it!

Groom your fantasy animal

If we are going to transform this cuddly unicorn into a ferocious hippogriff, that rainbow tail has to go, along with rainbow mane, ear, and horn! You can use the Erase tool, but you might find using the Select tool to delete parts of sprites easier and quicker.

    1. Click the Erase tool.

    2. Use the Line Width slider to increase the size of the eraser.

3. Click the Zoom In button once to zoom to 200%.

4. Click and drag to erase the tail, mane, ear, and horn (unless you want a *unigriff!?!*).

   Reduce the size of the eraser when you need to remove smaller areas.

 If you are using a laptop trackpad, you might find it easer to draw and erase more accurately if you use both hands. I am right-handed, so I click and hold the trackpad button with my left index finger and then use my right middle finger to control the cursor. It's a bit like finger-painting. Try it out.

Add a new tail

When the cutesy bits of your sprite are gone, you can change the color from white to a more hippogriff color and use the Brush tool to draw a tail back in, erase the head and front hooves with the Erase tool, and then draw eagle parts to your beast.

1. Click the Fill with Color tool.

2. Choose the Solid option.

3. Pick the color swatch you wish to use. (I'll choose a bright yellow.)

4. Click the body to fill it with the selected color.

5. Click the Brush tool.

6. Use the Line Width slider to adjust the line thickness.

7. Click the black color swatch.

8. Click and drag to draw a new tail.

 9. To reuse a color in your costume (say the hippogriff body color), use the Pick Up Color tool (to the right of the color swatches).

10. Use the Fill with Color tool again to fill in the tail.

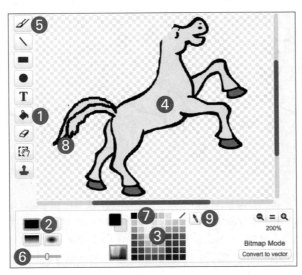

Paint the beak and claws

You should be getting the hang of the tools by now, so let's speed things up a bit.

1. Erase the front of the head and the front hooves.

2. Paint the outline of an eaglelike head and front claws.

3. Color in the new body parts.

Add wings and ferocious eyes

Your sprite should now be far more hippogriff than unicorn, but there are a couple more important touches: the wings and head features.

1. Draw the outline of the wings.

2. Color in the wings.

3. Choose the black color swatch.

4. Draw eagle eyes at an extreme slant to make your creature look more dangerous.

   The key to making your creature ferocious is to pay careful attention to the eyes.

Since it is your hippogriff, you can add as many additional details as you want (such as drawing a feathery texture across the front and horselike hair across the back).

Add Code for the Hippogriff's Whinny

Since we added a bit of code to the turtle, it would feel wrong to cheat your mighty hippogriff of the same treatment. Instead of movement, let's give the legendary creature a voice! You will choose a sound from the Sounds Library and then add the code blocks required to play the sound each time you click the spacebar.

1. Click the Sounds tab.

 2. Click the Choose Sound from Library button.

3. Click the Animal category and then double-click the *horse* sound.

4. Click the Scripts tab.

5. Add the following blocks and change the values to match.

 When you press the spacebar, you should hear a realistic horse sound play. If you want a more ferocious hippogriff sound, try recording your own by clicking the Record New Sound button on the Sounds tab.

Moving On

Once you've finished an animal or creature design, you can draw a backdrop for it or choose one from the Backdrop Library. Surely you can come up with something better than *mine!*

If you can design a realistic turtle and a fantastical hippogriff, you should have the confidence to create just about any animal you can imagine. And, you even used a bit of coding to bring your creations to life.

Here are some other animals whipped up in Scratch by my wonder-niece, Katelyn:

After you've shown off your new four-legged creatures to friends and family, turn the page and dive into Chapter 4! You can FINALLY try out those vector painting tools I've been teasing you with in the last couple chapters.

Making more accurate digital drawings

Are you having trouble drawing with your mouse or trackpad?

Tips for drawing with a mouse:

1. Use a wireless mouse.

2. Start drawing from the middle of your mousepad.

3. Use a larger mousepad. (You can make one from a piece of cardboard!)

Tips for drawing with a trackpad:

1. Click the lower-left corner with your left index finger and draw with your right index finger (or do the opposite if you're left-handed). This makes it feel like finger-painting.

2. Try drawing from the lower-left corner (or lower-right corner if you're left-handed).

3. A stylus for a touchscreen tablet might also work on your laptops with larger trackpads.

Another option for more accurate drawing is to use a drawing or painting app on an iPad or Android tablet (for best results, try a stylus) or using a graphics tablet, like a Boogie Board Sync or Wacom tablet. Then you can use the Upload Sprite from File icon to import your drawing into Scratch.

Build Vector Robots

Since I was a kid, I have been fascinated by robots, from the droids in *Star Wars* and the cylons in *Battlestar Galactica* to the robotic arm this geeky kid had in his bedroom on an old television show called *Whiz Kids*. Back then, I *really* wished I could have a robot of my own.

Robots may be less scarce today, but your parents are probably still more likely to buy you a Kindle than a life-sized WALL-E or EVE, or even a robotic arm. So why not design your own army of Scratch robots to fulfill all *your* robot dreams?

Diving into Vector Design

Using the design tools in Vector mode, you can quickly make robots as realistic as you want, then animate them with just a few more steps. You are only one button away from an entirely new way to design with Scratch!

1. Go to scratch.mit.edu or open the Scratch 2 Offline Editor.

2. If you are online, click Create. If offline, select File ⇨ New.

3. Name your project. (Online, select the title and type **Vector Robots**. Offline, select File ⇨ Save As and type **Vector Robots**.)

4. Delete the . . . WAIT! *Don't* delete the cat *YET!*

You may be thinking, "This dummy said we should ALWAYS start by deleting the cat. He has me all excited about building my own vector robot and then tells me NOT to delete the cat?!? Nothing could be LESS robotic than that cartoony cat!"

I know, I know, but let's look at the cat for just a minute. Would you believe the Scratch cat that I give such a hard time is actually

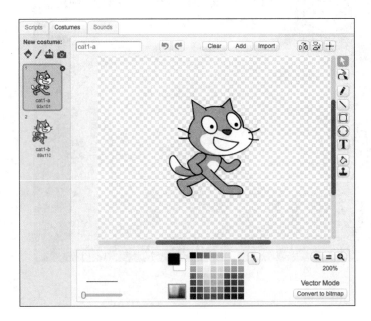

made up of vector graphics? How can you tell? Click the cat one time and then click the Costumes tab. Notice how the tools are going down the right side of the window instead of the left? Also, some of the icons are different from the ones that you may be used to from working through previous chapters. But, the real giveaway is the message *Vector Mode* appearing beneath the Zoom buttons.

Okay, now you can delete that awful cat! (Use the Scissors or right-click the cat and select *Delete*.)

What's the big deal about Vector mode?

I design almost all my sprites in Vector mode. Why? Because the design tools in Vector mode allow modification of shapes and lines in many more ways than can be done with bitmap graphics. Another advantage of vector graphics is being able to zoom in or increase the size of a sprite as much as you want without losing any of the detail. Bye-bye pixelation!

Best of all for Scratchers, vector graphics give you much more control of the individual parts of your sprite, so you can select and move any part of your robot or game character or scenery at any time. Remember how tricky it was to delete some of the smaller parts of the unicorn in the last chapter? Wait until you see how easy it is to make such changes in Vector mode!

TIP

DO NOT SKIP SECTIONS JUST BECAUSE YOU THINK MY ROBOT LOOKS TOTALLY LAME! The publisher did not choose me for my fantastic art skills. (Look no further than my hippogriff in the last chapter.) These projects have been set up to walk you through all the design tools in Vector mode and to present techniques you *MIGHT* find helpful. I am *POSITIVE* you can design better robots than I can, but going through these steps may provide a few tricks to make *your* robots even *COOLER!*

Sculpting Robot Shapes

Sculpting is a word I have not used before in this book, and a word you might not expect to be associated with Scratch, or computers for that matter. How do you "sculpt" something on a computer? In the previous version of Scratch (version 1.4), once you painted a bitmap sprite, you would need to completely repaint the costumes to make significant changes. With the addition of vector graphics, modifying costumes and backdrops is a snap!

1. Click the Paint New Sprite icon.

2. Click the Costumes tab.

3. Click the Convert to Vector button.

4. Zoom to 100%.

5. Click the Rectangle tool.

6. Choose the Outline option.

7. Select the black color swatch.

8. Click where you want the rectangle to start.

9. Drag the corner and release the mouse or trackpad button where you want the rectangle to end.

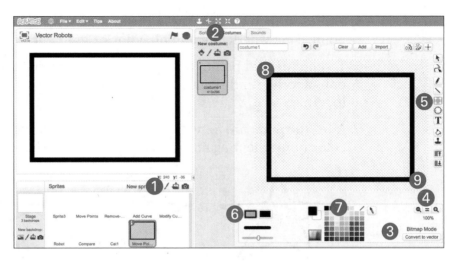

Ta-dah! Aren't you impressed? Look at that awesome rectangle! I know, lame, right? But, didn't I say something about sculpting shapes?

Use reshape on straight edges

1. Click the Reshape tool.

2. Click any corner of your rectangle and drag it around. Then another corner, and another . . . .

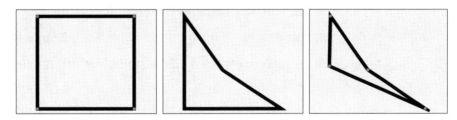

Add and remove points

In addition to moving corners, the Reshape tool also allows you to add new points to make more complex shapes and remove points.

1. Click between points to add a point on any line.

2. Click and drag the new point to change your shape.

3. Repeat Steps 1 and 2 to create a five-pointed star.

4. Click an existing point to delete it.

5. To break open a shape, hold the Shift key while clicking a point. This will delete any fill color or gradient.

6. To join the end points of lines, click one end point and drag it onto another end point (like welding two ends of a wire together).

7. After the ends are joined, you can fill your shape with a solid color or gradient again by using the Color a Shape tool.

Use reshape on curves

To get a real sense of sculpting shapes, you just GOTTA try the Reshape tool on an ellipse!

1. Click the Ellipse tool and draw a medium-sized circle.

2. Click the Reshape tool.

3. Click the ellipse one time to select it.

4. Click and drag a point on your ellipse to change the shape.

5. Click between points to add a point and then drag it to change the shape.

6. Double-click an existing point to delete it and simplify your shape.

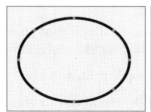  

As with rectangular shapes, you can Shift-click points to break open your curvaceous shape and drag end points together to allow you to fill the shape again.

 I like to fill my shapes before using the Reshape tool to sculpt them; it feels a bit more like sculpting with clay versus messing around with a hollow shape.

Add curves to rectangles

You've used the Reshape tool to move corners, add corners, remove corners, sculpt curved shapes, and even break shapes open. As if those were not enough uses, you can even add a curve to a straight line, too. Try this:

1. Click the Reshape tool.

2. Shift-click BETWEEN two existing points on a straight line and drag to make a new curve.

   You may need to click just inside the edge of a solid shape. If it doesn't work the first time, try Shift-clicking a different spot on the line, then drag it wherever you want.

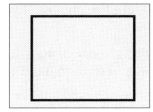 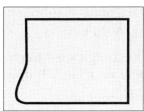 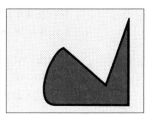

Combine vector shapes

Another cool way to make a complex shape is to break open a rectangle, break open an oval, and then drag the end points together.

1. Draw a rectangle and an ellipse side-by-side.

2. Shift-click points to cut open the rectangle and ellipse.

3. Click and drag end points from one shape to the other to weld lines together.

4. Click and drag to adjust the lines on either side of the intersection points between the original shapes.

5. Fill the final shape with color.

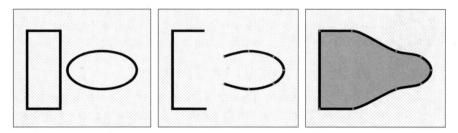

 Remember how after you finished painting part of your sprite in Bitmap mode you could only modify that part right away? Vector mode lets you go back and make changes to any part of the sprite any time you want, a few minutes or even a few weeks later!

Start Your Robot Design

Here are the steps I took to design the robot at the beginning of this chapter. Feel free to use the shapes you have already created to make a customized robot or delete the shapes if you wish to follow along more closely.

Begin with rectangles for parts with sharp corners and ellipses for parts that will be round. It may also help to expand the size of the Paint canvas.

 1. Click the Paint New Sprite icon.

 2. Click the Toggle button to expand the Paint canvas (or choose Edit ⇨ Small Stage Layout.

 3. Click the Convert to Vector button.

 4. Drag the Line Width slider to adjust the line width.

5. Draw several mechanical parts using the Rectangle and Ellipse tools.

6. Use the Reshape tool to sculpt parts into more irregular shapes.

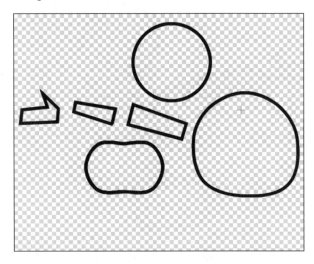

7. Choose a gray color swatch and use the Color a Shape tool to fill in the parts.

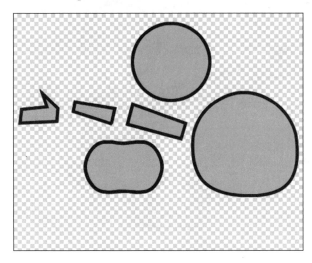

8. Use the Select tool to click and drag the parts into position.

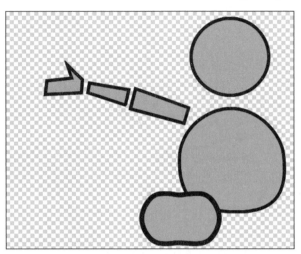

9. Use the Ellipse tool and hold the Shift button to draw solid circles for joints at the wrist, elbow, shoulder, and neck.

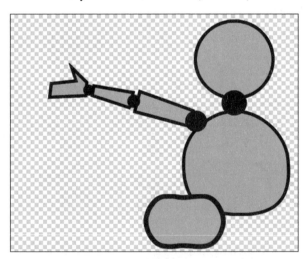

Move parts to different layers

If you went through the previous chapter, you may be wondering why I didn't have you begin drawing the turtle or the hippogriff as a bunch of separate parts. I didn't because it's much harder to select and move parts of images in Bitmap mode.

In Vector mode, each shape you draw in a costume or backdrop gets its own layer (just as each sprite on the Stage is on a different layer). In addition to moving vector shapes across the Paint canvas, you can also move objects behind other objects, or bring them above other objects by using the Back a Layer and Forward a Layer buttons.

The Forward a Layer and Back a Layer buttons are hidden until after you select a shape.

1. Click one of the robot joints with the Select tool.

2. Hold the Shift key while clicking the Back a Layer button.

   Shift-clicking sends the object all the way to the back, while clicking without the Shift button would only send the object back one layer at a time (which works for the Forward a Layer button, too).

Repeat Steps 2 and 3 to send all the joints back, so they appear inside the robot body parts.

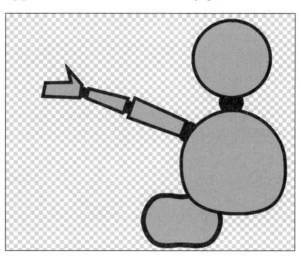

Group shapes together

Vector graphics also enable you to group shapes together. I bet I know what you're thinking: "Hey dummy, aren't all the parts grouped together since they are in the same sprite?" Yes, but can you guess why it might be helpful to have groups of objects within one sprite? What can you do if all the parts of the arm are grouped? Let's find out!

1. Click the Select tool.

2. You can select multiple objects two ways:

   a. Click beside the first object (like the hand) and drag over all the objects you want to group. This works well when parts are isolated, making it easier to select them without dragging over other parts.

   b. Hold the Shift key and click each object you want to group. This ensures you get each part, but you might have trouble selecting smaller objects, hollow shapes with thin outlines, or objects that are behind other objects.

3. Click the Group button.

   Notice how the shoulder that you sent to the back layer now appears to be in front of the robot body again? That's because when you group objects, the group is automatically moved to the top layer.

   The Group tool is hidden until you select more than one shape.

4. Click any object in the group to drag all grouped objects to a new location. Drag the group away from the robot body for now.

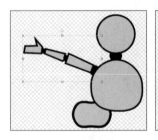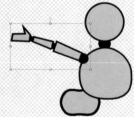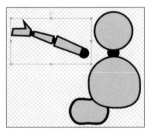

If you find you've grouped more objects than you meant to, you can use the Ungroup button and then try to reselect just the ones you meant to move. If you're still having trouble, you may need to drag objects out of the way and then try to select and group them again.

What can you do with that arm group besides just moving? You can rotate or resize all grouped objects at once. Can you see why this would make a sprite made of vector shapes so much better than bitmap graphics for animating?

I'm guessing you may want more than one arm and one leg for your robot. But don't race ahead and start drawing more parts because I have a shortcut for you!

Duplicate groups of body parts

Have you already guessed why I would have you draw just the left arm and leg? It's because you can use the Duplicate tool to copy groups and then use the Flip buttons to flip the new limbs vertically or horizontally. This not only saves time, but also ensures parts on each side of the body are exactly the same shape and size.

1. Click the Duplicate tool.

2. Click and drag the arm group to copy it to a new position.

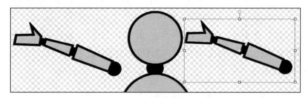

3. Click the Flip Left-Right button and adjust the arm position again.

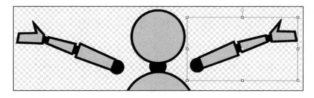

4. Click and drag both arms back into the robot body.

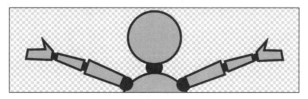

5. Select each arm group and Shift-click the Back a Layer button so the shoulder joints appear inside the body.

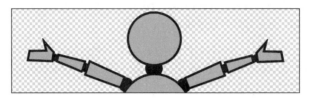

See how much time you saved? Now you can use the same technique on the left and any other parts that you wish to appear on both sides of the robot. In design, having the same parts on each side of the object is referred to as being *symmetrical*. The Flip Left-Right and Flip Up-Down buttons make it easy to create symmetrical backdrops and sprites. This is particularly handy for drawing people, animals, and mechanical objects.

Use gradients for a metallic look

What makes metal look like metal? If a shape is filled with a solid color, it will look flat, like a cartoon or simple illustration. A way to simulate the reflective nature of metal is to use a gradient fill. You can blend gray and white for a bright look or gray and black for a darker shade.

1. Click the Fill with Color tool.

2. Choose a medium gray color swatch.

3. Click the swatch behind your current gray swatch to swap colors, and then choose the white swatch.

   You will find the order of the colors (which color is on top and which on the bottom) can make a big difference on how the gradient turns out.

4. Click the Radial Fill button for round shapes or one of the Linear Fill buttons for more rigid shapes (with sharp corners).

5. Move your cursor into each object and click to fill.

6. If you do not like the gradient, swap the foreground and background colors and click to fill the shape again.

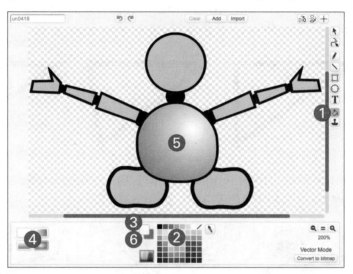

The circular gradient has an advantage over the other gradient options: If you click and drag inside a shape, you can specify where the center of your circular gradient will appear. This is a handy way to specify exactly where a highlight or dark spot should appear.

Add details with the Line tool

If you went through the previous chapter, you learned how to use the Line tool to draw straight lines between two points. It appears to work the same way in Vector mode, clicking to start the line and dragging to the end point, then releasing your mouse or trackpad button to finish the line. But if you continue to click and drag, you create a continuous outline that you can close by clicking back on the beginning point.

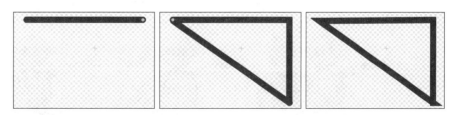

Once a shape is closed, you may find a corner appears messy (like the bottom-right corner of my triangle). You can usually fix these corners by selecting the Reshape tool, clicking the points of the corners, and dragging them into place.

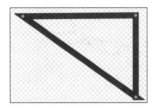 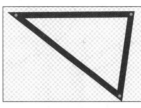 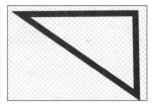

Use the Line tool, along with the Ellipse, Rectangle, and Reshape tools to add more details to your robot.

You can adjust the width of any line (including shape outlines) in Vector mode by selecting the line or shape and using the Line Width slider (to the left of the color swatches).

The last details to add are shadows to offset the gradient highlights.

Add shadows to vector shapes

A quick way to add a shadow is to duplicate a shape part (as I have with the body and head shapes), fill it with a darker color, make the edges the same color, use the Reshape tool to squish them, and then select and drag back onto the object.

What's a Robot Without Code?

Half the fun of drawing and painting stuff in Scratch is using code to make them interactive.

Move the robot with arrow keys

Go to the Scripts tab on your robot and add the following code:

```
when left arrow ▼ key pressed        when right arrow ▼ key pressed
change x by -10                      change x by 10

when up arrow ▼ key pressed          when down arrow ▼ key pressed
change y by 2                        change y by -2
change size by -2                    change size by 2
```

You don't have to click the Green Flag button on the Stage to test this code; just click the arrow keys on your keyboard. You may need to adjust the values on the blocks beneath WHEN UP ARROW and WHEN DOWN ARROW to make those motions appear more natural against your backdrop (as if the robot is moving into the distance or closer to the viewer).

Add robot sounds

Another thing that distinguishes robots from one another are the bleeps and blurps some make in place of human words. In the previous chapter, I walk you through adding (or recording) a sound from the Sounds Library for your Hippogriff. Here's a different approach for your robotic sounds:

```
when space ▼ key pressed
set instrument to 20▼
play note pick random 65 to 85 for .1 beats
```

You can hold down the spacebar for a stream of random beeps or clickity-click the spacebar for your own intermittent beeps (like melodic Morse code). Try changing the values in the RANDOM block to get a different mood. Additionally, you can change the BEATS value to extend or cut off the beeps.

Finishing Your Project

Although the Sprite Library contains many vector characters, animals, and objects, the Backdrops Library only has bitmap graphics. Go ahead and pick a backdrop. I like mine because it's kind of funny to see a robot in the middle of the desert (although C-3PO wouldn't think so).

Ryan decided to skip the backdrop for his vector robot, so you can see all the detail he put into his more realistic creation.

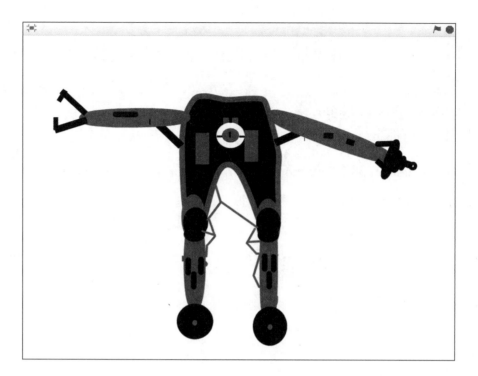

If you skip ahead to the animation chapters (Chapters 6–10), you'll find many more vector design and Scratch coding techniques.

Those of you with a careful eye may have noticed that the desert backdrop I chose looks a bit fuzzy compared to the robot. That fuzziness is, you guessed it, *pixelation,* which is a dead giveaway that a graphic is bitmap versus vector. Design your own vector backdrops to ensure your scene looks sharp at any Stage size.

Way more robot stuff

There are many other ways to create robots in Scratch using the design tools in Vector mode:

Design a humanoid bot or cyborg: Since you can have layers, why not start with a photo of yourself or a friend (or even a pet), convert the photo to a vector graphic, and then draw robotic parts over the image.

Build a robot factory: Create a starter robot sprite that contains many different shapes, which can be mixed and matched to quickly create a bunch of bots.

Activate your robot: After you finish your robot design, duplicate the costume and make subtle changes, such as the arms retracting or weapons popping out.

Digital Collages

"So what?" That's what some kids (maybe a bunch of kids) thought when they raced past this chapter to get to other projects they thought might be cooler. Maybe you were even one of those kids. Have you returned to Chapter 5 wondering, "What does this guy mean by digital collages? I have created tons of collages, some for school, and some for fun. What's different about a digital collage made in Scratch?"

When I was a kid, I might have skipped right past this chapter, too. But, can I share another secret with you? This is now one of my FAVORITE chapters. I actually LOVE the idea that only a select few of my Dummies readers will even look at it, because that means YOU must take collage pretty seriously. Well, now you get to explore some SERIOUSLY SENSATIONAL techniques for collaging right inside Scratch.

The Diary of Anne Frank

Before you create your Scratch collage project, choose a theme or central idea that you wish to convey with your unique blend of images (unless your teacher already has chosen one for you in the form of HOMEWORK!). I will use one of my favorite themes: *potato salad.* Don't you just love how that blend of mayo and mustard and chopped spuds mixed with. . . . Just kidding! My first collage theme will be a bit more universal: friendship.

Create a New Project

1. Go to scratch.mit.edu or open the Scratch 2 Offline Editor.

2. If you are online, click Create. If offline, select File⇨New.

3. Name your project. (Online, just select the title and type **Digital Collage**; offline, select File⇨Save As and type **Digital Collage**.)

4. Delete the cat by selecting the Scissors and clicking the cat or by right-clicking the cat and choosing *Delete.* (Come on, you didn't think I would want that annoying cat to be part of my COLLAGE, did you!?)

Choose sprites

You will start by whipping up a quick collage using images contained in the Sprite Library. (Feel free to skip ahead a few pages if you'd rather jump to importing your own images.)

1. Click Choose Sprite from Library.

2. Click People, so you only see human beings, and then Bitmap, so you can use the bitmap painting tools. (You will be using vector tools a bit later.)

3. Double-click any sprite you want. (I will stick to people for now, starting with *Cassy Dance* because I like her pose.)

4. Select several more people the same way. (I will add *Amon, Jodi,* and *Breakdancer2* because they already look like they could be friends.)

 Browsing for images can be one of the really fun parts of designing a collage. BUT, browsing for images also can swallow HUGE chunks of time. Limit your image searches to 10 or 15 minutes at first, start your collage, and then go back to browsing after you have a better idea of how images might go together.

Start Composing Elements

Composition is the arrangement of stuff on a page, canvas, or the Scratch Stage, and *elements* are the stuff. (These are the kinds of words that make you sound smarter than the average dummy, not to mention a professional digital artist.) Take a few minutes to move the different characters around. If you click each sprite and click the Costumes tab, you might find that some have multiple costumes with a different pose.

As a digital artist, I am looking at two elements while trying out different arrangements of sprites. And by elements, I mean different compositions! The first is obvious. I'm looking at which poses work and how the figures might fit together. The second is less obvious but REALLY important, especially in collage. In art school, they call this second element *negative space*. In dummy terms, that's the empty space around and between sprites.

Why would all that negative space be important for a collage? Because that's where all the stuff that is not your main characters can fit. In art lingo, the characters are *foreground elements,* or the stuff you want to stay in the front. That's why it makes sense to start with the foreground sprites and then gradually fill in the background.

Choose a background

I'm having trouble deciding exactly where I want the people in my friendship collage to appear. Before messing around with rotation and flipping and other ways to change costumes, maybe putting in a backdrop will help me figure out the best way to arrange them.

1. Click the Choose Backdrop from Library icon (below the Stage).

2. You can choose any backdrop you like, but I suggest going with a photograph (versus an illustration). I'll go with *Brick Wall2* because I think the characters will look good against it.

See, don't my characters look great against the brick wall? Well, okay, not yet. But, if I put a few more minutes into arranging them against the new backdrop. . . .

Hey, I like the idea of stacking them, a bit like cheerleaders. Now, I wish there were more people sprites that I liked.

Duplicate sprites

Something about the poses of *Cassy* and *Amon* gives me the idea of duplicating and flipping both of them. Using copies of some of the elements is a common collage technique.

1. Duplicate a few of your characters by right-clicking the sprite or by holding the Shift button while you click the sprite and then choosing *Duplicate*.

2. To flip a character, select its Costumes tab and then click the Flip Left-Right button.

3. See whether the doubled poses give you any new "composition" ideas for your collage.

   I'll duplicate all but one sprite, *Jodi,* so she can be the center of attention. This gives the sense everybody else is *her* friend.

In case you haven't noticed, clicking and dragging a sprite across the stage brings it to the front layer. This is how I decide whether you see these friends' hands on feet or feet on hands (or heads). If you want to bring a sprite to the front layer without changing its position, click and hold the cursor in place for a few seconds.

Add more elements

Before adding new elements, take a moment to think about your theme again. Close your eyes if it helps. Heck, go ahead and hum a song. (The first one that comes to my mind is "With a Little Help From My Friends" by The Beatles — and YES, they REALLY DID spell their band name that way!)

 Are you back? Now make your stage full-screen to see how it looks without all the Scratch buttons and tools and window stuff in the way.

I think I have enough people. I'd like to add an object or two. Back to the Sprite Library!

1. Click Choose Sprite from Library.

2. Click Things and Bitmap.

3. Double-click a sprite that fits your theme or evolving composition. The *Fortune Cookie* sprite gives me an idea. . . .

4. Click and drag your sprite(s) into position on the Stage.

Replacing *Jodi*'s head with a giant fortune cookie was not my *first* idea, but I could not resist. This brings to mind the idea of scale.

Transform Your Sprites

By *transform,* I don't mean turning your people into robots (that's *so* last chapter!). On the Paint canvas, you can use the Select tool to rotate and resize sprites. I want to resize and rotate the fortune cookie.

1. Select the sprite you want to transform and click the Costumes tab.

2. Click the Select tool.

3. Click and drag across the image on the Paint canvas.

4. Hold the Shift key while clicking and dragging a corner to evenly resize the selected image. (I am decreasing the size a bit.)

5. Click and drag left or right on the top handle (small circle) to rotate the selection.

6. Click another tool or click directly on the Stage to see the changes applied to your composition.

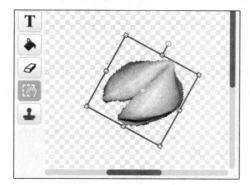

When working with bitmap graphics, you should avoid increasing the size because the more you scale up, the lower the image quality will be, due to pixelation.

Now I bet you're thinking, "What does that fortune cookie have to do with the theme of friendship?"

Adding Vector Graphics

The idea I had for the fortune cookie is to add a paper fortune about friendship. Vector graphics are a better choice than bitmap graphics for this because I will have more control of the paper background and the text.

Bitmap sprites and vector sprites handle text very differently. In Vector mode, you have much more control. You can resize text at any time, edit your text whenever you want, and increase the text size without it ever becoming pixelated or blurry.

You can save time by typing your fortune message first and then drawing the paper rectangle behind it (rather than trying to guess how big you will need the fortune paper to be).

1. Click the Paint New Sprite icon.

Convert to vector

2. Click the Convert to Vector button in the Paint Editor.

T

3. Click the Text tool, select a font (I'll choose *Donegal*), and choose a dark color swatch (I'll go with black).

4. Click near the left edge of the Paint canvas and type your fortune.

   If you need to resize your text, click the Select tool, hold the Shift key (to resize evenly), and then click and drag any corner.

5. Click the Rectangle tool, choose the Solid option, and select the white color swatch.

6. Click, drag, and release with the left mouse or trackpad button to draw the fortune paper right over the text message.

7. Click the Back a Layer button to send the paper behind the text message.

8. On the Stage, click and drag the cookie to the left side of the message (so it appears to be coming out of the cookie).

I had a bit of trouble getting the text into exactly the right spot on the paper and next to the fortune cookie. A great solution is to click the text with the Select tool on the Paint canvas, look at the cookie and text on the Stage, and click the arrow keys to nudge your text just one pixel (a tiny bit) at a time until it is in exactly the right place.

Make your Stage full screen again and see how your collage looks. I see so many things I could improve (like the bits of white around some of my characters and how jagged some parts are). Adding a vector graphic can make the bitmap graphics look pretty bad, especially when you zoom to full screen. Rather than spending more time fixing or adding elements, let's jump to a VITAL TOPIC for designing collages: importing your own images into Scratch!

Friends are the ones who always support you

Designing Advanced Collages

If you compare the basic collage from the previous section with the Anne Frank collage at the beginning of the chapter, you will notice many differences. I do not want to say one is better than the other is (especially because I am the one who designed BOTH of them), but you can imagine which one I put more time and effort into, right?

Friends are the ones who always support you

I want to share many of the techniques I have developed through the years (along with a few I've kept secret until now) so you can create more sophisticated collages, too. Rather than building on the friendship collage, it will be easier to start from, you guessed it: from SCRATCH!

Getting into a Great Collage

One key difference between my two collages is that one relies almost entirely on sprites from the Sprite Library while the other is composed mostly of imported images. I found the images in my second collage where most people go for photos these days, the World Wide Web.

Many of you probably have learned about piracy at school. I'm not talking about Captain Jack Sparrow and his drunken sailors. I mean the kind of piracy where you download movies or music or photographs that you have not paid for. It is illegal to use most images found online unless you have been given permission. This can all get pretty complicated, so I thought I would give you a few links to websites where you have permission to download and use the images any way you want. (These images are called *public domain;* they're free for the public to use.)

✔ Wikimedia Commons: `commons.wikimedia.org`

✔ The Library of Congress: `loc.gov/pictures`

✔ Pics4Learning: `pics4learning.com`

I found most of the photos in the Anne Frank collage on Wikimedia Commons (which is tied to Wikipedia). The other photographs I found using Google Image search. (You can use a filter to see just public domain images on Google.com. Type in the topic you are searching for and then choose Images⇨Search Tools⇨Usage Rights⇨Labeled for Reuse.)

Importing images

You do not have to create the same collage as mine. You can follow along with the steps I take to make the Anne Frank collage while using your own photos to create a more personalized collage. This could become a great gift for a friend or somebody special in your family (and might come in handy for future school family tree projects, too).

So STOP using Scratch RIGHT NOW. STEP AWAY FROM THE COMPUTER! Go find a family album or pull a few framed photos off the wall (carefully, please). Some of you might be able to find some good shots on Facebook or Flickr or some other website if you have enterprising people who have done the hard work for you. If you know of famous people that you are related to, perhaps you could find them online, too.

If your photos are already digital and you have access to them on your computer, you can skip to the "Upload sprite images" section. Those of you who do not have the photos on your computer yet have three options:

1. If they are on a digital camera, phone, or tablet, transfer them to your computer via a USB cable, flash media, or email to yourself.

2. If they are in a photo album or framed photograph, remove them and use a scanner or digital camera to capture your images and then transfer them as in Step 1.

3. If your laptop or computer has a webcam, you can hold a photo in front of the camera and click the New Sprite from Camera icon.

Having trouble using the webcam? You may need to follow a few extra steps the first time you use a webcam with Scratch. You can find more specific instructions on how to set up a webcam at the end of Chapter 2.

Upload sprite images

The Scratch team made it easy to upload images as new sprites, additional costumes inside a sprite, or backdrop images for the stage. For collages, I find importing each image as a new sprite gives you the most flexibility in laying out your composition.

1. Click Upload Sprite from File.

2. Navigate to where the photo is on your computer and double-click to import.

Try the Photos or Downloads folder or on your desktop because many photos end up in one of those places.

When you add images to Scratch, they will automatically be resized to fit the stage (which is 480 pixels wide and 360 pixels tall). Most smartphones and digital cameras create images WAY larger than this. So, if you are taking photos specifically for a Scratch project, get as close to the subject as you can and orient your photo horizontally (landscape) if you want it to fill the Stage.

Erase Part of an Image

Is there anything you want to remove from your photograph? I'm sure you know which tool you need. Yes, the Erase tool.

1. Right-click or Shift-click *Costume1* and then choose *Duplicate* to preserve the original copy.

2. Use the Erase tool to remove unwanted portions of the photo.

You might find the Select tool handy for removing larger portions.

 3. Click the Select tool, click and drag over the area you want to remove, and then click the Delete key on your keyboard.

Hide and show sprites

If you have a bunch of images (I'll have eight), hiding some of them at first might be helpful. Shift-click each sprite you want to hide and select *Hide*. Now, you can move the remaining images around the Stage and gradually unhide sprites when you are ready to include them in your composition.

Erase around jagged edges

Any dummy can use the Erase tool on the Paint canvas to erase part of a sprite, right? When I began my collage, the photo I chose of Anne Frank looked like this:

What if I want to erase the background of the photo, the gray area around Anne's head? Have you noticed one of the hardest things to erase around is hair? Another is grass or trees — pretty much anything with jagged edges.

1. Expand the Paint canvas by clicking the small triangle on the border beside the Stage (or choose Edit⇨Small Stage Layout).

2. Click the sprite you want to edit, click the Costumes tab, Shift-click the costume you want to modify, and select *Duplicate*.

   You will make all changes to the copy, preserving the original in case you go too far with the changes and want to start over.

3. Click the Erase tool.

4. Drag the slider to increase the eraser size.

5. Click and drag in the photo to remove larger areas.

6. Gradually reduce the size of the eraser to match the smallest areas you want to remove.

   For tight areas, move your eraser into place and click one time (rather than dragging across). Then you can move your eraser to another spot and click again. If you're removing outer parts, move your cursor to the area where you want to start erasing and then click and move toward the edge of the image.

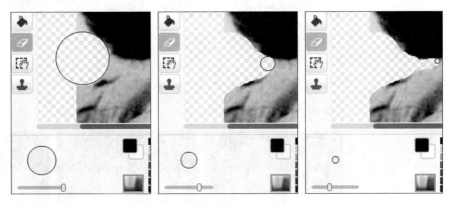

Erase complex shapes from bitmaps

This one will REALLY impress your friends! Do you know you can convert a bitmap graphic into a vector graphic? To cut out the area around the Star of David image, I need to convert the bitmap photograph into a vector graphic and then convert the vector graphic back into a bitmap graphic.

If you are creating your own collage with custom images, you can use this trick to cut out images or create different-shaped holes to see through an image to the layer beneath.

1. Click one of your bitmap sprites. (I'll click the star photograph.)

2. Click the Costumes tab, Shift-click the costume (there will be only one if you imported the image), and then select *Duplicate*.

Convert to vector 3. Click the Convert to Vector button.

 4. Click the Rectangle tool, choose the Outline option, and select a green color swatch (or a color that is not in your image).

5. Click, drag, and release with the left mouse or trackpad button to draw a rectangle that covers the top half of the image.

6. Click the Reshape tool, click one time inside the shape to select it, and then click and drag each corner of the rectangle to fit one corner of the star.

 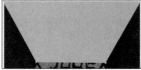 

7. Click between line points on the edge of the shape to add a new line point.

8. Drag that line point outward to a point on the star.

9. Continue until the top half of the star is covered.

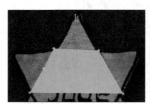  

Now turn your shape inside-out. WHAT?! How can you turn a two-dimensional (2D) shape inside out? Remember what I said about negative space? You want to modify your shape from being on the top half of the star to cover the top half of the emptiness you will be erasing.

1. Still using the Reshape tool, click the bottom edge of your shape to create a new point and then click again for a second point.

2. Drag the two new line points above the star, right off the Paint canvas.

3. Click near the edge to add another line point on each side.

Now, how do you select the rest of the background on the top half of the image? Why did we add another line point on each side?

1. Click and drag the new line points down and out.

2. Add a new point for each remaining star corner, dragging each to the corner on the star.

Great work! Now just one more point and then it's time for the real magic.

1. Click to create the last line point and drag it to the bottom of the star.

2. You may need to drag the outer corner points off the canvas to make sure you have selected the entire background.

3. Shift-click the costume you have been working on and duplicate it.

Duplicate it again? That's not MAGICAL! Nevertheless, you just did all that work and if something goes wrong with the "trick," you do not want to have to do it again, do you? Plus, that shape might come in handy later. Okay, NOW for the MAGIC! (I REALLY mean it this time.)

Remember how I said you would be converting a bitmap graphic to a vector graphic and then back to bitmap? Have you figured out why yet? Just one more second. Watch THIS:

1. Click the Convert to Bitmap button. (It may take several seconds. You'll know it's finished when your tools jump to the left side.)

2. Click the Fill with Color tool and select the Fill option and the Empty color swatch (white with red diagonal line).

3. Move the cursor into the shape and click one time.

Now THAT'S what I'm TALKING ABOUT! Isn't that COOL? I know it was a lot of steps, but doing the same thing with the Erase tool in Bitmap mode would take WAY longer, WAY more steps, and would not look nearly as sharp.

If you still see thin lines of the original background, just use the Erase or Select tool to remove them quickly. If there is a bit of color on the edge, that will be less noticeable after the next collage technique on blending sprites.

That vector shape you created to cover part of the image is a *mask,* just like masking tape, which you use to cover edges of windows while painting your bedroom wall. Now, don't go telling your parents I gave you permission to repaint your bedroom (unless it's a virtual makeover inside Scratch)!

Modify Sprites with Visual Effects

Did you happen to notice how some of the foreground sprites were a bit transparent, so you could see part of the image behind them? This method of blending photographs and other graphics together takes a tiny bit of programming in Scratch, but the results are totally worth it!

Make sprites transparent

For now, you will just make two elements of your collage transparent. (I will stick with Anne Frank's portrait and the star image.)

1. Click the first sprite you want to make transparent (I'll click Anne's portrait) and then click the Scripts tab.

2. Drag the WHEN GREEN FLAG CLICKED and SET EFFECT TO blocks into the Scripts Area.

3. Inside the SET EFFECT TO block, click where it says *Color* and select *Ghost.*

4. In the same block, click the *0* (zero) and type **30**.

Now, if you click the Green Flag button above the Stage, your sprite should suddenly appear transparent. (See why they call it the "ghost" effect?)

When you click the Stop button above the Stage, the sprite effects turn off until you click the Green Flag button again.

You could follow the same steps to make your next sprite transparent, too, but here is a shortcut.

1. Go to the Scripts area on the sprite you just modified, click the WHEN GREEN FLAG CLICKED block, and drag the code blocks over to the icon of the other sprite (beneath the Stage) that you wish to make transparent.

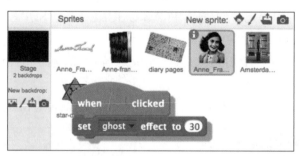

2. Click the second sprite, and you should see that the WHEN GREEN FLAG CLICKED and SET EFFECT TO blocks have been copied.

3. Change the value from *30* to *50* so the second sprite (the star for me) will blend a bit more.

4. Click the Green Flag button to see your changes.

 You can drag as many code blocks from one sprite to another, but they must be snapped together to copy over. You also can drag costumes and sounds from one sprite to another.

Adjust sprite brightness

I included the image of Anne Frank's signature in the previous images to show the importance of color. See how it almost pops out at you when placed in front of the transparent images?

Another way to draw attention to specific images or to make others less noticeable is by adjusting brightness. I would like to draw a bit more attention to Anne Frank's portrait by making the building behind her (where she hid with her family) appear darker.

1. Click the sprite you want to adjust.

2. Drag the following blocks into the Scripts Area and change the values to match.

3. Click the Green Flag button (or click right on the code block) to see the change.

4. Keep adjusting the brightness value for your sprite until you find the look that works best for your image.

Making the photograph of the building a bit darker made it blend better with the bookcase, so there is not such a distinct line between them. You also can use the brightness effect to draw attention to your most important element. What happens if I add a SET BRIGHTNESS EFFECT TO block with a value of *20* to the Anne portrait?

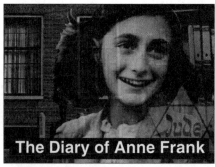 

Adjust sprite color

A SET EFFECT TO block also enables you to adjust the color of sprites. It works best on brightly colored sprites.

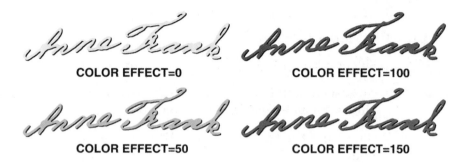

COLOR EFFECT=0   COLOR EFFECT=100

COLOR EFFECT=50   COLOR EFFECT=150

For black-and-white sprites (or *grayscale*), the color effect adds a subtle tint.

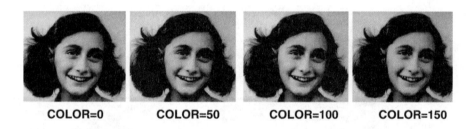

COLOR=0   COLOR=50   COLOR=100   COLOR=150

Remember how you hid some of your sprites? Now, you can gradually unhide each one (Shift-click the icons beneath the Stage and select *Unhide*) and try out different color, brightness, and ghost effects. Isn't this a blast? (Or am I having too much fun? I'm a Scratch nerd, aren't I?)

If you wish to reset sprites to their original appearance while your project is still running, use the CLEAR GRAPHIC EFFECTS block.

Use Vector Text for Title

The image of the signature in my collage is actually a vector graphic. But, just for you, I will hide the signature (by Shift-clicking and choosing *Hide*) and create a new sprite using the Vector Text tool.

1. Click Paint New Sprite.

2. Click the Costumes tab.

3. Click the Convert to Vector button.

4. Click the Text tool.

5. Select a font. (I'll use Helvetica for my title.)

6. Choose your color swatch. (I'll go with yellow because it shows up well against a dark background.)

7. Click near the left edge of the Paint canvas and type a title for your collage. (You can edit the title later since it's a vector sprite!)

8. If you need to resize your text, click the Select tool, hold the Shift key (to resize evenly), and then click and drag any corner.

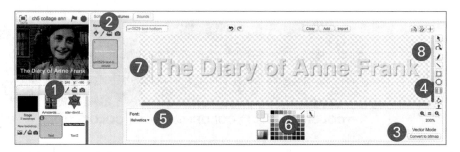

You may need to drag your text sprite into position on the Stage and then adjust it again on the Paint canvas. I often go back and forth until it's just right. I positioned my title near the bottom so as not to obstruct Anne's face or the writing on the star.

It can be hard to choose a text color when there is a mix of light and dark colors in the background. You can solve this problem by placing a contrasting rectangle behind your text (dark rectangle with light-colored text or light-colored rectangle with dark text).

1. Select the sprite that contains your title and click the Costumes tab.

  2. Click the Rectangle tool.

3. Choose the Outline option.

4. Click a color swatch that contrasts your text color.

5. Click outside the top left of the text and drag past the lower-right corner to completely contain the text.

6. Click the Color a Shape tool and click inside the rectangle to fill it in.

7. Click the Select tool and click the rectangle to select it.

8. Click the Back a Layer button.

Finish Up Your Collage

After reviewing my progress, I noticed I forgot to include one of the most important photographs: Anne Frank's diary. Studying the composition of the other sprites on the Stage, I see more images on the right side, so I'll unhide the diary photo and arrange it on the left side. I'm deciding against making the journal transparent, too, so it seems a bit more real.

I am almost satisfied, but I have one more idea. I need to rearrange some of the sprites to finally come up with my favorite layout.

The Diary of Anne Frank

I just gotta say that I am really happy with my Anne Frank collage. I think the quality of the work is a reflection of the deep admiration I have for such a heroic girl (and a FANTASTIC writer).

Ryan doesn't have anything against Anne Frank, but he's not too likely to do entire collages around a girl's photograph. He did a REALLY cool collage about one of HIS heroes, Harry Houdini. His project shows an entirely different approach of compositing images together so the whole becomes more meaningful than the parts.

Use collage techniques for . . .

These techniques can be used for more than just making collages. You can also:

- Combine different elements like sky, clouds, trees, hills, and grass for really classy backdrops.

- Change the color of sprites from the library for more diversity.

- Have text effects change over time, such as for animated cards and school or club presentations.

- Combine vector and bitmap graphics to change character outfits.

- Gradually add weapons, tools, and other items to game characters by adding vector shapes to additional costumes.

Part 2

Become a Scratch Animator . . .

Animation Essentials... 129

Animate Great Characters.............................. 152

Location, Location, Location........................... 176

Sounds Good to Me 197

Lights, Camera, ACTION! 217

You can watch completed animations and even scan through the sprites, costumes, backdrops, sounds, and code that brings them all to life at www.scratch4kids.com/animation.

Animation
Essentials

This is where I am supposed to talk about the history of animation and describe all the different kinds and give a bunch of examples and . . . [yawn] . . . NO THANKS! Maybe I am a complete dummy, but wouldn't you rather start animating right NOW?

In this chapter, you begin with one of the simplest forms of animation, stick figures, to tell a short story. An obvious advantage of stick figures is they are almost as easy to animate as they are to draw (especially in Vector Mode).

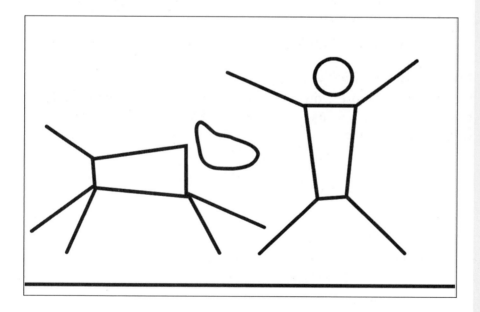

Draw Your First Character

In the old days, before computers, an artist had to hand draw or paint ten or more images for every SECOND of animation. If you wanted to make a one-minute animation, then you would need to create at least 600 pictures! I don't know about you, but it would take me many weeks to do that. Fortunately, several Scratch tricks and shortcuts enable you to draw just a few images and then modify them with either the vector tools or various code blocks.

Create new project

1. Go to `scratch.mit.edu` or open the Scratch 2 Offline Editor.

2. If you are online, click Create. If offline, select File⇨New.

3. Name your project. (Online, select the title and type **Stick Figure Animation**. Offline, select File⇨Save As and type **Stick Figure Animation**.)

4. Delete the cat. (Shift-click and select *Delete*.)

Draw body parts

For your stick figure, you need a circle for a head, a rectangle for a body, and lines for arms and legs. Initially, drawing the parts separately might be easier.

1. Click the Paint New Sprite icon.

2. Click the Costumes tab.

3. Click the Convert to Vector button (bottom-right corner of the Paint Editor).

4. Click the Zoom In button one time for 200% scale. (This makes it easier to work on your character.)

5. Click the Ellipse tool.

6. Click the Outline option to the left of the color swatches.

7. Drag the Line Width slider to adjust the line thickness.

8. Choose the black color swatch.

9. Click and drag to draw a small, hollow head.

   Remember you can hold the Shift key to draw a perfect circle.

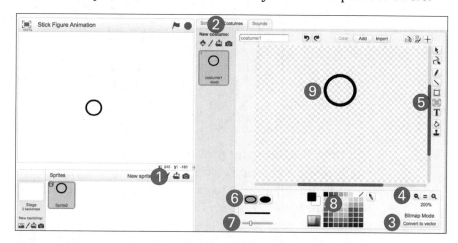

 10. Use the Rectangle tool to draw a hollow body.

 11. Use the Line tool to draw the arms and legs.

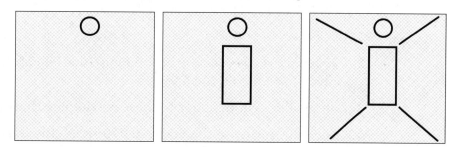

I would never want to animate a stick figure in Bitmap Mode because I would miss out on using one of the most valuable tools: the Reshape tool.

Sculpt the body with the Reshape tool

Here's how to make the rectangle more of a human shape and connect the arms and legs.

 1. Click the Reshape tool and click the body outline.

2. Click and drag each corner of the body into a new position.

3. Click and drag the end of each arm onto the top body corners where the shoulders would be.

4. Click and drag the top of each leg onto the bottom body corners.

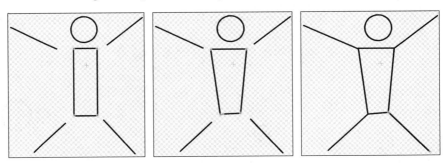

See how the Reshape tool helps you modify your stick figure easily? Because you have been working zoomed in to 200% on the Paint Editor canvas, check to see how your figure looks on the Stage. My lines appear a bit too thin.

Adjust the thickness of multiple lines

Fortunately, there is a quick way to adjust all the lines that make up your sprite as long as you are in Vector Mode. In Bitmap Mode, you would have to trace each line.

 1. Click the Select tool.

2. Click and drag across the entire figure on the Paint Editor canvas to select all the lines.

 3. Use the Line Width slider to increase the line thickness.

4. Check the sprite on the Stage to determine the best thickness for your figure.

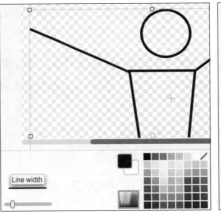 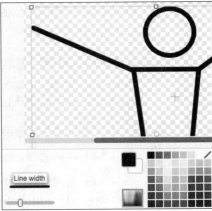

Animate the Stick Figure

In Scratch, you can animate your character two ways: Changing its position on the Stage or switching costumes within a sprite. Say you want your character to do a few jumping jacks; you already have the arms-and-legs-out pose, so you just need to create the arms-and-legs-in pose.

1. Shift-click *Costume1* and select *Duplicate*.

 2. Select the Reshape tool, click the left arm, and then click and drag the hand end down.

3. Repeat Step 2 for the other arm and both legs.

4. Click back and forth between *Costume1* and *Costume2* to see the change.

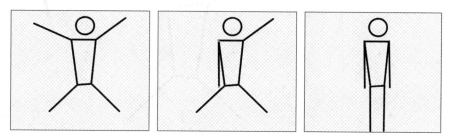

When I alternate clicking between *Costume1* and *Costume2,* something looks wrong. Instead of looking like jumping jacks, it's more as though my character is lying down and making snow angels.

When you do a jumping jack, you are not just waving your arms and your legs. Your body moves, too. How do you show the entire body moving? You need something that remains stationary while the body moves up and down.

Draw a simple backdrop

I hope you are ready for this. . . . Draw a straight line! Just one line representing the ground will make a big difference. Trust me. I suggest using Vector Mode to keep your graphics consistent and to modify the backdrop later, if you desire.

1. Click the Stage icon to the left of your stick figure sprite.

 2. Click the Convert to Vector button.

 3. Use the Line tool to draw a black line all the way across the Paint Editor canvas near the bottom of the window. Hold the Shift key to avoid a slanted line.

4. You may need to use the Line Width slider to adjust the line thickness the way you did for your stick figure. (Compare your figure and the new line on the Stage.)

Adjust movement against the backdrop

In each jumping jack pose, the feet should be on the ground. What if you treat the bottom of the Paint Editor canvas as the ground for all your costumes?

1. Click your stick figure sprite and then click *Costume1* on the Scripts tab.

 2. Use the Select tool to click and drag over the entire figure.

3. Click the Down-Arrow key on your keyboard several times until the stick figure's feet line up with the bottom of the Paint Editor canvas.

4. You may need to use the Reshape tool to align the bottom of each leg with the bottom of the window.

5. Repeat Steps 1–4 for *Costume2*.

Why use the Down-Arrow key when you can just click and drag? Because you don't want to move the sprite left or right accidentally (which would make the animation appear jittery).

Return to the Stage, click your stick figure, and then drag it so that the bottom of each leg aligns with the ground. If you alternate between *Costume1* and *Costume2,* the feet should now remain on the ground.

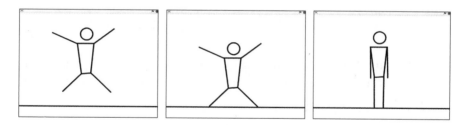

But, something is still missing. . . . Stand up and do a few jumping jacks. Seriously! One thing you need to do as an animator is act out each movement.

Do your feet stay in contact with the floor the entire time? Of course not. Why do they call them *jumping* jacks? Because you jump up!

Putting the jump in jacks

Right now, if you alternate costumes, it's like the feet just slide across the floor. You need to add a pose between *Costume1* and *Costume2* with the arms and legs midway between the other poses and the body above the ground. This also is a good time to rename the costumes so you don't get confused.

1. Click *Costume1*, select the costume name, and type **Arms Up**.

2. Click *Costume2* and rename it **Arms Down**.

3. Shift-click the *Arms Up* costume and select *Duplicate*.

4. Click and drag the new costume up so it comes between *Arms Up* and *Arms Down*.

5. Rename the middle costume **Arms Mid**.

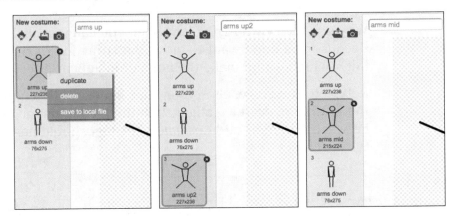

Since the feet are at the bottom of the canvas, you need to select and move the entire figure up before repositioning the legs.

1. Click the Select tool.

2. Click and drag over the entire stick figure to select all the body parts.

3. Click the Up Arrow key 50 times.

4. Use the Reshape tool to drag the ends of the arms and legs closer together.

The bottom of the legs should remain above the floor for the jump. If you want the man to jump a bit higher, reselect all the parts and click the Up-Arrow key several more times.

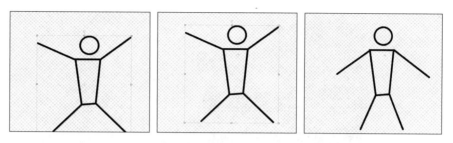

Now that there are three costumes, it's more of a challenge to click through them to see the animation, so this is a good place to add a bit of code to your character.

Animate with Code Blocks

The more familiar you are with Scratch code blocks, the quicker you can finish animation. You will start by creating a loop (just like the turtle in Chapter 2), which will allow you to repeat part of your animation as many times as you want. For ten jumping jacks, follow these steps:

1. Click the Scripts tab for *Sprite1*.

2. Drag the following blocks into the Scripts Area and change the values to match.

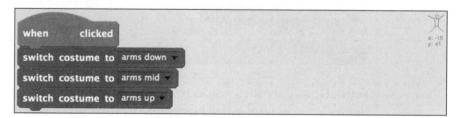

If you click the Green Flag button to test your code, what happens? Nothing *appears* to happen because the costume changes appear so fast you can't see them. You need to add WAIT blocks between the SWITCH COSTUME blocks to slow the change down enough for you to see it. The default of *1* second is too long, so try changing the value to **.25** for each block (for a quarter of a second).

Now when you click the Green Flag button, you should be able to see the costume changes. If you want your figure to do ten jumping jacks, you could drag a whole lot more blocks over or add just one REPEAT block.

Your stick figure should do ten jumping jacks, but they don't look right. Can you spot what is missing in the code? The figure starts in the arms down position, switches to arms mid, then arms up, and then skips back to arms down for the repeat. You need to add another arms mid position to smoothen the animation between each repeat. And each SWITCH COSTUME needs a WAIT block, too.

```
when       clicked
repeat 10
    switch costume to  arms down ▾
    wait .25 secs
    switch costume to  arms mid ▾
    wait .25 secs
    switch costume to  arms up ▾
    wait .25 secs
    switch costume to  arms mid ▾
    wait .25 secs
```

Click the Green Flag button and you should now see all the costume changes through ten jumping jacks. But there's still one more problem. When you do jumping jacks, don't you pause a moment in both your arms up and arms down positions? There should be a longer WAIT after those poses, right? I spent a few minutes trying different WAIT values and found these ones work best:

```
when       clicked
repeat 10
    switch costume to  arms down ▾
    wait .5 secs
    switch costume to  arms mid ▾
    wait .125 secs
    switch costume to  arms up ▾
    wait .5 secs
    switch costume to  arms mid ▾
    wait .125 secs
```

The jumping jacks should look much better when you click the Green Flag button. But, notice how it freezes on the last jumping jack mid-jump. You need one more SWITCH COSTUME block *after* the REPEAT block to bring your figure back to the upright position.

 Maybe I am in too much of a rush, but I don't want to have to sit through ten jumping jacks every time I make a change in my code. I usually use a smaller number while coding and then raise the value to ten (or 100) when I am happy with how the jumping jacks look.

Bring Humor to Your Animation

If you search YouTube or other online video sites, you can find thousands of hilarious stick figure animations. What do they all have in common? Like any story, your animation should have a beginning, a middle, and an end. But, what makes most of them funny? Usually, the element of surprise!

I know there is nothing surprising about a stick figure who does ten jumping jacks. If you want to make it funny, what could you add to surprise the audience? Right now, the jumping jacks are like a story that's just a middle (no beginning or ending).

To transform this scene into a funny story, you need to answer two questions:

1. Why is a stick figure doing jumping jacks?!

2. What could prevent the stick figure from finishing jumping jacks?

Watch just about any humorous scene and you will notice there is a character who really wants something and an obstacle preventing the character from getting it. In the Pixar movie *Up,* a grumpy old man wants to get away from everybody, so he straps all these balloons on his house and then takes off. What goes wrong? An annoying little Boy Scout flies off with him.

A stick figure doing a bunch of jumping jacks. . . . What if each jumping jack made his head a little bigger until it flies off like a balloon? What if his big balloon head whisks the rest of his body up, up, and away? Surprising, yes, but not exactly hilarious.

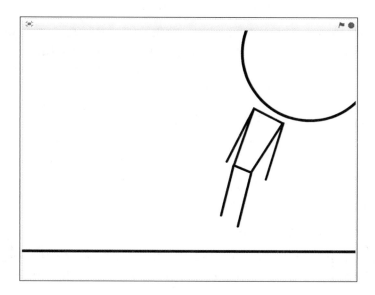

Maybe you need a second character, like the little boy in *Up,* or Batman in *The Lego Movie,* or Donkey in the *Shrek* movies, or the dog in . . . THAT'S IT! Let's give our stick person a stick pet! A dog that prevents him from finishing his morning exercises!

Add Stick Man's Best Friend

Here's another of my favorite Scratch stick-figure animation tricks. Instead of drawing a new character, you can duplicate your first character and reassemble the body parts (a bit like Dr. Frankenstein). This way, you make sure the characters are the right scale and look good together, too. And since there will be more than one character, you should give each a unique name.

1. Shift-click *Sprite1* and choose *Duplicate.*

2. To rename the two sprites, choose *Info* and then change the names.

   I will call the man *Sticky* and the second sprite *Woof.*

3. Click the Back button to exit Info view.

Surely you can come up with better names for your animation characters. I've been writing about Scratch animation all day. I'm just about out of creative juice, man!

You should now have two sprites. Click the *Woof* sprite's icon, go to the Costumes tab, and delete all but the first costume by clicking the small X on each costume's icon. The first costume will be the basis for the new character.

Modify parts to create a new character

You will use the Select tool to rotate the body and drag the other body parts into position. Then use the Reshape tool to sculpt the dog's head.

1. Click the Select tool.

2. Click the body shape.

3. Click the rotate handle (the small circle above the selected shape) and drag to rotate the body into a horizontal position.

4. Click and drag the arms and legs into position.

5. Click the Reshape tool.

6. Click the head, then click and drag the control points to sculpt it into more of a dog head shape.

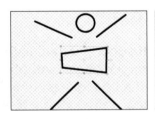 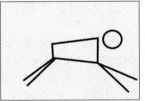 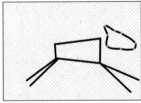

Develop your humorous story

The dog will be the obstacle to *Sticky* finishing morning exercise, but how can you start the story? Why is *Sticky* exercising? I can think of all kinds of reasons, but what would be a simple one that you could show quickly (so you do not have to spend HOURS animating)? Why do people work out and what might be funny? What if *Sticky* puts up a new poster of muscle stick man? It might be funny to see a skinny stick figure walk across the Stage and put up a poster of a stick figure with crazy muscles, eh?

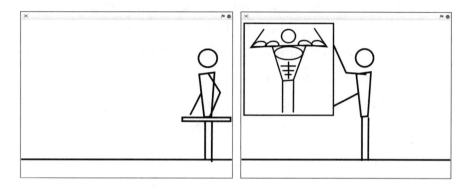

Then *Sticky* starts doing jumping jacks, but the dog runs over and nags him. *Sticky* ignores the dog until it jumps up and tears part of the poster, and *Sticky* ends up chasing the dog for so long, he ends up with huge leg muscles instead of arms, chest, and six-pack abs. That COULD be funny.

But, can you make it even easier so we can finish this first animation and get into even cooler techniques in the coming chapters? What if the poster is already on the wall when *Sticky* enters? The dog could be there, too. Then you just need to have the man enter the scene.

Walk Like a Man

Let's get *Sticky* onto the Stage as fast as possible, okay? Wait, he's already on the Stage. Get him OFF OF THERE!

1. Hide *Woof* for now by Shift-clicking the sprite and selecting *Hide*.

2. Select *Sticky* and change his costume to *Arms Down*.

3. Click and drag *Sticky* to the far-right side of the Stage.

You want *Sticky* to walk onto the Stage BEFORE doing the jumping jacks, so the new code needs to go between WHEN GREEN FLAG CLICKED and the REPEAT block. Snap the following code blocks right under WHEN GREEN FLAG CLICKED and change the values to match:

```
when      clicked
switch costume to  arms down ▾
go to x: 260  y: 38
glide 3 secs to x: 100  y: 38
wait 1 secs
```

If you click the Green Flag button to test your code, *Sticky* should begin at the right side of the screen, slowly move toward the middle, pause for one second, and then do the set of ten jumping jacks.

What if you add a sleeping pose to *Woof* and have the dog wake up when the man begins exercising?

Rotate parts with the Select tool

When working in Vector Mode, you have two primary tools for modifying the shapes within sprites: Select and Reshape. You used the Reshape tool on *Sticky* to move the end points of his arms and legs, which some people find faster and easier when using stick figures. The problem with this method is the lengths of the arms and legs are likely to change as you move points.

To preserve the length of lines while rotating, use the Select tool. With Vector shapes, you can even change the point around which they rotate by following these steps.

1. Shift-click the *Woof* icon and select *Show*.

2. Click *Woof* to select the sprite and then click the Costumes tab.

3. Shift-click the costume and select *Duplicate* (in case you want to use the original pose later).

4. Click to select the new costume and rename it *sleeping*.

 5. Click the Select tool and click one of the hind legs.

6. Shift-click the small circle in the center of the selection square and then drag it to the end of the leg where it meets the dog's hip.

7. Move your cursor to the circle outside the box until it turns into a circular arrow.

8. Click and drag the circular arrow to rotate the leg forward until it is under the dog's body.

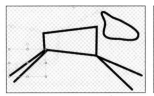 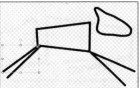 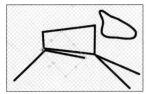

Go ahead and rotate the remaining three legs using the same steps, lower the head and the tail to look more like a sleeping dog, and then click and drag the sprite into position on the left side of the Stage.

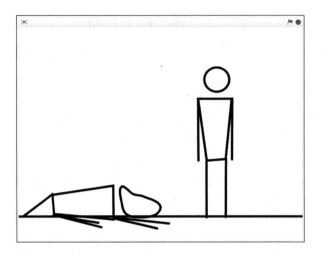

Animate the Dog

I think it's finally time to bring the dog to life, don't you? Design an awake costume for *Woof*.

1. Shift-click *Woof's* sleeping costume and choose *Duplicate*.

2. Rename the costume *wake*.

3. Click the Select tool.

4. Click and drag the dog's head up a bit (or you can use the Up-Arrow key for more precise movement).

5. Click and drag to rotate the tail up.

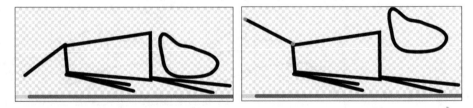

Add code to animate the stick dog

Timing is essential in animation, especially when you have two or more characters interacting. Can you figure out how many seconds the dog should wait until waking up? Look back at the code on *Sticky:* three seconds to glide in and then a one-second pause before starting the jumping jacks. So the dog should wait about five seconds, right?

1. Click the Scripts tab.

   If you duplicated the stick figure sprite to make the dog as I did, there will already be jumping-jack code there. Shift-click the WHEN GREEN FLAG CLICKED block and choose *Delete.*

2. Drag the following code blocks to the Scripts Area and change the values to match:

Click the Green Flag button and the dog should sleep for five seconds, then appear to wake up by lifting its head and tail. What might the dog do next? When I enter a room and a dog there wakes up, if it knows me, it usually starts wagging its tail.

Animate tail wagging

What would be a quick way to wag the tail? Just duplicate the *Wake* costume, rename the new costume *Wag,* and use the Select tool to rotate the tail again.

Use a REPEAT block to switch between the *Wake* and *Wag* costumes. I think we also should add a two-second delay between the dog first waking and then wagging its tail. (Surely dogs need a few seconds between waking and showing excitement.)

If you click the Green Flag button, the stick figure should glide across to the dog and start doing jumping jacks, and the dog's head should lift. The dog should wait two seconds and then wag its tail five times. I don't know about your animation, but mine doesn't look right.

```
when      clicked
switch costume to  sleep ▾
wait  5  secs
switch costume to  wake ▾
wait  2  secs
repeat  5
    switch costume to  wag ▾
    wait  0.25  secs
    switch costume to  wake ▾
    wait  0.25  secs
```

Talk Like a Man

The characters are stick figures, so I think it works best to "stick" (pretty hilarious, right?) to speech bubbles, rather than recorded sounds and voices. (You use digital audio in Chapter 9.) You could draw a speech bubble into a new costume or make a separate sprite, but I find using the SAY blocks easier.

I want my figure to speak WHILE doing jumping jacks. If I put a SAY block inside the REPEAT block, then *Sticky* will keep saying the same thing over and over until the last jumping jack is finished.

What is a poor little animator to do?

If you have done any of the game projects in this book, you may have noticed you can have different chunks of code running at the same time on different sprites and even within the same sprite. This means you can keep your current gliding and jumping jacks code blocks on the stick figure, add a second WHEN GREEN FLAG CLICKED block, and then use some more WAIT blocks to time your speaking.

1. Click the *Sticky* sprite icon and then click the Scripts tab.

2. Drag the new blocks into the Scripts Area to the right of the current set of blocks.

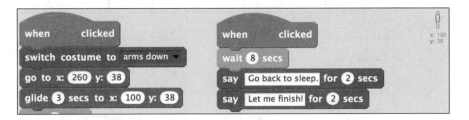

3. Click inside each SAY block and replace *Hello!* with whatever you want your stick figure to say (unless you want your character to say, "Hello. . . Hello!").

I will have my guy say, "Go back to sleep" and then "Let me finish!"

I am going to let you finish the animation on your own. You have all the tools and techniques you need to make *Woof* sit up, bark, do jumping jacks, and attack *Sticky*. The remaining choices are more about the story. What is the story you want to tell? How long do you want your story to go on? How funny can you make it?

If you get stuck, you can watch my completed version and review all the sprites, costumes, and code blocks at www.scratch4kids.com.

Improve your stick figure animation

You will be learning more about animating characters, designing complex backgrounds, and adding sound and special effects over the next several chapters. But, if you feel invested in your current animation and want to improve it even more, you could:

✔ **Add another character or two:** I could imagine a cat and/ or a parent adding to the hilarity.

✔ **Add a few props:** We touched on the idea of a poster earlier. What else could you add for *Sticky* or *Woof* (or other characters) to interact with?

✔ **Change the location:** What if the scene took place outside or in a more public place?

✔ **Add sound:** The more crazy the action gets, the more your scene may benefit from sound effects (such as growling, barking, and crashing).

CHAPTER

7

Animate Great Characters

You don't have to be Walt Disney or Seth MacFarlane or the *South Park* animators to make memorable characters. No matter how old you may be, I bet you know enough cool, weird, and funny people to fill ten animated films. Or maybe YOU should be the star of YOUR OWN!

In this chapter, you will create a unique cast of characters using vector drawing tools and learn a few design techniques to help bring them to life.

Keep It Simple, Stupid

When I was younger, I learned KISS means more than just smacking your lips into somebody. It can stand for Keep It Simple, Stupid. The more complex your characters are, the harder it is to animate them. So keep your character design simple, dummy!

If your goal is to create simple characters, doesn't it make sense to begin with a few simple shapes? When designing a new character, I often start with just three circles.

What do you see? A face, right? Now what happens if I move the eyes around?

Although the three circles are the same size, placing the eyes in different locations already begins to suggest three different characters. Add two smaller circles to each set of eyes . . .

. . . draw a simple line for a mouth . . .

. . . and then fill each face with a different color.

Wow, I don't know what you see, but I see a zombie, a person, and a werewolf!

I didn't start with the intention of drawing two monsters and an ordinary person. I just started moving around some circles and drew a few lines to see what kind of faces might emerge. To keep it simple, I will work with these faces, come up with a story that involves three characters, and explore ways to bring the characters and their world to life.

Getting a Head Start

Before starting, take a moment to think about the story you want to tell and the characters who would be the most fun to bring to life. If you don't have a good idea yet, don't worry, you can start messing around with a few characters and see where they lead you.

If you have never used the vector drawing tools before it may help to review Chapter 4, which provides a great introduction.

Create a new project

1. Go to `scratch.mit.edu` or open the Scratch 2 Offline Editor.

2. If you are online, click Create. If offline, select File➪New.

3. Name your project. (Online, select the title and type **Animation Characters**. Offline, select File➪Save As and type **Animation Characters**.)

4. Delete the cat!

Paint a new sprite

1. Click the Paint New Sprite icon.

2. Click the Costumes tab.

3. Click the Convert to Vector button.

4. Click the Ellipse tool.

5. Click the Outline option.

6. Choose the black color swatch.

7. Click and drag to draw a head and two eyes.

   You can hold the Shift key to draw a perfect circle.

8. Draw two more ellipses for eye pupils.

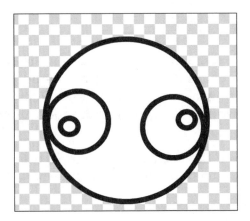

 If you want your eyes to be exactly the same size, you can use the Duplicate tool to make exact copies.

Is your character beginning to emerge? If not, perhaps a bit of hair will help.

Quick hair styling

You can draw hair with the Pencil tool or sculpt it by using the Reshape tool on an ellipse or rectangle. I will combine techniques to get a unique hairstyle for my zombie.

 1. Click the Ellipse tool.

2. Click the Solid option.

3. Choose a color swatch for your hair color.

4. Click and drag right over your character's face.

 5. Shift-click the Back a Layer button to send the hair to the bottom layer (behind the head and eyes).

Every time you use a new tool to draw a shape in Vector Mode, a new layer is created. This makes it easier to select individual shapes and to arrange which shapes appear over other shapes.

 6. Click the Reshape tool.

7. Click the hair to select it.

8. Click and drag control points to style your hair.

 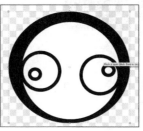 

The Pencil tool is better at drawing jagged shapes, like zombie hair bangs! (Zombie hair bangs sounds like a British punk band or a new weapon in *Plants vs. Zombies!*)

 1. Click the Pencil tool.

2. Choose a color swatch.

3. Click and drag to start drawing.

4. Drag the pencil back to the starting point to create a closed shape that can be filled with color.

 5. Click the Color a Shape tool and then click inside the new shape to fill it.

 Using the Pencil tool generally creates many more control points than the Line, Ellipse, or Rectangle tools do. Fortunately, you can use the Reshape tool to smoothen lines, which reduces the number of points and makes sculpting shapes and animating them later easier. Click any vector shape with the Reshape tool and the Smooth button will appear above the Line Width slider.

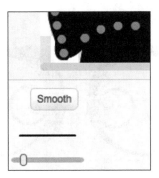

Open wide

What fun is a zombie without a mouth to bite off your arm or munch on your brains? Animating later will be easier if you begin with an open mouth, so draw an ellipse in the open position first.

 1. Click the Ellipse tool to draw the mouth open.

 2. Click the Reshape tool, click the mouth one time, and then click and drag points into the shape you want.

 3. Click the Color a Shape tool, choose a lip color, and click the edge of the mouth to create lips.

 4. Click the Select tool, click the mouth, and use the Line Width slider to adjust the line thickness.

Give 'em a nose job

Although some zombies may have lost a nose in their travels, I think my little ghoul could use a petite schnoz. Use the Pencil tool to draw yours and then the Reshape tool to smoothen it.

Nose placement can affect your character as much as the eyes and mouth, so you might want to try out a few positions before you lock in your face for all eternity.

A Little Body Work

When it comes to body parts, I usually prefer mine attached — unless I am getting ready to animate! Having the body, arms, and legs as separate objects within your sprite will allow you more movement options when it comes time to tell your story. And, to avoid getting in trouble for naked characters in my book, be sure to include clothing.

 1. Click the Ellipse tool, choose your outline color (I'll choose classic black), and draw an oval the approximate size you want for the body.

 2. Click the Color a Shape tool, choose a color for the character's shirt or dress, and click inside the initial body shape.

 3. Click the Reshape tool, click the body to select it, then click and drag points into the shape that looks best to you.

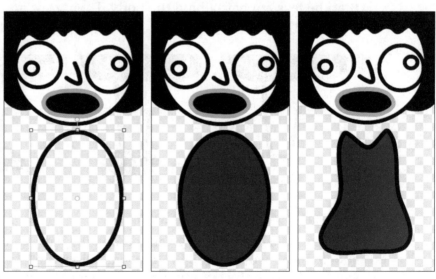

Add simple legs

You are about to see just how lazy I am. Although you can draw separate legs if you wish, I am going to invoke the KISS rule and take the easy way out!

You can use the Rectangle tool to draw the legs together, the Reshape tool to taper them at the ankles, and then fill them in with the pants, tights, or zombie skin color of your choice.

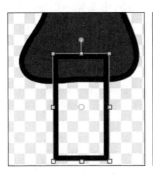  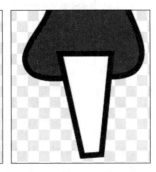

 Something doesn't look right. . . . Oh yeah! I don't want the zombie's dress to be too short. Shift-click the Back a Layer button so that the legs appear behind the body. Then draw an ellipse and reshape it into shoes.

 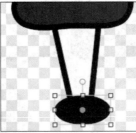 

Arming your characters

Although you can get away with combining legs, your character should have two arms, right? You can follow the lazy animator way by drawing the left arm and then using the ole' one-two punch of duplicate and flip.

1. Use the Ellipse tool to draw the left arm.

 2. Use the Reshape tool to refine the shape.

 3. Fill the shape with skin color. (I'll choose zombie-white).

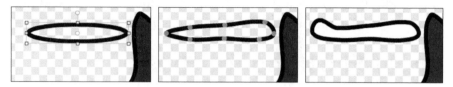

 4. Click the Duplicate tool, click the arm, and then drag the copy to the other side.

 5. Click the Flip Left-Right button.

 6. Click the Select tool and then drag the arm into the correct position.

Oops, I just noticed my character is missing a neck! Why not duplicate the leg shape and flip it vertically?

 1. Click the Duplicate tool, click the legs, and drag the new legs to where the neck should be.

 2. Click the Flip Up-Down button.

3. Shift-click the Back a Layer button.

I usually Shift-click the Back a Layer and Forward a Layer buttons while working on character designs. Otherwise, you could be click-click-clicking dozens of times because a layer is created for every object. To move several objects at once to another layer, you must first select and group them (the Group button will only appear when more than one object has been selected on the canvas).

Apply Finishing Touches

Take a moment to look at your new character on the Stage. Are there any little details you can add to make it stand out? I used the Reshape button to give the bottom of my zombie dress more of a torn look and decided to go with bluish skin and dull gray pupils. What do you think?

I know exactly what you are thinking: "That is so much work. How the heck will I be able to finish the other characters for my animation?"

The good news is you have already done a lot of the work for your other characters. The same way you duplicated parts of your character, you can now duplicate your entire character and simply apply a few changes to make a completely different person for your animation.

It's Okay to Clone Scratch People

In later chapters, you learn how to use CLONE blocks, but for now, you will just use the Duplicate tool.

1. Shift-click your first character sprite on the Stage and choose *Duplicate*.

2. Shift-click the first sprite again, click the Info button, and then rename the character. (I will call my zombie girl *Zomberta*.)

3. Rename the duplicate sprite. (This will be my werewolf, so I will name it *Werewoof*).

It took more than seven pages to get through the first character; let's see if we can pull off creating the next character in just one! Make sure you have your clone selected and then follow along.

From Dead Skin to Furry Beast

Some of the quickest ways to change a character are to swap colors, change the hair shape, and give the face a makeover.

1. Click the Color a Shape tool, choose your color, and click inside the shapes you wish to change.

My second character kind of looks like a chocolate zombie at this point. I think it's time to make that face a bit more ferocious!

 2. Click the Select tool, then click and drag the eyes and pupils into new positions.

 3. Click the Reshape tool, click each shape you wish to modify, then click and drag the points to create your character's new appearance.

4. Use the Reshape tool to change the eye and hair shapes.

Well, *Werewoof* is definitely headed in the right direction. But, with that empty mouth, it's hardly a ferocious beast.

Fangs Make the Beast

When drawing detailed shapes, like sharp teeth, either zoom in or draw the shape large and then shrink it to size.

1. Click the Line tool.

2. Click the Outline option.

3. Click the black color swatch.

4. Click and drag to draw one side of fangs.

5. Click back on first point to close the shape.

6. Click the Color a Shape tool, click the white swatch and click inside the shape.

 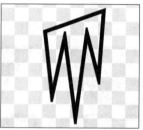 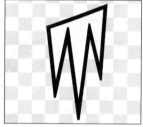

7. Click the Duplicate tool, click the first set of fangs, and drag them to the other side of the snout.

8. Click the Flip Left-Right button to flip the fangs.

9. Use the Select tool to drag the fangs into position.

10. Use the Reshape tool to adjust the mouth to fit the new snappers.

Ah, the fangs make my character much more ferocious, but he looks like he still looks like he's wearing a furry dress. Well who says *Werewoof* is a boy? Okay, then SHE looks like she's wearing a furry dress!

Undress the Beast

Before you just delete the dress (or some other body part), take a moment to think about whether it could serve another purpose. It occurs to me that if I resize it and move it up to the shoulders, it could look more like fur.

 1. Click the Select tool, click the dress, and then drag the bottom side up to make it shorter.

 2. Click and drag the fur up to the shoulder area.

 3. Click the Ellipse tool and then draw a new body shape.

 4. Click the Reshape tool, click the body, and then drag the points to make ribs.

 5. Click the Select tool, click the legs shape, and then resize the legs to fit.

Strike a Pose

I'm satisfied with the shape of my (somewhat cheesy) werewolf, but it looks weird with the arms outstretched in the zombie's pose. Quickly repositioning body parts is one of the reasons we went with Vector Mode. Not only can you move and rotate objects, but you can also change the center point around which body parts rotate (as you may have learned in the previous chapter).

 Duplicate a character's costume (Shift-click ⇨ *Duplicate*) before changing any pose to make returning to the original pose easy. Unless you WANT to re-create poses all week long.

1. Click the Select tool and then click the left arm.

2. Shift-click the small circle in the center of the selection square and drag it to the shoulder.

3. Move your cursor to the small circle above the selection box until it turns into a circular arrow.

4. Click and drag the circular arrow to rotate the arm.

5. Repeat Steps 1–4 for the right arm.

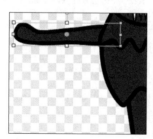 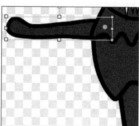 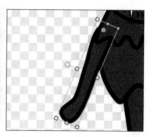

 You will have to readjust the center of rotation each time you rotate a body part, even if you moved it on a part before.

Add Finishing Touches

I may have gone a bit over my goal of transforming the zombie into a werewolf in just one page, but notice how much quicker it is than starting all over. Remember how we added a few details to make the zombie stand out? What would make the werewolf more *werewolfy?* Instead of standing up tall, how about changing to a crouching position?

1. Click the Reshape tool and then click the legs.

2. Shift-click and drag a new point and curve on each side.

3. Click the Select tool, click the legs, and drag up.

4. Click the feet and drag up to the new leg position.

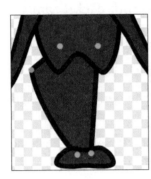 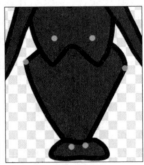 

Rotating the arms was not enough. Now that the werewolf is crouching, I want to bend the arms and add some claws! You could draw new claws, but your lazy author will simply duplicate the fangs and reshape them to fit each paw.

1. Click the Reshape tool and click the left arm.

2. Click and drag points into a bent arm position.

3. Click the Duplicate tool, click one set of fangs, and drag them to the left paw.

4. Click the Reshape tool, select the claws, and adjust the points.

5. Repeat Steps 5–8 for the right arm (or duplicate and flip the left arm and claw).

Create a Third Character

If you look at the two characters side-by-side, you would hardly guess they came from the same basic figure (unless you did all the work).

I set out to design three unique figures. The one remaining character is the regular person — who should have a lot to worry about in this company.

Now that you have two characters, decide which one is closer in shape to the new character you wish to create. In my case, *Zomberta* is more like a person than my crouching, snarling werewolf is, so I will duplicate her.

1. Shift-click the sprite you wish to copy and then choose *Duplicate*.

2. Shift-click the new sprite, click the Info button, and change the name. (I will name my person *Hector*. Why not?).

3. Click the Costumes tab.

From zombie girl to bland boy

You already transformed one character into another character, so I am going to move quickly this time. I will start by changing the skin and hair colors from zombie girl to ordinary boy. Then I will draw more boyish hair (you can use the Pencil or the old Reshape-on-an-Ellipse technique), reshape the nose, and move the pupils to the middle of his eyes.

 I am not saying there is anything wrong with a boy wearing a dress, but I want my character to have a bit more traditional boyish outfit to go with the story I have in mind. The dress shape is all wrong, so I will delete it, create a new shirt, and then color the legs to look like long pants.

Design character clothing

 I may want to create a regular girl character later (perhaps showing *Zomberta* before her zombie transformation) so, before changing the dress, I will duplicate the costume. You can even create a new sprite and drag the boy-in-a-dress costume to it if you plan to create a new character soon.

Using the Advanced Color Palette

Skin color can be a tricky thing to get right. By default, there are only 56 color swatches to choose from in the Paint Editor.

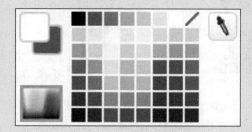

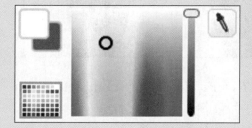 Fortunately, Scratch has a bunch more color options just a click away. Click the Switch Color Palette button at the bottom of the Paint Editor, just to the left of the color swatches, to switch to the Advanced Color Palette.

Click and drag that small circle inside the blended colors until you get the color you want and then use the Shade slider on the right side to make the color darker or lighter. You can use the Pick Up Color tool (the dropper beside each color palette) to select a color from any object on the Paint Editor canvas. This is important when using custom colors because they do not have an easy-to-find color swatch. To return to the basic swatches, click the Switch Color Palette button again.

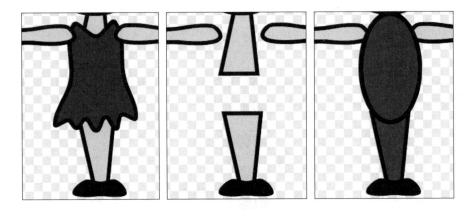

Use the Reshape tool to sculpt the ellipse into a t-shirt. You can click anywhere on the outline to add more points. I will add two points to each shoulder to get the sleeves right.

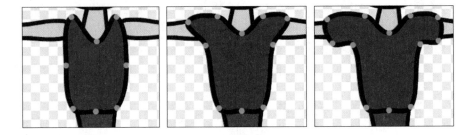

Now that *Hector's* clothes are complete, I'm no longer happy with how his face looks.

Tweak facial features

Use the Reshape and Select tools to experiment with different eyes and noses. It might also help to add eyebrows (tweaking the hair if you need more room for them).

I am much happier with how the eyes and nose look now. But, that mouth is kinda freakin' me out, man. It looks like somebody knocked the boy's teeth out. TEETH!

Add a set of teeth

Is there an easy way to add teeth? Of course!

1. Shift-click the costume and choose *Duplicate* (in case you want to use the wide-open-in-terror mouth shape later).

2. Click the Color a Shape tool and then choose the white color swatch.

3. Click inside the mouth to fill it with white.

4. Click the Line tool, choose the black color swatch, and then draw a straight line across the middle of the mouth.

5. Click the Reshape tool, click the mouth, and adjust the shape.

What an improvement a set of teeth can make to a face! So keep brushing your teeth or you'll end up looking like *Zomberta* some day!

Posing clothed figures

Although you already posed arms and legs with the werewolf figure, moving clothed characters involves a few extra steps. You can still use the Select tool to rotate the arms (remember to move the center of rotation), but you will also need to use the Reshape tool to adjust the shirt after the arms have been moved. Don't forget to duplicate the costume first in case you want the arms raised later!

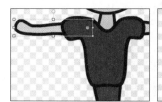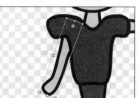

Assembling Your Cast

After following the same steps for the right arm, I wanted to see how the boy looks in comparison to his more gruesome animation mates, so I dragged all three into position on the Stage.

Even though I am proud of my design work, I see so many ways I could make the characters better. One of the hardest things in design is to decide whether your work is "good enough."

Katelyn and Ryan are better about saying, "It's done" than I am. They knocked out the following characters in 15 minutes for a puppet show set in the world of MINDcraft! That was before Ryan discovered *Terraria* and left his *Minecraft* addiction behind. Katelyn still has hers.

You can spend as much time as you want refining your character designs, but this section is about animation, so let's move on to building your scenes, adding sound, and using special effects to make your cartoons even more memorable.

Quick character improvements

If you simply MUST spend a bit more time working on your characters, here are some tips that might help.

✔ **Compare to other animation characters:** Spend a few minutes reviewing a few of your favorite characters from animated films or shows with a critical eye. What details help distinguish one character from another?

✔ **Add texture:** Bring your design skills to clothing by adding patterns, shapes, and texture. A few wavy lines can also make for a better hairstyle.

✔ **Add shading:** Review the end of Chapter 4, where I add subtle shading in the Vector Mode's Paint Editor.

✔ **Add a more striking pose:** Rather than just having your characters stand around, experiment with more dramatic poses, which helps you express their personalities.

✔ **Add drama:** Choose a specific scene from the story you have in mind and adjust the characters' poses and expressions to match the tone/mood you wish to express.

Location, Location, Location

Every animation takes place somewhere, from a family basement to the far reaches of outer space, from South America to South Park, Colorado. The last chapter walked you through the creation of three different animated characters. In this chapter, you create immersive scenes — object-filled locations that grab your senses — for your characters to explore.

Enough of those flat backdrops. Get building your own immersive animation WORLD!

Planning Animation Scenes

Before a movie or television show is made, somebody writes a script, which includes all the scenes. Each scene starts with a location. While you are thinking about the story that you want to tell, you should also start to think about where the story will take place. I will stick with the three characters I designed in Chapter 7. It might be funny if I find a way to force all three of them together. What if they are strangers who must share a room? Where is that likely to happen? How about summer camp?

Every location is going to be either inside or outside, an interior scene or an exterior scene. Let's begin inside. In previous chapters, I had you create a new project. If you plan to use your characters from the previous chapter (or from another project you have created), it will be easier to open that project so your characters will be available. If you wish to use sprites from the Sprite Library or design new ones later, you can create a new project (and delete the Scratch cat).

1. Go to `scratch.mit.edu` or open the Scratch 2 Offline Editor.

2. If you are online, browse and open the project you want to copy. If offline, select File⇨Open and then select your project.

3. If Online, click the File menu and choose Save a Copy. Offline, select File⇨Save As.

4. Name your project as you wish. I'll name my project *Animation Backgrounds*.

Design an Interior Scene

In Chapter 6, I presented the most basic kind of interior scene, a single horizontal line to indicate the floor. Even for a more complicated scene, determining the intersection of floor and wall is a great place to start.

I recommend designing your backdrops in Vector Mode to take advantage of the vector drawing tools and have the capability to modify lines and shapes at any time. (For more about using vector graphics, see Chapters 4, 6, and 7.) If you just draw a line, you will not be able to use the Color a Shape tool, so draw rectangles for the floor and wall.

1. Click the Stage icon to the left of the character sprites.

 2. On the Backdrops tab, click the Convert to Vector button.

 3. Click the Rectangle tool, choose the black color swatch, and then adjust the line thickness with the Line Width slider to the left of the color palette.

4. Click just off the top-left edge of the Paint Editor canvas, and then click and drag approximately two-thirds of the way down the Paint Editor canvas for your wall.

5. For your floor, click off the bottom-left edge of the Paint Editor canvas and then drag toward the lower-right corner of the wall.

 6. Click the Color a Shape tool, select the color you wish to use, and then fill the wall and floor shapes. (I chose dark brown for the floor and light tan for the wall.)

Most of the walls in my house have either a window or a door. Windows have the advantage of helping to indicate the time of day, weather, or a vicious monster looking for its next meal.

 1. Click the Rectangle tool, choose the black color swatch, and drag the Line Width slider to adjust the line thickness.

2. Click and drag to draw the outer part of the window.

 3. Click the Line tool, hold the Shift key, and drag across the middle of the rectangle to divide the shape into two parts.

4. Shift-click and drag down the middle of the top section to indicate two panes of glass in the upper window.

 5. Click the Color a Shape tool, choose the light gray color swatch, and click inside the window to fill it with color.

Share sprites between projects

What if you want to bring in characters from more than one project or start with a blank project, work on your backdrops, and then bring characters in later? Whether working online or offline, Scratch allows you to export sprites, individual costumes, and backdrops from one project and then import them into another project.

Shift-click a sprite, costume, or backdrop and select *Save to Local File*.

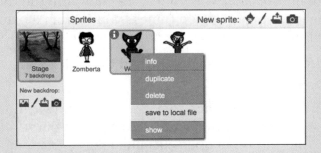

 Use the Upload Sprite from File or Upload Costume from File button to load your character into a new project.

If you are working online and do not have permission to save files to your computer, fear not! You can use the Scratch Backpack (at the bottom of your Scripts/Costumes/Sounds page when working online).

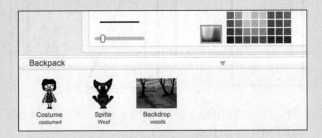

You can drag sprites, backdrops, costumes, scripts, and sounds into and out of your Backpack. To date, the offline version of Scratch does not include a Backpack.

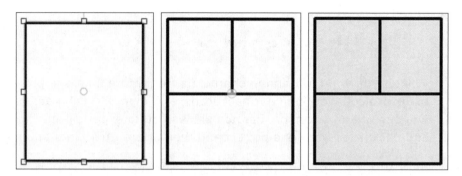

Adding curtains will bring more color into the room and make it obvious you are inside (unless you're from a place where people put their curtains on the outside of their house!?!).

1. Click the Rectangle tool and then click and drag across the left side of the window.

2. Click the Reshape tool, Shift-click midway down the right side of the rectangle to add a point and a curve, and then drag to the left for an open-curtain look.

3. Click and drag to adjust the top-right and bottom-right points.

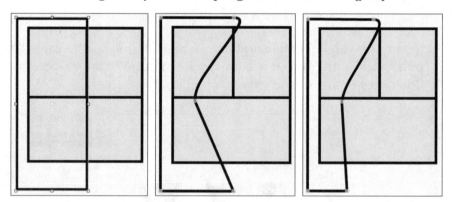

4. Click the Color a Shape tool, choose a curtain color, and click inside the curtain.

5. Click the Duplicate tool, click the curtain, and drag the copy to the right side of the window.

6. Click the Flip Left-Right button.

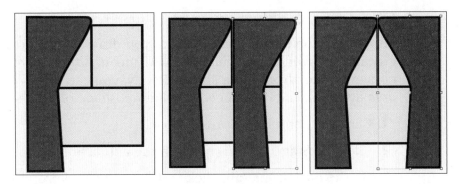

At this point, you may want to use the Reshape tool again to adjust each side to change the length of the curtain or reveal more of the window to look like a familiar curtain. You can also use the Select tool to move the curtains up or down.

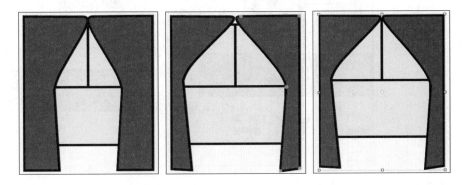

Make Scenes More Immersive

Backdrops are always on the very back layer, so technically, you cannot have anything behind your backdrop. But, what if you want viewers to see objects through a window or have characters enter and exit through doors, or hide behind trees?

You make a scene more *immersive* by including foreground and background objects, like props on a stage.

Instead of putting the walls, windows, floors, and doors all in one backdrop, you can put them in a sprite! Scratch sprites are far more flexible than backdrops; sprites can move behind and in front of each other, move from side-to-side, and get smaller and larger.

Change a backdrop into a sprite

I hope you don't think that I'd make you draw the window and curtains all over again. I am not THAT mean! Although you cannot convert a backdrop into a sprite exactly, you can drag a backdrop *onto* a sprite, which will become a new *costume* on that sprite.

1. Click the Paint New Sprite button.

2. Click the Stage button (beneath the actual Stage).

3. On the Backdrops tab, click and drag the backdrop that includes your window onto the new sprite.

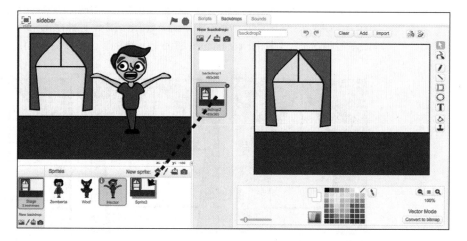

4. While you are still on the Backdrops panel, select the plain white backdrop (if you do not have one click the Paint New Backdrop button).

   Otherwise it may be confusing to have a backdrop and sprite with the same image.

5. Click and drag the new wall sprite into position on the Stage.

Design see-through windows

You can enable seeing other sprites through windows a few ways. One way is to delete the color inside the window panes, but that won't work here. Can you figure out why? You drew the wall rectangle first and *then* drew the window *over* it? Because it's a vector sprite, each object is on its own layer.

You will need to draw a new wall that goes to the left, right, top, and bottom edges of the window, then clear out the glass.

1. Select the wall/floor/window sprite and click the Costumes tab.

2. On the Paint Editor canvas, click anywhere on the wall and then click the Delete key on your keyboard.

 3. Click the Color a Shape tool, click the empty color swatch, and then click the glass.

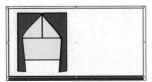 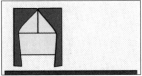 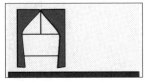

Why did you need to fill the window with an empty color rather than just clicking and deleting the glass? Because the glass color and the black edge were part of the same object, so using the Delete key would delete both. This way, you should see your character(s) as though the wall were invisible.

To make a character appear through the window, move the sprite into position, and then send it behind the window/wall sprite.

1. On the Stage, click and drag the character(s) to overlap with the window.

2. Click anywhere on the curtain or floor and hold your mouse or trackpad button for a few seconds to make that sprite move to the front layer.

I know it looks weird, if not lame, but after you add a new wall and backdrop, it should look much better.

To keep the window transparent, you will need to draw the wall in four sections and leave a hole around the window.

1. On the Paint Editor canvas, click the Rectangle tool and then click the Solid option and choose the color of your wall in the Paint Editor.

2. Click and drag from just above the top-right corner across the canvas to the right side of the curtain and down to the floor. (It's okay to overlap the curtain and the floor a bit.)

3. Hold the Shift key while you click the Back a Layer button.

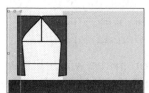 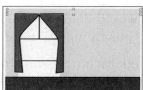 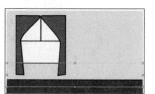

4. Repeat Steps 2 and 3 for the remaining three sections of the wall. Click off the canvas to ensure the section fills each area.

 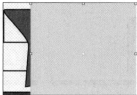 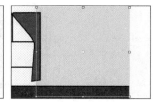

After your new wall is filled, your scene should give the illusion that your character is outside the room looking in through the window. To give viewers a better sense of depth, add a character to the inside and have it react to the character (or monster) outside.

You should now have a room with a window through which you can see outside. To make the scene more immersive, you need to add something inside the room that the character can move behind. In theater, film, and television, these objects are called *props*. I have *just* decided the first scene of my animation will take place in this boy's home, where a werewolf and a zombie will appear through his living room window.

Build your own furniture

Nothing quite says "living room" like a big fluffy couch. You can follow along or draw a different prop that fits your room (and your story) better.

The simplest way to draw furniture (in this case, a couch) is to break it down into the major parts and utilize the Duplicate tool for common features, such as cushions, arms, and pillows. Even though most couch cushions are rectangular, it is better to begin with an ellipse and then use the Reshape tool to get the rounded corners right.

1. Click the Paint New Sprite icon beneath the Stage.

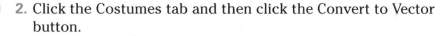
2. Click the Costumes tab and then click the Convert to Vector button.

3. Click the Ellipse tool, choose the black color swatch, drag the Line Width slider to adjust the line thickness, and choose the Outline option.

4. Click and drag to draw the first cushion. (Leave enough room for the arms and two more cushions.)

5. Click the Reshape tool, select the cushion, then click and drag the middle edge points inward to form a rounded rectangle.

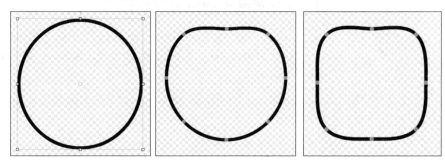

6. Click the Color a Shape tool, click the color you think will look good in your room, and then click inside the cushion. The color should contrast the color of the wall and the character's skin, hair, and clothing.

7. Click the Duplicate tool, click the first cushion, and drag the copy into place beside it. Repeat for the third cushion.

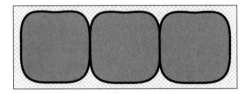

If you hold down the Shift key, you can keep making duplicates of the shape without having to reselect the Duplicate button each time. Release the Shift key before dragging the final copy into place.

8. Click the Select tool and then Shift-click each cushion until all three are selected. Don't worry about the gaps; you can fill them in later.

9. Click the Group button.

10. Click the Duplicate tool, click the group of cushions, and drag them to where the seat cushions should be.

11. Click the Select tool and click the bottom-center control point to shorten the group of cushions.

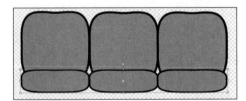

12. Click the Ellipse tool, choose the black color swatch, drag the Line Width slider to adjust the line thickness, and choose the Outline option.

13. Click and drag to draw an oval where the left couch arm should be.

14. Click the Reshape tool, select the arm, and then click and drag points to sculpt a thick couch arm shape.

 15. Click the Color a Shape tool, choose the same color you used for the cushions, and then click inside the arm.

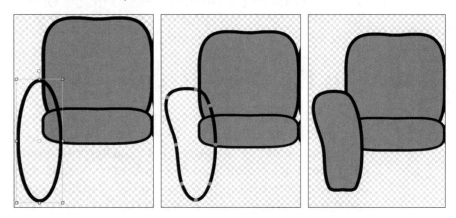

The viewer will not see the other couch arm or the legs in my scene, so I will just draw a rectangle beneath the cushions, fill it with green, bring the seat cushion group to the front layer (Shift-click the Forward a Layer button), and then have my character run for cover!

Study your finished scene to make sure sprites do not have too many similar colors. In case you didn't notice, I changed the wall color from tan to a bright yellow after I noticed the previous color was almost the same shade as my character's skin (though he probably wishes he could blend right into the wall!). I also changed the backdrop color to a dark gray so it looks like the werewolf is outside in the dark.

Design an Exterior Scene

The couch in the living room scene would be considered a foreground element, while the window and any objects (or werewolves you can see through it) are background elements. You can vary your background and foreground to design any interior you want, from a bedroom to a gym to the control room of a flying saucer. But, eventually, your characters (and your story) will want to go outside, right?

To include interior and exterior scenes in the same Scratch project, hide all the sprites (Shift-click and select *Hide*) except for whichever character(s) will be in the scene you are about to design.

I haven't used my zombie girl, *Zomberta,* in awhile; she could use a little fresh air. Let's make her first scene arriving at summer camp. Begin with a new backdrop:

1. Click the Stage icon to the left of the character sprites.

Convert to vector 2. On the Backdrops tab, click the Convert to Vector button in the bottom-right corner.

 3. Click the Rectangle tool, click the Solid option, and then choose a light blue color swatch for the sky.

4. Click just off the top-left edge of the Paint Editor canvas and then click and drag to approximately halfway down the canvas.

5. Choose a shade of green for the grass, click just off the bottom-left corner of the Paint Editor canvas, and drag up to the bottom edge of the sky. (It's okay to overlap a bit.)

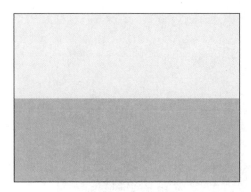

That's it! I mean what more do you need than a blue sky and green grass? Just call it my zombie at camp field scene . . . or not!

If you went through Chapter 1 and got as far as creating the sky for your *Flappy Bat* game, you may remember the trick I shared for making a more realistic sky: using a *gradient* (blending between two colors).

1. Click the Color a Shape tool.

2. Click the Horizontal Gradient option.

3. Click the white color swatch.

4. Click the Swap Colors button to swap the foreground and background color.

5. Click a sky blue color swatch.

6. Click inside the sky rectangle to replace the flat blue color with the gradient.

    You can reverse the two colors by clicking the Swap Colors button and clicking inside the rectangle again.

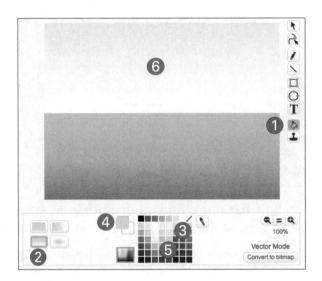

Generally, you will want the sky to be brightest near the horizon and darkest toward the top of the canvas. You can also experiment with gradients on the ground. (I chose a light and darker green.)

Yet another advantage of using vector graphics over bitmap graphics is vector graphics allow you to change the gradient at any time. Vector Mode also allows you to preview your object before applying the gradient.

Draw scenes with perspective

As it applies to drawing and animation, *perspective* is a set of techniques that make some objects appear far away while others appear to be closer to the viewer. You can see perspective in action by adding a road to your scene.

Click the Rectangle tool, select a dark gray color swatch, and then click and drag from the horizon (the border between your sky and ground rectangles) down to the bottom of the canvas.

Ewww! That does not look like a road; it ruins the nice sky over grass gradient effect and looks more like a flag than a landscape.

You may be thinking, "What if I add a gradient to the road?" Go ahead, try, I dare you! It may help a little, but what would really help is for us to employ a bit of perspective.

 Click the Reshape tool, click the road rectangle to select it, and then click and drag the top points closer together.

 If you are having trouble getting the top corners of the road to line up with the straight horizon or you just want to be lazy like me, try this simple trick. Select the sky rectangle, bring it to the front layer (Shift-click on the Forward a Layer button), then drag the bottom down to cover the top of the grass and road rectangles. Voilà! A nice and straight horizon line!

You can adjust the distance between the left and right corners to give a sense of how wide and how long the road is. The best part is the road acts as a guide for the rest of the objects in your scene. Trees, buildings, and anything outside the road need to be smaller the further "down" the road it is placed. (And by "down," I mean toward the top of your scene!)

I know you are thinking, "What's with the lame trees, man, they look more like mushrooms?!" Buddy, my answer to you is K.I.S.S.!

To give the illusion of distance, the mushroomy trees are not only smaller but are also closer together and higher on the canvas the further down the road you go.

Even if your scene is not going to have a road, it might be helpful to draw one initially as a guide for positioning and scaling your objects. I often start with a backdrop like this:

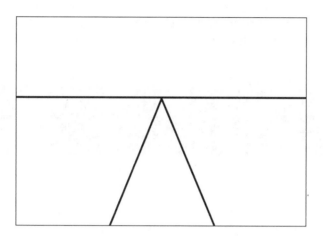

If you want to space the same objects (trees, streetlights, chickens waiting to cross the highway) equally on both sides of the road, follow this simple formula: draw, duplicate, reposition, and resize.

1. Use the Paint Editor tools to draw your first tree (or other object).

2. Use the Duplicate tool to drag copy to align with the road.

3. Click the Back a Layer button until it appears behind the first object.

4. Use the Shrink tool to make the object appear smaller than the previous.

5. Repeat Steps 2–4 until you have one side of the road lined with objects.

After you have one side of the road complete, rather than going through those steps again for the other side, you can select and group the first set, duplicate the group, and then flip it horizontally and drag it into place on the other side of the road.

Scale characters inside a scene

Another REALLY important element you should use to help lay out your scene is the person/people who are going to be in it! I've been building roads and planting mushroomy trees without giving any thought to how large the objects should be in relation to my little zombie.

Unless this is going to be *Attack of the 60-Foot Zombie Girl*, it would be better to figure out how large I want her to appear in the scene, and then leave her on the Stage as a visual reference while adding objects.

I'm going to delete the trees and the road and start over. This time, I'll add objects in relation to both my road (the driveway leading into the summer camp) and *Zomberta*. Use the same steps that you used for the interior scene: Start with basic shapes and then modify and combine them to make more complex objects.

1. If your character is still hidden, Shift-click the sprite and select Unhide.

2. Use the Grow and Shrink buttons to resize your character. The smaller your character, the harder it is to see its expression (not a big deal for zombies but important for most characters).

3. Use the Reshape tool to adjust the width of your road in relation to your character.

4. Begin adding objects in proportion to the road and the character.

Mushroomy trees aside, the scene is looking better. If I had more time, I would try to hide the horizon line with more outdoor objects, but this will do for now.

When I am ready to animate *Zomberta* in the scene, I will use perspective to gauge how large she should appear based on how far down the road she goes. Perspective will also dictate when she should be in front of or behind other objects.

There will be PLENTY of time to build up your immersive scene-building skills (balancing color, placing objects, creating foreground and background) and to play with perspective while you continue with your animation career (as well as future chapters in this very book).

Quick scenery improvements

Here are a few tips to enhance your scenes:

✔ **Use reference photographs:** You can use the web or your own camera to grab interior and exterior images. If you want to trace over them, be sure to convert to Vector Mode after you import your photo as a sprite or backdrop.

✔ **Apply more gradients:** Gradients are not just for sky, ground, and road. Try horizontal, vertical, and radial gradients on trees, buildings, or your favorite breakfast cereal. Radial gradients work best on circular objects, and horizontal and vertical gradients work better inside rectangular shapes.

✔ **Add shadows:** You will learn a few shadow techniques in Chapter 10. For now, think about how you might duplicate a sprite, fill it with a dark gray color, and reshape it (like the trees in the first image in this chapter). Be warned: After you put a shadow on one object, you have to put one on all the other objects or your scene may look incomplete.

✔ **Consider the weather:** Is it a cloudy day? Rainy? Or BRAINY?!

✔ **Consider the time:** Especially for exterior scenes, it is important to choose whether it is morning, afternoon, or evening. (You revisit this in Chapter 10.)

Sounds Good to Me

If you are anything like my niece and nephew, half the time you are supposedly "watching" television, your eyes are not even on the screen. You're texting somebody with your phone or looking up something on your tablet or playing a game on your laptop or even doing homework. One of the easiest ways to catch your attention, though, is to hit the Mute button on the remote, right? "Hey, I was *watching* that!" This should illustrate how important sound is to conveying a story.

That's What He Said

In previous chapters, you began thinking about your story, designed some characters, and created an interior and an exterior scene. The next step in the animation process is to add dialogue.

Dialogue is so important to the animation process that actors are recorded before almost any animation begins because synchronizing character animation to sound is easier than trying to fit sound into finished animation. In the animation world, this initial sound recording is the *scratch* track. How perfect is that?

Although this chapter is about recording and playing audio, there is another way to have your characters speak to one another in Scratch. In Chapter 6, I introduce the SAY block. If you add this block to a character, any text you type into the block will appear in a speech bubble. You can even control how long the speech bubble appears by using a SAY FOR SECONDS block.

Write dialogue for your characters

Okay, don't *hate* me, but even if you are going to provide the voice for all your characters, writing your dialogue before you begin recording is best. You don't have to make it look like a script or anything, just something like this:

```
Hector: Since I got here first, I should get to
    choose which bunk I sleep in.
Zomberta: Brains... brrrraaaaaiiiiinsssss!
Hector: Okaaay... Well, I'd like the top bunk.
Werewoof: Grrrrrrrrrr!
Hector: Does that mean great or what, dog boy?
Werewoof: Aaarrrrgggghhhh!
Hector: Hey, I'm not arguing, I'm just telling you
    how I feel.
Zomberta: Brrrrrr...
Hector: Heh, are you cold, too? Let me get that
    window! I'm more of a DOER than a brainy type.
Werewoof: AAAHHHWWWHHHOOOOOOO!
Hector: Okay, chill out a little, poochie. Boy, you
    could really use a breath mint. What did you
    have for lunch?
Zomberta: Brains!
Hector: Like a grilled brains sandwich or do you eat
    'em right out of the skull? I'm just askin'...
```

I'm not saying you have to type it out as I did. You can write it on a napkin with a purple crayon if that makes you happy, *Harold*. You just need to put a bit of thought into what your characters are going to say (even if it's just "Grrrrrrrr!") before hitting the Record button. And, if you are going to record anybody else's voice, the actor will need something to read from.

Record Dialogue in Scratch

Okay, do you have your dialogue written down? Ready to record? In the previous chapter, I suggested you open a Scratch project containing the character (or characters) you want to use. If you created your own scene, doesn't it make sense to open *that* project now (because it should have your characters, too)?

If you'd rather record your dialogue first and then bring characters, backdrops, or scene sprites into your project, refer to the first tip in Chapter 8 about importing sprites, costumes, and backdrops.

1. Go to `scratch.mit.edu` or open the Scratch 2 Offline Editor.

2. If you are online, browse and open the project you want to copy. If offline, choose File⇨Open and select your project.

3. Name your project. If online, click the File menu and choose *Save a Copy*. Offline, select File⇨Save As. I will name my version *Animation Soundtrack*.

4. Delete the cat.

You can add sound to a Scratch project three ways:

✔ You can choose a sound from the Sound Library.

✔ Import a sound file (.mp3 or .wav format).

✔ Record a sound directly in Scratch.

Although the Sound Library has a bunch of music and sound effects to choose from, there is no dialogue — the MIT geniuses left the talking to you.

Find the Record button

In the previous chapters, you spent most of your time in the Paint Editor. As you may have guessed, in this chapter you will be spending more time in the Sound Editor.

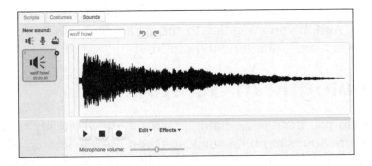

Click the Sounds tab (to the right of the Costumes tab) to get to the Sound Editor. But WAIT! Before you start clicking, recording, and playing, it's important to decide where each sound should go.

In Scratch, sounds are handled the same way as costumes and scripts. Just as each sprite can have several different costumes and code blocks, each sprite can also contain several different sounds. Because my character, *Hector,* has the first line of dialogue, I will select his sprite before recording.

1. Click the sprite of the character who will be speaking (or growling or moaning) and then click the Sounds tab.

2. By default, each sprite has the *Pop* sound. Unless you are planning to have your character pop (or have it attack a roll of bubble wrap), Shift-click the sound and choose Delete. You can also click the X on the Sound icon to delete it.

3. Click the Record New Sound button.

   Note: If you do not have a microphone connected to your computer or you want to use audio recorded on a different device (like a phone or digital recorder), click the Upload Sound from File button and skip ahead to the "Edit Sound Waves" section.

You might think that as soon as you click the Record New Sound button Scratch would start recording. Nope! That button works like the Paint New Costume button; it creates a sound *object* that appears in the New Sound column of the Sound Editor. Like using the Paint tools (Rectangle, Line, and so) to add shapes to a costume, recording adds sound to a sound object.

If you have more than one character in your animation, it is generally a good idea to record each of their lines separately. Later, you will learn how to use code blocks to control when each sound will play.

1. With the new *Recording1* sound object selected, click the Record button.

2. If you are using Scratch in a web browser, you may get a message that reads "If you click Allow, you may be recorded." DUH! Of course you may be recorded; you just clicked the RECORD BUTTON! Click Allow to allow Scratch to record.

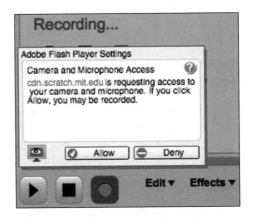

The same message will come up the first time you try to use a webcam. This happens in case you're on a website where *you* did *not* click a Record button, but somebody else may be trying to record sound or images from your computer. I know it sounds creepy, but at least in Scratch *you* are the one *in control.* (Cue sound of a power-hungry dictator's *maniacal laugh: Booowhahahaha!*)

If the microphone is enabled, the word *Recording* should appear in orange. While you are speaking/growling/moaning, a vertical green bar should appear to the left of the recording controls.

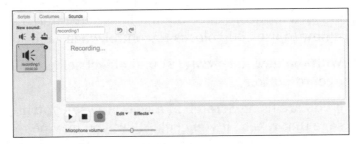

3. Click the Stop button to end your recording.

That vertical green bar shows how loud your voice sounds through the microphone. As your voice gets louder, you may see yellow or even red appear near the top of the line. This means the sound is too loud and may be distorted. You can either lower your voice or adjust the Microphone Volume slider beneath the Record button. (Move the slider to the left for a real loudmouth or to the right for that friend you are always asking, "Say what?")

Edit Audio Clips

Editing your sound recordings is one of the COOLEST features of Scratch! Imagine that you bribe your big sister to act as the voice of a mad scientist in your cartoon; you go to all the trouble of writing down her dialogue, you hit Record, and she makes a mistake or just pauses too long between two words. Instead of recording the lines again, you can just cut out the part you don't want, which is as easy as selecting and deleting a shape on the Paint Editor canvas.

After you finish recording your sound, something like this should appear in the sound canvas:

That row of black, squiggly shapes is called a *sound wave,* which is a visual version of the sound you just recorded.

Why call it a sound *wave?*

Why call that thick, blotchy shape a wave? If you could zoom in on the audio the same way you can zoom in on a sprite, you would see that the shape is actually a continuous wave. The louder you speak the taller the wave appears, and the faster you speak the narrower the wave appears.

  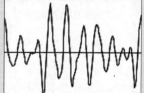

Do I *really* need to tell you to click the Play button to hear your recording? Seriously? In case you have trouble finding the button, it's beside Stop and Record.

Now that you have recording and playing sound out of the way, let's get to the cool part: editing sound clips!

 When editing a long sound clip, you might find it helpful to expand the Sound Editor. Choose Edit↩Small Stage Layout or click the small, gray triangle located between the Stage and the Sound Editor to expand and contract your work area.

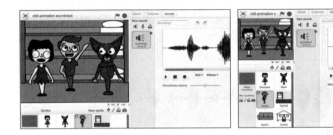

Trim Beginning of Sound

Start by deleting the extra silence (where the line is completely flat) at the beginning of the sound wave.

1. Select the sprite you recorded audio on and then click the Sounds tab.

2. If you have more than one sound, click the one you want to edit.

3. Use the horizontal scroll bar to find the beginning of the sound you wish to use.

4. Click the sound wave right at the point where the silence *ends* and drag *left,* all the way to the beginning of the sound wave.

5. Beneath the sound wave, click the Edit menu and choose Delete.

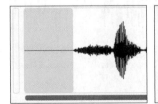 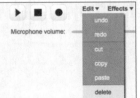 

Okay, maybe you don't think it's that cool to delete silence. A bit like deleting nothing, right? But, check this out: Each of the blobs represents one word, and the flat lines are the bits of silence in-between (unless you talk as fast as my friends in New York City whose words practically overlap!).

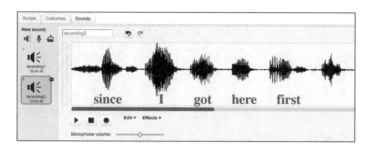

You can delete a word the same way you deleted silence, by clicking and dragging over the word and then choosing Edit⇨Delete. The Edit menu also enables you to undo and redo edits, copy part of your audio and paste it somewhere else, and select the entire sound wave.

Before recording, tell your actor(s) that making a mistake is okay (to put them at ease). Then tell them, if they do mess up, to take a breath and repeat that part. This way, you do not have to keep stopping and starting the recording. After the actor finishes, you can find the mistakes and delete those portions of the sound wave. It's easier to find mistakes and words you're looking for in shorter sound waves so make several short recordings rather than one, long recording.

Use sound editing effects

I almost titled this section "Using sound effects," but that would have been misleading. *Sound effects* usually refer to all the non-spoken sounds in your animation, such as doors slamming, explosions, and toilets flushing. (If you combine all three, you have the makings of a hilarious scene!) *Sound Editor effects* are just ways to modify the volume of any part (or all) of your sound wave, as well as reversing a sound (fun to try out, but not very useful for recorded dialogue unless you want a character possessed by a demon who speaks in tongues).

Try making one of the words in your recording louder.

1. Click and drag to select the part of the sound wave you wish to make louder.

2. Beneath the sound wave, click the Effects menu and choose *Louder*.

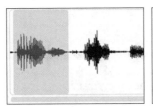 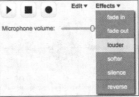 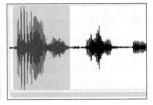

Notice how that part of the sound wave appears taller after the effect is applied. In the real world, sound may be invisible, but not inside Scratch!

Play Sound with Code Blocks

You know how to play sound in the Sound Editor, but how do you get the sound to play along with the animation? Two code blocks make the recorded dialogue start when the Green Flag button on the Stage is clicked.

1. Click the sprite of the character you recorded dialogue for.

2. Click the Scripts tab.

3. Click the *Sound* category.

4. Drag the PLAY SOUND block *or* the PLAY SOUND UNTIL DONE block into the Scripts Area.

5. Click the *Events* category and then drag and snap the WHEN GREEN FLAG CLICKED block onto the top of the PLAY SOUND block.

If you have more than one sound stored in your character sprite, you can choose which one to play using the drop-down menu in the PLAY SOUND block. Then, when you click the Green Flag button, the selected sound should play.

What's the difference between PLAY SOUND and PLAY SOUND UNTIL DONE? If you have more code blocks snapped into place beneath the PLAY SOUND block, those commands will run *while* the sound is playing. If you use PLAY SOUND UNTIL DONE, the other blocks will *not* run until the sound has finished playing.

What if you do not want your sound to play right away? You can snap a WAIT block above it and set the number of seconds to wait, or have something other than pressing the Green Flag button make the sound play (more on that later).

Animate Character Speech

If you've recorded dialogue for one of your characters, the next logical step is to make them look like they are speaking. There are several ways to achieve this:

- Show the character while playing the recorded voice. (Duh!)

- Animate the character's mouth. (Easier said than done, right?)

- Show who or what the character is speaking to. (Like how you only see Charlie Brown while some invisible adult is saying, "Whuh wuh wh wh whaughhh.")

- Use a *voiceover,* where you see the character but when he or she starts talking, you show something else. (You often see this in a flashback, where a character tells you about something that already happened, while you see some of the stuff he or she is describing.)

✔ Show an unbearably cute photo of your cat while we hear your character talking about something completely unrelated to unbearably cute cats.

Aside from the last one, you will see a combination of all these techniques used in animation, sometimes even in the same scene.

So where is a young Scratcher to begin? I'm a dummy, so I say begin with the very *hardest,* animating the character's mouth! If you can master that one, the rest will be a breeze.

In previous chapters, I showed how to drag both costumes and code blocks from one sprite to another. You can also drag sounds between sprites. This is handy if you ever record audio onto the wrong sprite (or if you are animating identical twins)!

Mouthing the words

The more time you are willing to put into animating characters' mouth, the better they are likely to look while speaking. Animators refer to this as *lip-synching.* Synch is short for *synchronization,* which means matching the picture with the sound.

Synching does not have to be hard or too time consuming. I bet you've seen the easy way, where a character's mouth just opens and closes repeatedly while talking and stays closed while *not* talking. A classic hand puppet or marionette works like this.

Did you notice how all the characters I designed in Chapter 7 start with an open mouth? This lets me add teeth and/or a tongue. Then I can just duplicate the costume and reshape the mouth for the closed-mouth view.

1. Select the sprite that will be talking and then click the Costumes tab.

2. Shift-click the costume with the character's mouth open and select *Duplicate*.

3. Rename the first costume to *Mouth Open* and the second costume to *Mouth Closed*.

4. Select the *Mouth Closed* costume.

5. Use the Reshape tool to modify the mouth so it appears closed.

You should now have a character sprite with at least two costumes (*Mouth Open* and *Mouth Closed*), recorded dialogue, and a short script (two code blocks) that makes the audio play as soon as somebody clicks the Green Flag button.

Easy lip-synching

How do you get Scratch to alternate between the open- and closed-mouth costumes while the audio is playing? If you went through Chapter 1 or Chapter 3, you may remember the blocks used to alternate between different costumes (to make flapping wings or a crawling turtle). If not, check out the *Looks* category of code blocks.

1. Select the sprite that will be talking and then click the Scripts tab.

2. Drag and snap these blocks (SWITCH COSTUME TO, WAIT, and REPEAT) to the bottom of the other two blocks in the Scripts Area:

```
when     clicked
wait  5  secs
play sound  recording2 ▼
repeat  8
    switch costume to  open ▼
    wait  0.25  secs
    switch costume to  closed ▼
    wait  0.25  secs
```

I used the drop-down menu to choose Open in one SWITCH COSTUME TO block and Closed in the other. I also changed the WAIT time from the default 1 second to .25 seconds and the REPEAT value to 8. At the least, you will probably have to tweak the REPEAT value for your character. Can you figure out why?

When the Green Flag button is pressed, I want the mouth to open and close for as *long* as the audio plays. I didn't automatically know it would take 8 times of opening and closing to match the audio. The first time I guessed 10. When that was too long, I tried 6, and then, finally, 8. You will have to adjust this based on the length of *your* audio. You can also try different times for the WAIT block until you get the look you want.

If you do not use the WAIT blocks, the costumes will swap so fast you will not be able to see the costume change.

Achieve more realistic lip-synching

Go to a mirror, stand really close, fix your gaze on your mouth, and say the word *donut* as slowly as you can. Notice how it's not just your lips, but also your teeth and even your tongue that combine in different ways depending on which letters or sounds you are forming. For the *D* your teeth start together and your tongue is at the roof of your mouth. When you get to *O,* your mouth is open and then it closes part way while your tongue bends up to the roof of your mouth for the *N.* Your mouth opens for the *U* and returns to the same position as the *N* for the *T.*

DON'T WORRY: You DO NOT have to draw EVERY SINGLE LETTER of your dialogue (that would take FOREVER)! Most people talk so fast you only see a few of the distinct mouth shapes. If you don't believe me, go back to that mirror and say, "I love donuts," the way you normally speak.

The key to getting more realistic speaking animation is to animate the shapes the mouth makes at key times, otherwise known as *keyframes* (frames in which something important changes). Animators refer to the basic shapes your mouth makes to form the vowel and consonant sounds as *phonemes.* Although the English alphabet has 26 letters, there are far fewer phonemes because many letters overlap, such as M, P, and B (lips together) and D and T (tongue against upper teeth).

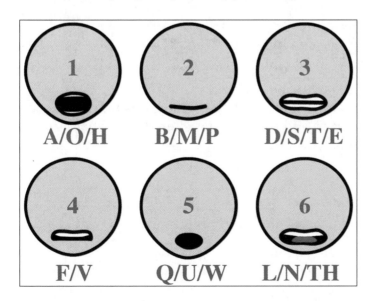

So that you're on the same page as I am, let's all make our characters say, "I love donuts." (I mean, who *doesn't* love donuts?) I'm going to switch to *Zomberta* because I'm getting a bit tired of *Hector*. Surely, zombies would love those gory jelly donuts if they tried them.

1. Click the sprite of the character who will be speaking and then click the Sounds tab.

 2. Click the Record New Sound button.

3. Rename the new sound object *Donuts*.

 4. Click the Record button and say, "I love donuts."

5. Click the Stop button.

6. Select any silence at the beginning of your sound wave and choose Edit⇨Delete.

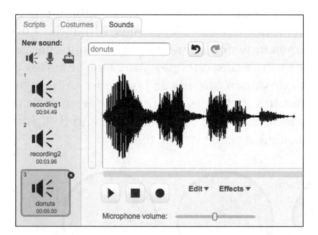

When your donut recording is ready, it is time to choose the key phonemes to add to your character. Here's what I think will work best:

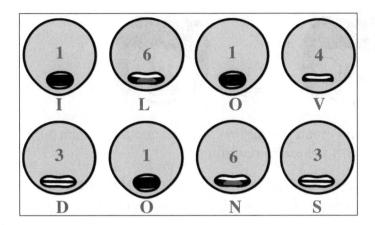

See what I mean about duplicate phonemes (using #1 three times and #'s 3 and 6 twice)? I did not create phonemes for the U or the T in donuts. Can you figure out why? The T and S are the same phoneme, and when I say *donuts,* the emphasis is on the first syllable (*DO-nuts*), so my mouth barely opens for the u.

Create custom phoneme costumes

You only need phonemes 1, 3, 4, and 6 for your sentence. If you want to use your *Mouth Open* costume for #1, then you only need to create three more mouth shapes.

1. Select the character you want to animate and then click the Costumes tab.

2. Shift-click the *Mouth Open* costume and choose *Duplicate.*

3. Rename the new costume to correspond to the phoneme (F/V, L/N/TH, or D/S/T/E).

4. Use the Reshape tool to change the mouth to the desired phoneme shape.

5. Repeat Steps 2–4 for each remaining phoneme.

 Wanna save yourself a TON of animation time? Why not make a new sprite named *Talking* with each phoneme as a different costume. Then, you can place that mouth over any character on the Stage. This will allow you to animate your character's body separate from its mouth and then duplicate the sprite instead of creating a different set of phonemes for every character.

After you create the phonemes you need, all that's left is to synch them with the audio recording.

Switch costumes to match phonemes

Make sure you renamed all your costumes or coding will be tricky.

1. Select the sprite containing the phoneme costumes.

2. Click the Scripts tab.

3. Drag the following blocks into the Scripts Area:

> when clicked
> play sound donuts ▾
> switch costume to L, N, TH ▾
> wait ❶ secs
>
> x: -161
> y: 28

4. Shift-click the SWITCH COSTUME TO block, choose *Duplicate,* and drag and snap the copies to the bottom of the current blocks.

> when clicked
> play sound donuts ▾
> switch costume to L, N, TH ▾
> wait ❶ secs
> switch costume to L, N, TH ▾
> wait ❶ secs
>
> x: -7
> y: 20

5. Repeat #4 until you have a SWITCH COSTUME TO block and a WAIT block for each phoneme.

6. Select the phoneme in each SWITCH COSTUME block.

7. Adjust the values of the WAIT block so phoneme costumes come at the proper time while playing audio.

My final script looks like this (I added red letters *outside* of Scratch to show which blocks correspond to each part of my donuts audio):

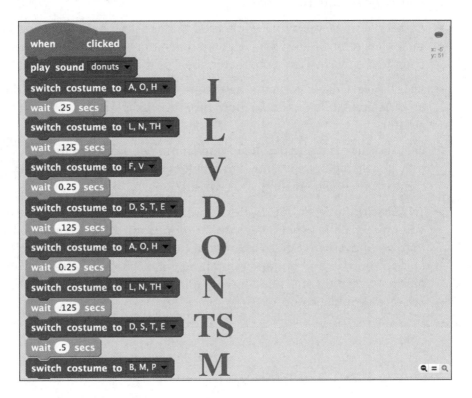

After you master the phonemes in *donuts,* you should be able to lip-synch all your animation characters. The key is finding the most important mouth shapes for any given word/phrase. And the faster your character talks, the fewer phonemes you should use or his or her mouth will be moving like crazy!

More dialogue tips

↙ **Animate the jaw:** When you speak, it's not just about your lips, teeth, and tongue. Head back to the mirror and see where your jaw is when you go through the phonemes. It's easy to add, just use the Reshape tool to tweak the bottom of the head.

↙ **Animate the eyes/eyebrows:** People tend to raise their eyebrows and open their eyes a bit wider when asking a question. What other ways can you change the eyes when a character speaks? (Your mirror beckons.)

↙ **Add blinking:** Unless your characters are in a staring contest, try adding an occasional blink to make them more realistic (or a wink to get them a date).

↙ **Animate hands:** Have you noticed how some people move their hands as they speak, almost as if they are conducting an orchestra (or trying to distract you while stealing your wallet)?

↙ **Try Audacity:** Audacity (`audacity.sourceforge.net`) is a free audio-editing application that gives you far more control over audio editing than you have with Scratch. Some of the biggest advantages are being able to zoom in and out on your sound wave, show precise time information, speed up and slow down audio, and apply sound effects that are more sophisticated.

Lights, Camera, ACTION!

After you have come up with a story, casted your characters, created your backdrops, and recorded some dialogue, you can put all the elements together into an animation. The mix of design and programming tips in this chapter can streamline your animation process. I'm no Brad Bird (his films *Iron Giant* and *The Incredibles* are two of my very favorites), but I can provide you many techniques to help you produce your own ANIMASTERPIECE!

(Not) Starting from Scratch

Unless you skipped the previous chapters in this part of the book, you should begin by opening a project that contains any characters, backdrops, or sounds (preferably all three) that you want to include in your animation. It's a good idea to save a copy of your project each time you are preparing to make major changes. That way, you can start over if your project spirals out of control.

 If you have never animated with Scratch before and want to create your own animated story, skim Chapter 6, where I lead you through the creation of a stick-figure animation.

1. Go to www.scratch.mit.edu or open the Scratch 2 Offline Editor.

2. If you are online, browse for and open the project you want to copy. If offline, choose File ⇨ Open and select your project.

3. If online, choose File ⇨ Save a Copy; offline, select File ⇨ Save As.

4. Name your project as you wish. I'll name my project *Camp Freaks*.

If you wish to start over or just use sprites, backdrops, and sounds from the Scratch libraries, follow these steps:

1. Go to scratch.mit.edu or open the Scratch 2 Offline Editor.

2. If you are online, click Create. If offline, choose File ⇨ New.

3. Name your project. (If online, select the title and type your new project name. If using the offline version of Scratch, choose File ⇨ Save As and type your new project name.)

4. Delete the cat with the Scissors (or Shift-click the cat and choose *Delete*) unless that's the first character you want in your animation.

 5. Use the Choose Backdrop from Library and Choose Sprite from Library icons to load sprites and backdrop(s) for your animation.

If you worked through Chapter 7, you designed three new Scratch characters. I created a zombie girl *(Zomberta)*, a werewolf *(Werewoof)*, and an ordinary boy *(Hector)*.

In Chapter 8, I showed you how to design interior and exterior scenes as immersive locations in which your stories can unfold.

In Chapter 9, I presented steps to record dialogue directly into Scratch and create different mouth positions (called phonemes) that make characters look like they are speaking.

I'll be using *my* characters, backdrops, and sounds throughout this chapter, while you should be using *yours*.

Lights (or What Time Is It?)

In a professional screenplay, each scene begins a certain way:

INT. *HECTOR*'S APARTMENT. NIGHT.

INT is short for *interior*. I want my first scene to be an interior of *Hector*'s apartment at night. But what if the character and the backdrop I designed look like this:

Does that look like a nighttime scene? It looks like high noon on a sunny day. What could I change to make it look like night and make the scene more dramatic?

Create a night scene

Surely there must be a few Scratch tricks that could save you time changing a bright sunny scene to a dramatic nighttime one, right? For starters, that window is a big giveaway: It should be dark outside. In Chapter 8, I show you the importance of having back walls be sprites instead of backdrops so you can put other graphics behind the wall, like so:

What if I told you just one code block can make it look even LATER outside? I will hide *Hector,* his couch, and the wall by

Shift-clicking each sprite icon beneath the Stage and choosing _Hide._ (I'll unhide them later.)

Some Scratchers don't even think to add code to their backdrop, but several blocks in the _Looks_ category work on backdrops. One of them can help you transform day into night.

1. Click the Stage button located to the left of your sprite icons.

2. Click the Scripts tab.

3. Click the _Looks_ category.

4. Click one time on the SET EFFECT TO block in the Scripts Area.

Inside the SET EFFECT TO block, click the drop-down menu, which by default reads _Color._ You should see six more options in addition to Color. Which effect do you think would help make a backdrop darker to give a sense of nighttime? Test it for yourself by choosing an option and changing the value from 0 to some other number (the maximum being 100 for any effect).

You can use the CLEAR GRAPHIC EFFECTS block to reset any backdrop or sprite to its original brightness or color.

The _Brightness_ effect seems to me like a good place to start. If you choose _Brightness,_ change the value to 50 and then click one time on the block. What happens to the backdrop? The backdrop gets quite a bit brighter. If you changed the value to the maximum of 100, the backdrop would be completely white. So how would you make it darker? Try a negative number!

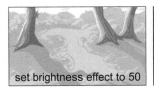  

I find –35 works well for my exterior scene. I'll unhide (Shift-click and select *Show*) the wall, couch, and *Hector* to see how the scene looks now.

Better. But what if I want it to be darker *inside?* Let's say a bolt of lightning has knocked out the power? You could use the same effects block on all the sprites in your scene, but there is a far easier way.

Turn out the lights

Changing several effect values when you have a bunch of sprites in your scene can be a drag. Can you think of a way to change the brightness or darkness of a scene all at once? What if you could put a black curtain over the entire scene and then make it partially transparent? That's where the *Ghost* effect comes in! (***Hint:*** It's not just for ghosts.)

1. Beneath the Stage, click the Paint New Sprite icon.

2. Click the Costumes tab.

3. Click the Fill with Color tool.

4. Click the black color swatch.

5. Click the Solid option to the left of the color swatches.

6. Click the Paint Editor canvas to fill it with black.

7. Click and drag the new sprite to cover the Stage.

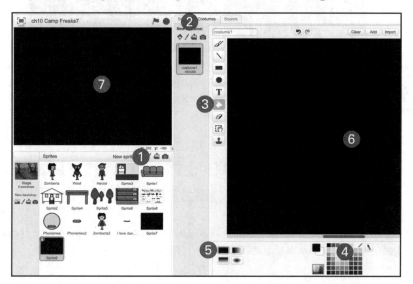

Unless you want complete darkness, you need to drag a SET EFFECT TO block into the new sprite's Scripts Area, along with a WHEN GREEN FLAG CLICKED block. Might as well add a GO TO X Y block, too, and set both values to *0* to ensure the sprite centers on the Stage.

When you change the SET EFFECT TO values to *Ghost* and *35* and click the Green Flag button, your scene becomes quite a bit darker. You can adjust the value to suit your taste.

TIP

Shift-click the new sprite and hide it when you need to see and move other sprites on the Stage.

Animate the effect for fade-in and fade-out

You can achieve a fade-in effect at the beginning of a scene by gradually changing the *Ghost* value from *0* to *100*.

```
set ghost effect to 0
repeat 100
    change ghost effect by 1
```

To fade to black at the end of a scene, set the *Ghost* value to *100* and change it by *–1*.

```
set ghost effect to 100
repeat 100
    change ghost effect by -1
```

Camera (or What Do I Focus On?)

For a live-action film or television show, the director and cinematographer determine what the audience will see by pointing the camera at a specific place. In Scratch, there is no camera. So how do you control what your audience sees? By selecting which sprites and backdrops to place on the Stage.

Have you noticed how animators alternate between wide shots that show you the entire scene and close-ups that may show only part of a character (most frequently, the face)?

In the following three images, I used the SET SIZE TO block to change the size of *Hector,* the window, and the couch from 100% to 250% to 500%:

Wait a minute! Why is there so little difference between the size of *Hector*'s face in the second and third image? Scratch has limitations on how much you can increase a sprite size when using LOOKS blocks.

Scratch imposes limits on the maximum size of each sprite based on the size of the original costume. For example, the Scratch cat can be increased to 535%. A costume the size of the Stage (480x360) can be increased to only 150%.

Fortunately, I can make *Hector* even larger in the Paint Editor.

Increase the costume size

In the Paint Editor, you can increase the size of a character's costume by grouping the shapes together and using the Grow tool near the very top of the screen. It is a good idea to duplicate a costume before changing its size so you can quickly switch back to its original size.

1. Click the Costumes tab.

2. Shift-click the current costume and choose *Duplicate*.

3. Click the new costume to select it. (A duplicate appears beneath the other costumes for the sprite.)

4. Change the costume name to *zoom in*.

5. Click the Select tool.

6. Click and drag across all the shapes in the costume. (Several new buttons appear to the right.)

7. Click the Group button.

8. Click the Grow tool and click several times on the costume to increase size.

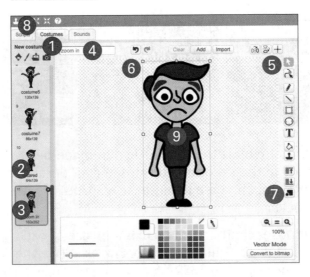

If you are using bitmap graphics, you will need to redraw your sprite or it will become pixelated. (Refer to the beginning of Chapter 4 to learn more about the differences between Bitmap Mode and Vector Mode.)

For interior scenes, you can cheat by filling the costume's background with the wall color (so you do not need to resize other sprites in the scene).

The more you alternate between camera views, the more you will learn to avoid placing characters in front of windows or other sprites that can be difficult to resize properly.

A camera is capable of more than only zooming in and out on characters. Another frequently employed camera technique is to alternate views, such as seeing a character from the front or from the side. In the previous chapters, the sprites and backdrops were drawn from the same point of view, with characters seen only from the front. There is no Scratch block to change the view of a sprite. Whether you are using Bitmap or Vector Mode, you must create each view yourself.

I have learned some tricks from watching *South Park* and other shows that can help you minimize the number of sprites in your animation. These tricks work best in Vector Mode because vector graphics are far easier to change than bitmap graphics.

Create a back view of characters

I ended a previous chapter with *Zomberta's* back to the viewer as she appeared to walk toward a camp cabin in the distance.

The following sequence of images shows how I modified the sprite from a front view to a rear view by pulling the hair over her face and then sending her arms to the back layer. (Refer to Chapter 4 or 7 to review using the Select tool and Layer buttons in Vector Mode.)

After you have a front and back view for each character, you can alternate between them during an encounter.

Notice I make the character who faces away from the camera appear larger than the character facing the camera. This is another example of perspective (covered in detail in Chapter 8). The smaller the difference in size, the closer together the sprites will appear. I also remembered to flip *Hector*'s hair swoop from righf to left for his rear view and used the Reshape tool to cover the back of his head.

Do you notice a problem when his head overlaps the floor? If I choose to use this view, I will have to add carpeting or something so his hair is not the same color as the floor! If you don't like having a black wall behind *Zomberta,* you could try flipping the wall sprite so the window appears on the other side.

Create a side view of characters

The most frequent use of a side view is for characters walking or running. Here's how you could change *Zomberta* to a side view when she walks into the room.

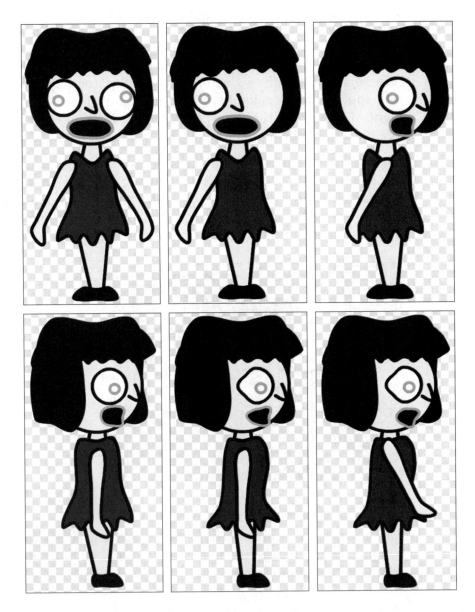

The Select tool allows you to quickly delete some body parts and move others. The Reshape tool is great for tweaking the eyes, mouth, hair, and body. Rather than just moving the line that indicates a nose, a character like *Hector* might look better if you added a few new points to the side of his head by clicking between two existing points with the Reshape tool and dragging to form the nose.

You can spend days (even weeks) tweaking each character view. Scratch makes it easy to swap costumes later, so don't spend too much time on views until you know your animation REALLY needs each one.

Action! (or Let's Get the Story Moving)

It is FINALLY time to bring your characters to life, tell your story, and impress your friends, family, and classmates. If you find yourself getting frustrated, check out the credits from any animated film to remind yourself how many people come together to make an animated tale. If you enjoy one part of the process much more than another, perhaps it's time to recruit a few collaborators.

Animate sprite entering the scene

To save a bit of time, I'm going to use the "cheap" walking technique, in which a character keeps facing the camera and bounces up and down.

1. Click and drag your sprite to the *ending* position on the Stage (where you want the character to stop once on the Stage).

2. Click the Scripts tab.

3. Drag the following blocks into the Scripts Area and change the values to better fit your sprite/scene:

```
when        clicked
go to x: 240 y: 36
glide 4 secs to x: -28 y: 36
```
x: -40
y: 36

When you click the Green Flag button, you should notice the character looks like it's being pulled across the floor rather than walking.

Add a (slightly) more realistic walk

When people walk, they do not just move horizontally across the floor. With each step, their entire bodies also move up and down. (Otherwise, balancing plates on your head would be easier, if you're into that sort of thing.) Sure, animating each step would be far more realistic, but replacing that GLIDE block with the following code blocks is a quick way to make your character more believable.

1. Click the Scripts tab for your character's sprite.

2. Delete the GLIDE block (Shift-click and choose *Delete*) below the GO TO X Y block.

3. Drag and snap the following blocks to the bottom of the GO TO block (shown) and change the values to match:

```
go to x: 240 y: 36
repeat until   x position  < -28
    change y by 3
    change x by -10
    wait .2 secs
    change y by -3
    change x by -10
    wait .2 secs
```

When you click the Green Flag button, your character has a more realistic walk. You can tweak the WAIT values to make your character a bit faster or slower and the X or Y values for a better-looking stride.

Can you figure out why I made the code repeat until X < –28 instead of X = –28? Because the X value is being changed twice, I did not want to take a chance of X skipping past –28 before repeating!

 An alternative to having your character walk across the Stage is having your character walk in place while the background scrolls. You cannot move a backdrop, but you can design a background image as a vector sprite (as I did with the wall), use a SET SIZE block to boost the size, and then use a GLIDE block to move it from one side of the Stage to another.

Broadcast Animation Messages

Various events will happen while your animated story progresses. In my story, *Hector* enters his living room, a flash of lightning reveals a werewolf outside his window right before knocking out the electricity.

When a character reaches its destination, how do you send a message to other sprites and backdrops to do their thing? That's where *broadcasting* comes in!

Send a broadcast message

Let me show you how I'd broadcast a message that *Hector* has entered the room to trigger the lightning flash, a sound effect, and the werewolf's sudden appearance.

1. Click the Scripts tab for your character's sprite and click the *Events* category.

2. Drag and snap a BROADCAST AND WAIT block to the bottom of the "walking" blocks (the REPEAT loop you created in the previous section).

3. Click *Message1* inside the BROADCAST AND WAIT block and select *New Message*.

4. Type **Lightning** and click OK to add a new broadcast message.

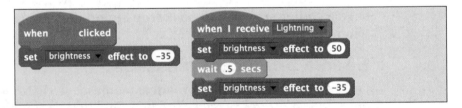

The sprite will broadcast the *Lightning* message after it finishes the blocks in the REPEAT loop. But sending a broadcast is only the first part. You need to tell sprites what to do when they *receive* a message.

Receive a broadcast message

You need to drag a WHEN I RECEIVE block into the Scripts Area for each sprite that you want to react to the broadcast message. When a broadcast message is received, any code blocks attached to the WHEN I RECEIVE block will execute.

Here's how to create a flash of lightning outside the window.

1. Click the Stage button and then click the Scripts tab.

2. Drag the following blocks into the Scripts Area and change the values to match:

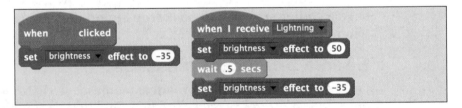

When you click the Green Flag button, the scene outside the window lights up for a moment as soon as the character finishes walking. You can trigger a sound effect at the same time by snapping a PLAY SOUND block between the WHEN I RECEIVE and the SET BRIGHTNESS EFFECT blocks. (Stick with the default *Pop* sound for now. You can replace it later with a more exciting thunder sound by following the steps in Chapter 9.)

> when I receive Lightning ▾
> play sound pop ▾
> set brightness ▾ effect to 50

To make it appear in the window, I'll add these blocks to *Werewoof:*

> when clicked
> go back 10 layers
> hide
>
> when I receive Lightning ▾
> show

 Click directly on the WHEN I RECEIVE block to test your code without having to wait for a broadcast. This can be quite handy in longer animations (and for impatient animators).

To make *Hector* turn around a split second later, he will need a few more blocks, too.

> when I receive Lightning ▾
> wait .25 secs
> switch costume to back view ▾
> wait 1 secs
> switch costume to scared ▾

If I want my first scene to end with the lights going out, then I can add another BROADCAST block with a new message: *Lights out* to *Hector:*

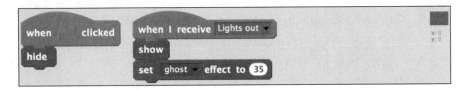

And add a WHEN I RECEIVE broadcast block and SHOW to the *Darkness* sprite with the GHOST EFFECT created earlier in this chapter. I also needed to add a WHEN GREEN FLAG CLICKED and HIDE block to hide the *Darkness* sprite until the *Lights Out* message is received:

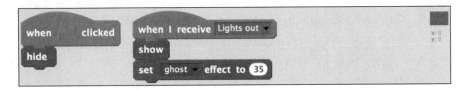

You get the idea? Each event in your story can trigger as many code blocks as you wish to use by broadcasting and receiving messages, like a director calling out instructions to actors and technicians during a rehearsal. And you can see from the SWITCH COSTUME TO blocks why it's important to use descriptive names, such as Back View and Scared.

Switch between Animation Scenes

To change scenes in your animation, you need a way to hide sprites that make up your first scene and show sprites which make up your second scene, as well as change any backdrops that may appear. For my story, this would mean hiding the couch, wall, *Hector*, and *Werewoof* sprites and showing the trees, camp sign, building, and *Zomberta* sprites that make up the next scene.

How do you send a message to hide or show several sprites and change backdrops? This is another ideal use of broadcasting.

1. Add the following code to each sprite you wish to appear at the beginning of your animation and then hide in your second scene:

2. In the WHEN I RECEIVE BLOCK, select *New Message,* type **Scene 2**, and click OK.

3. Add the following code to each sprite you wish to hide at the beginning of your animation and show in Scene 2:

4. If you need to change your backdrop between your first and second scene, click the Stage icon and add the following code to the Scripts tab.

```
when I receive Scene 2 ▾
switch backdrop to scene 2 backdrop ▾
```

5. Select the name of the backdrop you wish to use for Scene 2 in the SWITCH BACKDROP TO block.

Did you notice something missing? You need the block that *sends* the broadcast message! Where should the BROADCAST block go? It must go under the last block that executes in Scene 1.

What is the last thing that happens in Scene 1? In my story, the last thing I coded is the lights going out. So I need the BROADCAST *Scene2* block to go on the *Darkness* sprite:

But there's a problem. Can you see it? As is, the code will hide all my scene 1 sprites and show my scene 2 sprites immediately, so I will never see the darkened version of scene 1 *and* the scene 2 sprites will be darkened instead.

You could use a WAIT block to pause a few seconds on the darkened first scene, but there is a more dramatic way to handle this: Add music! I find just the right music in the Sound Library called *Spooky String*. I can add a PLAY SOUND UNTIL DONE block before BROADCAST Scene 2 and then hide the *Darkness* sprite to have a smooth transition to the next scene.

When I click the Green Flag button, my first scene plays out and then has a much smoother transition into scene 2.

 In a previous tip, I suggest clicking directly on a WHEN I RECEIVE block to test the attached code without having to wait for the broadcast. You can also click a BROADCAST block to trigger *all* the stuff you've set up for that broadcast, such as changing scenes. This is a great shortcut if you want to swap sprites and backdrops to work on a new scene!

And CUT!

There are so many possibilities in the world of animation. If you go to your favorite library or bookstore, you will find a bunch of books dedicated entirely to animation, from the classic hand-drawn approach to stop-motion and computer animation. Below you will find several great resources for inspiration and expanding your animation skills.

Learn more about animation online

The following websites offer tons of tips, techniques, and tutorials to expand your skills.

✔ www.scratch.mit.edu: Come on, I'm not the only Scratch animator out there (and I'm sure not the best, either!). If you search for animation tutorials, you'll find thousands of projects and hundreds of studios covering a wide range of styles.

✔ www.youtube.com: You get the best results when you are specific with a search on YouTube. Try searching for "scratch animation tutorial," "simple animation tutorial," or "2d animation tutorial." (If you are in a school that blocks access to YouTube, try www.schooltube.com.)

✔ www.vimeo.com: If you use the same search terms as YouTube you will find many unique tutorials. *The Six Steps of Animation* is a great introduction to more traditional animation techniques that can also be applied to Scratch.

✔ www.animatorisland.com: An animation community built to share animation techniques from storytelling to drawing to special effects.

✔ www.jerrysartarama.com/art-lessons/Skill-Level/ Kids/: Don't let the LONG web address scare you off. This site has a BUNCH of great art and design tutorials.

✔ diy.org/tags/animation: The online community for kids who like to make stuff, create all kinds of art, learn about the world around them, and experiment with everything from baking to beekeeping.

Part 3

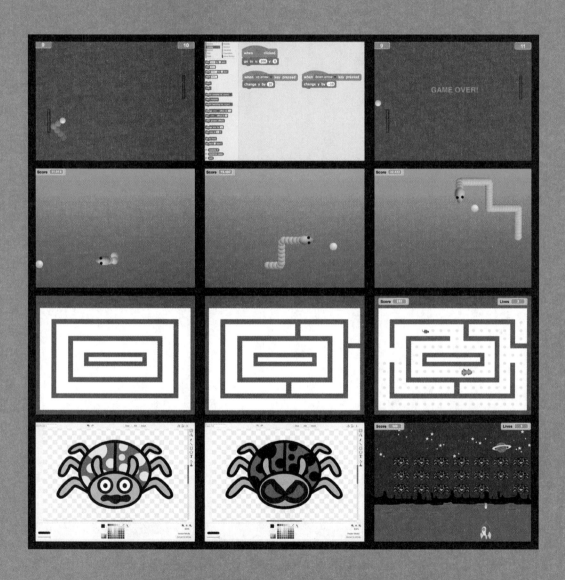

Become a Scratch Game Developer . . .

◼ Design a Classic Videogame 243

◼ Super Snake 266

◼ A-Maze-ing Game 289

◼ Attacking the Clones 319

◼ Game Not Over! 354

Play the completed games, review the code, or insert your own graphics, sound effects, and custom game features by remixing them at www.scratch4kids. com/games.

Design a Classic Videogame

Creating a classic *Pong*-style videogame is the game design equivalent to stick-figure animation. It's not so much about creating an awesome game as it is about covering the basic game design elements that you will need to create *your* awesome game. Most ball sports videogames (think tennis and soccer) evolved from *Pong,* so this is the perfect project for those of you who eventually want to design your own football, volleyball, basketball, or hockey game. Even if you don't want to create any kind of sports game, you will quickly learn how to move a character using keyboard keys, have stuff move around on its own, trigger sound effects, and keep track of score.

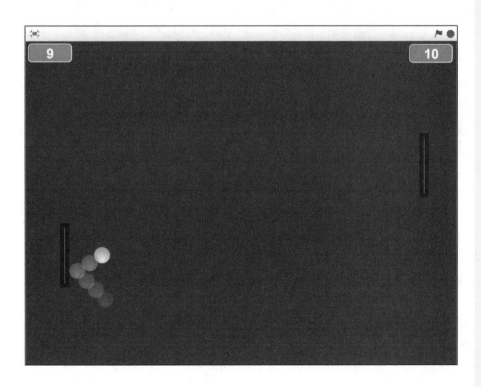

This Game Looks LAME!

Just because your friendly neighborhood author is starting off with simple graphics doesn't mean you have to. If you are not into the "retro" look of this game, Scratch makes it easy to change the background and sprites at any time by changing the backdrop or sprite costumes. You can choose from the many graphics included in the Scratch libraries or paint your own.

Ask anybody over 40 years old what the first videogame he or she ever played was and most will answer *"Pong."* Me, too! The original arcade game was produced by Atari, way back in 1972. It used a black-and-white television set from Walgreens, a coin mechanism designed for a laundromat, and a milk carton to catch the quarters. Atari went on to dominate arcades with huge hits including *Asteroids, Centipede, Missile Command,* and *Tempest.* Then the company brought popular videogames into homes with the Atari 2600, a precursor to Nintendo NES, PlayStation, and Xbox.

Create a New Project

Because the name *Pong* is short for Ping-Pong and a bunch of people have been sued (by the inventors of *Pong*) for calling their games Pong, you'll call your game *Ping-Pong.* (See how super-creative I am?)

1. Go to www.scratch.mit.edu or open the Scratch 2 Offline Editor.

2. If you are online, click Create. If you're offline, choose File ⇨ New.

3. Name your project. (If online, select the title and type **Ping-Pong**. If offline, chose File ⇨ Save As and type **Ping-Pong**.)

4. Delete that cat by selecting the Scissors and clicking the cat or by Shift-clicking the cat and choosing *Delete*.

With the cat gone, you have a world of possibilities! Since this is your game, you can paint the Stage any color you want.

Change the Background Color

I will make my backdrop dark green, just like a classic ping-pong table.

1. Click the Backdrops tab. (You may need to click the Stage icon if you have any sprites selected in your project.)

2. Click the Fill with Color tool.

3. Click the Fill option to the left of the color swatches.

4. Click the color swatch you wish to use.

5. Click inside the Paint Editor canvas to fill the backdrop with the new color.

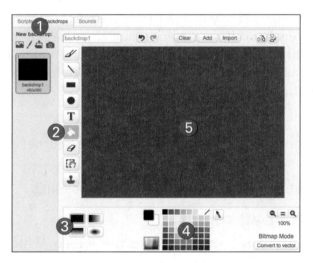

Add a Bouncing Ball

Even though it is not difficult to draw a ball, using the sprite named *Ball* in the Sprite Library will ensure everybody starts with the same sized sprite. If you don't want to be like everybody else, go ahead and paint your own Scratch ball.

1. In the New Sprite area beneath the Stage, click the first icon: Choose Sprite from Library.

2. Under Category, click *Things*.

3. Click the sprite named *Ball* and then click the OK button.

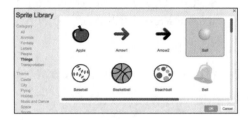

Change the ball color

On the Costumes tab, you see that the *Ball* sprite has five costumes, each a different color. Click any costume to change the ball to that color. Delete all but one of the costumes. I will use the original orange costume because I think it looks more like a real ping-pong ball.

1. Click the costume you wish to delete.

2. Click the X which appears on the top-left corner of the costume.

3. Repeat for the other costumes you're deleting.

Make the ball move

One block can move a sprite across the screen. Which category do you think will have that block?

1. Click the Scripts tab.

2. Click the *Motions* category.

3. Click the MOVE 10 STEPS block, drag it into the Scripts Area, and then release the mouse or trackpad button.

4. Click the block one time while watching the ball on the Stage.

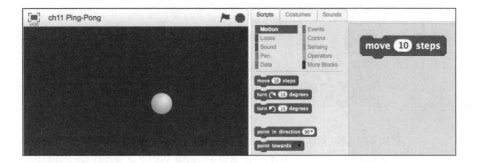

Each time you click the block, the ball should move ten steps to the right. But you don't want somebody to have to keep clicking a block to make something happen.

How should a player start the ball moving? Usually, people start a Scratch game by clicking the Green Flag button above the Stage. In the *Events* category, you should be able to find the block that checks to see whether the Green Flag has been clicked.

1. On the Scripts tab, click the *Events* category.

2. Click and drag the WHEN GREEN FLAG CLICKED block into the Scripts Area.

3. Snap the block onto the top of the MOVE block.

When you click the Green Flag button, the ball should move ten steps. But how you do tell a sprite to keep moving?

Make blocks repeat

Check out the *Control* category. Several blocks can make something happen over and over. Which one should you try?

1. In the *Control* category, find the FOREVER block.

2. Click and drag the FOREVER block over to snap beneath the WHEN GREEN FLAG CLICKED block.

   Notice how the FOREVER block stretches to surround the MOVE block.

3. Click the Green Flag button to test your code.

Any blocks inside the FOREVER block will keep running as long as the Green Flag is on. But your ball will move only until it reaches the right side of the Stage. You haven't given the ball the instruction to bounce!

The programming term for blocks like FOREVER and REPEAT is *loop*. Just like in music, a programming loop is whenever you have commands running over and over again. Loops are so important that you will find them in every programming language. If it weren't for loops, computer programs would be WAY longer, WAY slower, and WAY LESS efficient.

Bounce off edges

Check out the *Motion* category again. You just need one more block to make the ball bounce between edges of the Stage. Can you find it? Where should it go in your code?

1. Click and drag the IF ON EDGE, BOUNCE block from the *Motion* category to the Scripts Area.

2. Snap it into place inside the FOREVER block, just beneath the MOVE block.

3. Click the Green Flag Button to test your code.

Placing the IF ON EDGE, BOUNCE block inside the FOREVER block should make your ball bounce back and forth. But it's kinda boring to keep bouncing in a straight line. How do you change the angle the ball is moving? Surely there is a block for that.

Change the bounce angle

By default, all sprites are pointing in the same direction, to the right. In the *Motion* category, is the POINT IN DIRECTION block. If you click the value, the default is 90, the menu will show four values starting with (90), Right. If you change the direction to one of the other three values, the ball will still bounce in a straight line, back and forth. But you are not stuck with those four directions.

1. Click and drag the POINT IN DIRECTION block into the Scripts Area.

2. Snap the POINT IN DIRECTION block between WHEN GREEN FLAG CLICKED and FOREVER.

3. Click 90 to select it and type **45**.

If you click the Green Flag button to test your code, the ball should now start traveling diagonally and then bounce in a different direction each time it reaches the edge of the Stage.

Set the ball starting position and size

The ball should begin in the center of the screen and look a bit too large.

1. On the Scripts tab, click the *Motion* category, drag a GO TO X Y block into the Scripts Area, and then snap the GO TO X Y block to the bottom of the WHEN GREEN FLAG CLICKED block.

2. Change each number value to 0 (so the ball will start at X: 0, Y: 0).

Choosing direction for sprites

Because a circle is 360 degrees, you can enter any value between 0 and 360 to set the direction of your sprite. As you see in the pull-down menu of the POINT IN DIRECTION block, you also can enter negative values. So, to go left, you can either put –90 or 270. Confused? Don't blame *me*, I didn't invent *geometry!*

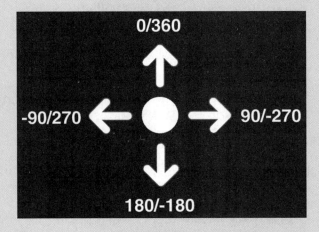

3. Click the *Looks* category and drag a SET SIZE TO block into the Scripts Area.

4. Snap the SET SIZE TO block between WHEN GREEN FLAG CLICKED and GO TO blocks.

5. Change the SET SIZE TO value to 40 to decrease the ball's size from 100% to 40%.

6. Click the Green Flag button to test your code.

The ball should be smaller and begin at the center of the screen when the Green Flag button is pressed.

Add the Paddles

If you are getting used to sprites and code blocks, you can pick up the pace a little when adding the game's paddles.

1. Beneath the Stage, click the Choose Sprite from Library icon.

2. Chose the *Things* category.

3. Click the sprite named *Paddle* and then click the OK button.

4. Click the Costumes tab, click the Color a Shape tool, choose a color swatch (I'll choose brown), and click inside the paddle.

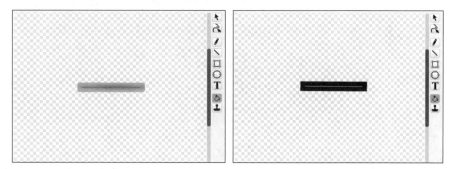

The paddle is the right shape and size, but needs to be rotated.

1. On the Costumes tab, click the Select tool.

2. On the Paint Editor canvas, click the paddle.

3. Click the small circle that appears directly above the paddle and rotate the paddle into a vertical position.

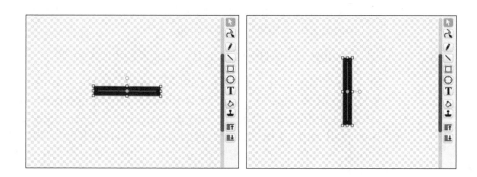

Move paddle with the keyboard

To play the game, players will use one key to move their paddle up and another key to move their paddle down. Before adding the code to enable this, you should position one paddle along one side of the screen.

1. On the Scripts tab, drag the WHEN GREEN FLAG CLICKED block into the Scripts Area.

2. From the *Motion* category, drag and snap a GO TO X Y block to the bottom of the WHEN GREEN FLAG CLICKED block.

3. Change the block values to X: *200* and Y: *0*.

4. Click the Green Flag button to test your code.

Your paddle should move to the middle of the right side of the screen, leaving a gap between the paddle and the edge of the screen so there is room for the ball to zoom by. Now comes the really cool part: interactivity!

1. Drag these blocks into the paddle's Scripts Area:

2. Inside the WHEN KEY PRESSED block, click the drop-down menu and choose *Up Arrow*.

3. Change the CHANGE Y BY block's value to 10.

See how the WHEN KEY PRESSED block is the same shape as the WHEN GREEN FLAG CLICKED block? These are both *hat blocks,* which are blocks that fit only on top of code blocks (and look like baseball caps, I mean *hats*). Because WHEN KEY PRESSED is a hat block, you do not need to click the Green Flag button to test your code. Just click the Up-Arrow key on your keyboard. If your code is correct, the paddle will move up while the key is pressed.

Instead of dragging more code blocks over for the Down-Arrow key, try this:

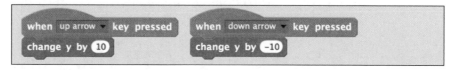

1. Shift-click the WHEN UP ARROW KEY PRESSED block inside the Scripts Area and select *Duplicate*.

2. Drag the duplicate away from the original and then release the mouse or trackpad to drop the set of blocks.

Find X and Y coordinates on the Stage

The Stage is 480 pixels wide by 360 pixels tall. The exact middle of the Stage is 0, 0 (X = 0 and Y = 0). So the largest X value you can have is 240 (the right edge of the Stage) and the lowest X value you can have is –240 (the left edge). The top edge would be Y = 180 and the bottom edge would be Y = –180. There is a handy X and Y coordinates backdrop in the Backdrops Library (the very last backdrop).

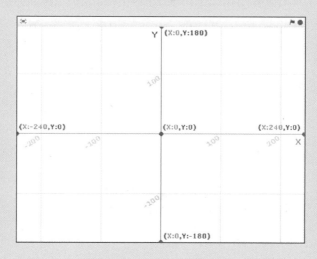

3. Change *Up Arrow* to *Down Arrow* in the new WHEN KEY PRESSED block and change 10 to –10 in the new CHANGE Y BY block.

Test your Up- and Down-Arrow keys to make sure your paddle moves up and down. If you want your paddle to move faster, what would you need to change? Increase the Y values until you have the speed you want.

Make the Ball Bounce Off the Paddle

When you click the Green Flag button, the ball bounces off the edges but passes right through the paddle. Similar to the way you instruct the ball to bounce off the edge of the Stage, you must also instruct the ball to bounce off other objects.

1. Click the *Ball* sprite and then click the Scripts tab.

2. Drag an IF THEN block from the *Control* category and a TOUCHING? block from the *Sensing* category into the Scripts Area.

3. Insert the TOUCHING? block into the IF THEN block.

4. Click the drop-down menu inside the TOUCHING? block and choose *Paddle*.

5. Drag and snap a TURN CLOCKWISE block from the *Motion* category into the Scripts Area and inside the IF THEN block.

6. Change the TURN value to *180* (so the ball will move in the opposite direction).

7. Click and drag the IF THEN block inside the FOREVER block, just beneath the IF ON EDGE BOUNCE block.

IF THEN blocks will often go inside a FOREVER block so your game or program will keep checking whether the condition is true (such as "Is ball touching paddle?"). When you click the Green Flag to test your game, the ball should bounce right off the paddle.

Add a Second Player

The game will surely be more fun with an opponent. Remember how to Shift-click a chunk of code to duplicate it? You can use the same technique to duplicate sprites, too. And, when you duplicate a sprite, all the code inside it is also duplicated. So it should be easy to create a second player.

1. Shift-click the paddle sprite, choose *Info,* and change the name to *Player Right* (since it is on the right side of the Stage).

2. Click the blue triangle to exit *Info.*

3. Shift-click *Player Right* and choose *Duplicate.*

4. Shift click the new sprite, choose *Info,* and change the name to *Player Left.*

5. Click the blue triangle to exit *Info.*

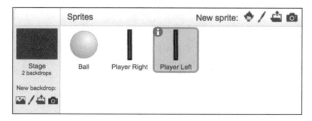

Go to the Scripts tab for *Player Left.* All the scripts from *Player Right* should be there, but you will need to change the horizontal (X) position and change the keyboard keys that will control the second paddle. (Both players cannot use the arrow keys at the same time, right?)

Update the Player Left code blocks

1. Change the GO TO X Y block's X value to –*200*.

2. Change WHEN UP ARROW KEY PRESSED to WHEN W KEY PRESSED.

3. Change WHEN DOWN ARROW KEY PRESSED to WHEN S KEY PRESSED.

4. Click the Green Flag button to test your game.

You probably noticed there's a problem: The ball bounces off *Player Right* but passes right through *Player Left*. Can you figure out why? I'll give you a hint: Check the code on the *Ball* sprite.

Update the ball code

Scratch updated the TOUCHING? block when you changed the name of the sprite from *Paddle* to *Player Right*. But the IF THEN block is only checking whether the ball is touching *Player Right*, not *Player Left*. What's the solution? How about a bit more duplicating?

1. Shift-click the IF THEN block, choose *Duplicate*, and drag the copy to snap beneath the original IF THEN block.

2. In the duplicate blocks, change *Player Right* to *Player Left*.

3. Click the Green Flag to test your code.

```
forever
    move 10 steps
    if on edge, bounce
    if        touching  Player Right ▼  ?    then
        turn ↻ 180 degrees

    if        touching  Player Left ▼  ?    then
        turn ↻ 180 degrees

                                                            x: -155
                                                            y: -58
```

The ball should bounce off both rackets. But you may find after a few volleys that the ball just bounces back and forth without needing to move either racket. This happens because the ball uses the same angle, 180 degrees, each time it bounces off either racket.

Make the bounce more random

Instead of using a single value, you can use the PICK RANDOM block to choose a number between two different values.

1. Click the *Ball* sprite.

2. Click the Scripts tab.

3. Drag a PICK RANDOM block inside each TURN CLOCKWISE block (replacing the *180* values inside each) and change the values to match the following image:

```
if        touching  Player Right ▼  ?    then
    play sound  pop ▼
    turn ↻ pick random 170 to 190 degrees

if        touching  Player Left ▼  ?    then
    play sound  pop ▼
    turn ↻ pick random 170 to 190 degrees

                                                            x: 14
                                                            y: 119
```

Now when you click the Green Flag button to test your code, the ball should bounce off each racket at a slightly different angle. This would be a good time to find an opponent to test your game with. But wouldn't it be more fun if your game could keep track of score?

Keep Track of Player Scores

So far, you have *Player Right* controlling one paddle and *Player Left* controlling a second paddle, with the ball just bouncing all over the place. If I am *Player Right* and you are *Player Left,* how do you score against me? I mean what's the point of this game, *man?!* (Or what's the point of this game, *lady!?*)

Check the X value of the ball

If you miss the ball, your opponent (me) scores a point, right? You used two IF THEN blocks to check whether the ball is touching *Player1* or *Player2*. Couldn't we use two more IF THEN blocks to check the X position of the ball? If the X value is too large, then the ball must have shot past the player on the right side of the Stage. Too small? The player on the left side must have missed the ball.

1. Click the *Ball* sprite and then click the Scripts tab.

2. Drag these three blocks into the Scripts Area:

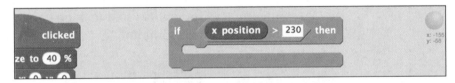

Player1's X position is 200 and the maximum value is 240, so your IF THEN block could check whether the ball's X position is greater than 230 (it's good to have a little leeway). Type **230** inside the second > slot (IF X > 230).

But we need somewhere to keep track of the score. *Scores,* really, because each player will need his or her own score.

Create score variables

Don't get all freaked out by the word *variables*. Some of you may have already learned about variables in math class; the rest of you Scratchers will quickly become variable masters!

Score variables provide a place for Scratch to keep track of the score for each player.

Since the score will be determined by the position of the *Ball* sprite on the Stage, all code for changing either player's score will be placed in the Scripts Area for *Ball*.

1. With the *Ball* sprite selected, click the *Data* category on the Scripts tab.

   Wait a minute! Where are all the code blocks? Because the blocks in this category require a variable, you will not see any until you have *created* your first variable.

2. Click the Make a Variable button.

3. Name the variable *Player Right Score,* leave *For All Sprites* checked, and click OK.

4. Repeat Steps 2 and 3 to create a second variable named *Player Left Score.*

   Both variables should appear on the Stage and you should now see several VARIABLE blocks listed under the *Data* category.

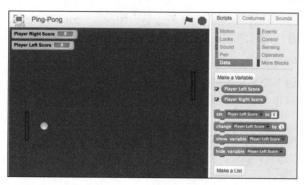

Adjust score display

The scores are taking up too much room on the Stage, and I don't like having them stacked one over the other. You can drag variable displays to a new position on the Stage just like sprites. If you place each score above the paddle it goes with, then you don't need to see *Player Left Score* and *Player Right Score;* you can just show the value.

1. On the Stage, click and drag each score into position above the corresponding paddle.

2. Double-click each score on the Stage to hide the name of the variable (it will just display the numeric value).

3. Re-adjust the score positions to take up the least room.

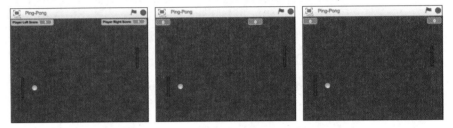

Increase the score

If *Player Left* misses the ball, then *Player Right*'s score should change by 1.

1. Drag and snap the CHANGE BY block from the *Data* category into the IF THEN block and change the values to *Player Left Score* and *1*.

2. Drag the IF THEN block into the FOREVER block so Scratch will continually check whether the ball has made it past *Player Right*.

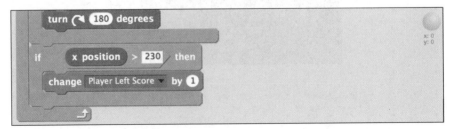

3. Click the Green Flag button to test your code.

If your code works like mine, then *Player Left*'s score keeps increasing whenever the ball is between *Player Right* and the edge of the screen instead of just assigning one point at a time. Can you think of a way to fix this?

One way is to reset the position of the ball after adding a point. Then you can have the game pause briefly before the ball moves again.

1. Drag and snap a GO TO X Y block to the bottom of the CHANGE BY block and set the values to X: 0 and Y: 0.

2. Drag and snap a WAIT SECS block from the *Control* category to the bottom of the GO TO X Y block and change the value to 1.

3. Click the Green Flag button to test your game.

Player 2's score should increase by 1 whenever the ball reaches the right side. Then the ball should jump to the center and wait 1 second before moving again.

You can follow the same steps to enable Player 1's score whenever Player 2 misses the ball. Or you can take a shortcut by duplicating the previous code and changing the values. (Be sure to replace the > block with a < block!)

Reset scores when the game starts

You will want to reset the score whenever somebody clicks the Green Flag button to start a new game. This is an *easy* one!

1. Click the *Ball* sprite and then click the Scripts tab.

2. Drag and snap these blocks into the Scripts Area beneath a WHEN GREEN FLAG CLICKED block and change the values to *Player Right Score* and *Player Left Score:*

Check for the Winning Score

Are you going to have people play hour-after-hour until they are so bored they want to pound their heads into the screen? I usually play *Ping-Pong* until somebody scores 11 points.

Create an end-of-game sprite

Create a new sprite named *Game Over,* which will check the score, display a "Game Over" message when either player score reaches 11, and then end the game.

1. Click the Paint New Sprite icon beneath the Stage.

2. Click the Costumes tab.

3. Click the Convert to Vector button.

4. Click the Text tool.

5. Select a font. (I'll select Helvetica.)

6. Choose a bright color swatch. (I'll choose orange to match the score color.)

7. Click near the center of the Paint Editor canvas and type **Game Over!**

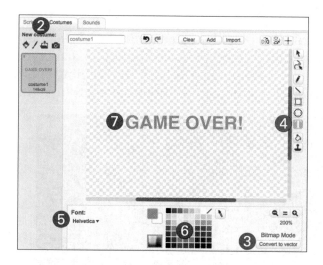

On the Stage, you will need to click and drag the message into the correct position (centered and a bit above the ball).

Add an end-of-game code

When one of the player's score reaches 11, the winning message should appear. This means you need to hide the end-of-game sprite's message at the beginning of the game. You will need one IF THEN block per player to check his or her score.

1. Click the Scripts tab for the *Game Over* sprite.

2. Add these blocks to the Scripts Area:

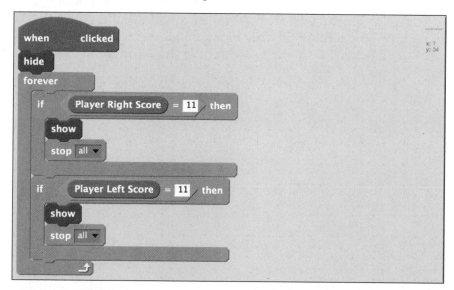

When you click the Green Flag button to test your code, you should be able to play the game until one of the players reaches 11, then the Game Over message should be displayed and the code should stop running. (Reduce the winning score if you want to check your code quickly without having to reach 11.)

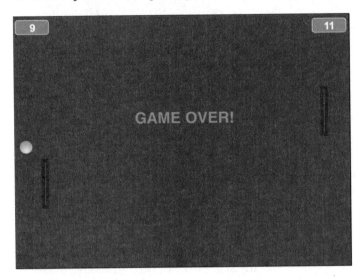

Add Sound Effects

An easy way to make your game your *Ping-Pong* game more authentic is to add a sound effect to the bouncing ball. You can use the default *Pop* sound whenever the ball hits a racket by adding a PLAY SOUND block inside each of the IF THEN blocks, which check if the ball is touching the paddle.

```
forever
    move 10 steps
    if on edge, bounce
    if     touching Player Right ▼ ?   then
        play sound pop ▼
        turn ↻ 180 degrees

    if     touching Player Left ▼ ?   then
        play sound pop ▼
        turn ↻ 180 degrees
```

x: 49
y: 49

See if you can figure out where you would put a different PLAY SOUND block to go along with your Game Over message (be careful where the STOP ALL block goes).

Improve your game

In game design, there is almost always room for improvement. In each of the next chapters, you will learn more game design techniques. In the meantime, see if you can figure out how to improve your *Ping-Pong* game. Here are a few ideas:

- **Make the goals smaller:** Instead of using the entire side you could create a smaller goal, as in ice hockey, to make it more difficult to score a point.

- **Add obstacles:** Add other sprites for the ball to bounce off between the two players.

- **Adjust game difficulty:** You can make the game more challenging by changing the length of the paddles, increasing the speed of the ball, or slowing down player movement.

- **Allow players to "catch" the ball:** Program an additional key players can press when the ball is close enough to catch. When they release the key, the ball could fly right across the Stage.

Super Snake

When I was a kid, I *REALLY* wanted a pet snake! I don't mean a cute little garter or grass snake, no thank you. I dreamed of having a boa constrictor or a python that could grow to be six feet or even longer!

Unfortunately, my stepfather is really scared of snakes, so I couldn't bring anything bigger than a nightcrawler into the house. The closest I ever came was playing various *Snake* games on my computer. Designing your own version of this classic game means you can have any kind of snake you want. Best of all, you can create the entire game with just two sprites and a dash of Scratch blocks!

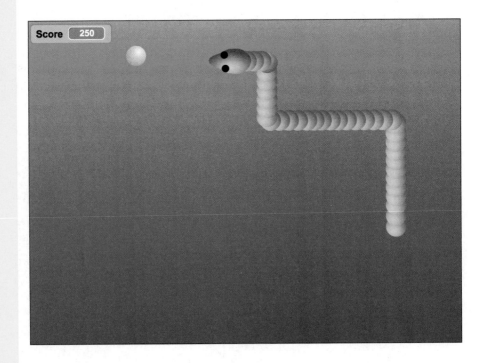

Create a New Project

This is one chapter where I could use the name *Snake* since that's the *type* of game (like *tag* or *board game*), not the original game title. But I think *Super Snake* might grab people's attention. If you're as afraid of snakes as my stepfather, feel free to make your game *Creepy Caterpillar* or *Wonder Earthworm* or *Seriously Slimy Slug*.

1. Go to `scratch.mit.edu` or open the Scratch 2 Offline Editor.

2. If you are online, click Create. If offline, select File⇨New.

3. Name your project. (If online, select the title and type **Super Snake**. If using the offline version of Scratch, select File⇨Save As and type **Super Snake**.)

4. Delete the cat by selecting the Scissors and clicking the sprite or holding the Shift key while clicking and then choosing *Delete*.

Use Gradient for Background

I will make my backdrop brown since I imagine my snake digging through the dirt in search of sniveling snacks (perhaps a shell-less snail or a scrumptious truffle). Instead of filling it in with a solid color, you can make your backdrop a bit more interesting by using a gradient to blend between a lighter and a darker shade.

1. Click the Backdrops tab.

 2. Click the Fill with Color tool.

3. Click one of the gradient options to the left of the color swatches.

4. Click a dark color swatch.

5. Click the current swatch to switch to the background color.

6. Choose a lighter color.

7. Click the Paint Editor canvas to fill the backdrop with your gradient.

8. If you wish to try a different gradient, click the Clear button and start over.

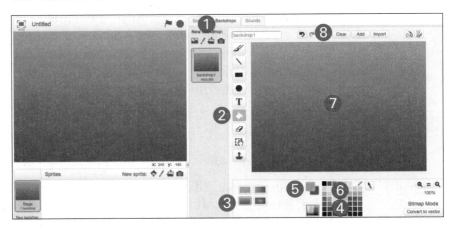

Construct Your Snake

If you browse the Sprite Library, you will find many animals, but no snakes. That's fine. Part of the fun of this project is designing a slithering snake out of a few simple shapes.

1. Click the Choose Sprite from Library icon beneath the Stage.

2. Choose the *Things* category.

3. Click the sprite named *Ball* and then click the OK button.

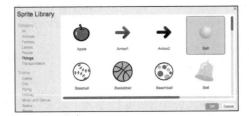

Don't worry. You are not in the wrong chapter. Wait until you see how Scratch lets you transform a simple ball into a sly serpent.

1. Rename the sprite *Snake*. (Click the blue Info button or Shift-click and choose *Info.*)

2. Check which direction the sprite is facing (90 degrees to the right) so you know which side of the shape is the front of the head.

3. Click the Back button (white triangle on blue circle) to close the Info window.

Select a sprite costume

On the Costumes tab, click the color you wish to use for your snake. (I think light green looks great against the brown background.) You can delete the other costumes. It will help later if you rename the costume to *Head*.

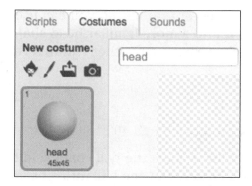

Create a snake body

I'm sure you could design a long, curvy snake using the Paint Editor tools, but this game requires a more flexible creature. Instead of drawing the entire snake, you will use a few Scratch blocks to clone a simple body segment into a longer snake. Begin by duplicating the head costume.

1. On the Costumes tab, Shift-click or right-click the first costume and choose *Duplicate*.

2. Rename the new costume *Body*.

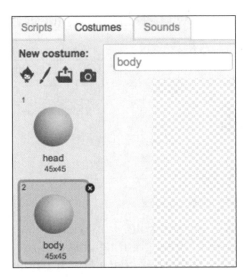

Sculpt the snake's head

The sprite you chose is a vector graphic, so you can use the Reshape tool to stretch it into a more familiar head shape. Then you can draw a few black eyes and any other features you want.

1. Click the *Head* costume.

 2. Click the Reshape tool.

 3. Click the Zoom In button twice to a 400% view.

4. On the Paint Editor canvas, click the ball shape and then click and drag control points to sculpt the ball into a head shape.

 5. Click the Ellipse tool, click the Solid option, select the black color swatch, and then click and drag to draw one of the eyes (hold the Shift key for a perfect circle).

 6. Click the Duplicate tool, click the eye, and drag the copy into place.

 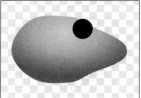 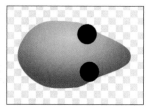

Set the Snake in Motion

In a typical snake game, the player is always moving forward at the same speed while clicking buttons to turn left or right in pursuit of food. It's like combining the constant motion of the *Ping-Pong* ball with the left and right movement of the paddle.

Make the sprite move forward

You must put the MOVE block inside a FOREVER block to create a loop that keeps the snake moving forward.

1. Click the Scripts tab for the snake sprite.

2. Drag these blocks into the Scripts Area and change the MOVE value to *2:*

Add turning blocks

To avoid slithering head first off the Stage, you need to add two sets of blocks to turn your snake in each direction.

1. Drag two WHEN KEY PRESSED blocks from the Events category into the Scripts Area.

2. Drag and snap a TURN block beneath each WHEN KEY PRESSED block and change the values to *90.*

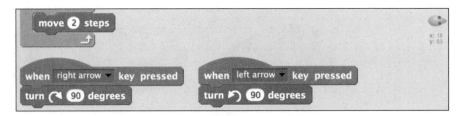

If you click the Green Flag button on the Stage, the snake moves forward on its own, turns left when you press the Left-Arrow key, and turns right when you press the Right-Arrow key.

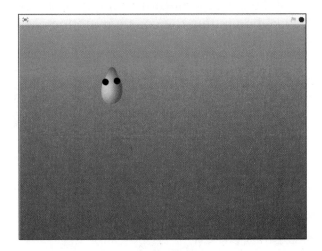

 Why have the snake turn 90 degrees each time? Because it will make the game harder if the snake can move only up, down, left, and right versus turning any way the player wants. The same thing applies to allowing only the Left- and Right-Arrow keys to control movement.

I know it's not too exciting to just move a head around the screen, especially if this is not your first Scratch game design project. But next comes one of the coolest parts: coding the body!

Add Body to the Snake

You duplicated the *Head* costume (when it was still just a green ball) to make a body costume. If the head always moves at a constant speed, you can use a neat cloning trick to create body segments that follow the head around each turn.

Create body cloning loop

You will need a WAIT block to slow down the creation of clones. So the next set of blocks needs to go under another WHEN GREEN FLAG CLICKED block or the new WAIT will slow down the snake movement, too.

1. Drag another WHEN GREEN FLAG CLICKED block into the Scripts Area beneath the previous blocks or to the right.

2. Drag and snap the remaining blocks pictured beneath WHEN GREEN FLAG CLICKED and change WAIT to *.25*.

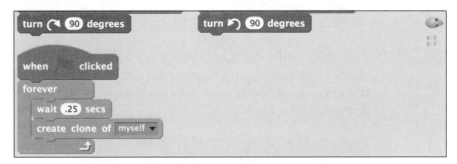

This is a great place to check your code. When you click the Green Flag button, the head moves the same way as before, but now a strange-looking body (made of several more *heads!?!*) trails behind. That's correct because you need to change the clone costume.

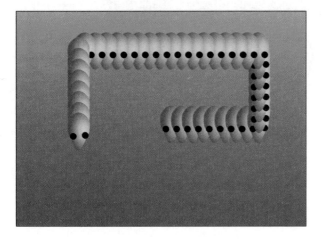

Make clones different

When you create a clone of a sprite, you can use the WHEN I START AS A CLONE block to give instructions to each new clone, such as changing the size or switching costumes.

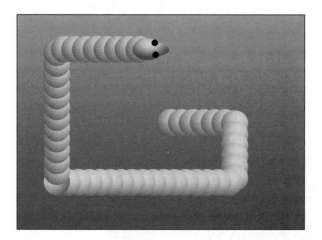

Test your code again and you have a much more suitable body shape. But since you sculpted the head, the body sections appear thicker, which looks more like a caterpillar. And the snake length appears to be endless.

You can fix both of those problems by adding three more blocks under WHEN I START AS A CLONE. The last block might surprise you.

The SET SIZE TO block makes the body sections a bit smaller than the head. But what's up with WAIT and DELETE THIS CLONE? Click the Green Flag button and see what happens.

Your snake moves the same way across the Stage, but now appears much shorter. Can you figure out why?

When the game starts, the head creates a clone of itself and then immediately moves two steps. But when the clone is created, it waits a quarter of a second (.25) before moving, so it's a few steps behind the head. Each clone is the same distance behind the previous one.

With the code you just added, the clone switches to the *Body* costume, is resized to 75% right away, and then moves along with the head and other clones for two seconds before being deleted. That two-second delay determines how many clones remain on the screen at one time, which is how long your snake is. Change the value to WAIT *5* SECS and see what happens. You get a much longer snake, right?

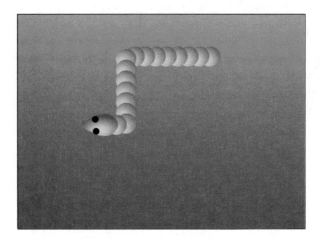

For this game, I'm thinking that each time the snake eats a yummy morsel, it will grow a bit longer. By using cloned body parts, you can increase that WAIT block value as the player gets more food. What do you say, want to add that food to the game?

Add Food for the Snake

In the snake game I remember best, a single bit of food randomly appears at the start of the game. Each time the snake eats it, the snake grows a bit longer and another snack appears somewhere else.

Create food sprite

You can choose any sprite you want or paint your own food. I'll use another ball and change the color and size to make the task easy.

1. Click the Choose Sprite from Library icon beneath the Stage.

2. Choose an object to act as food for the snake and then click OK.

3. Click the Info button on the sprite and change the name to *Food*.

4. Click the Costumes tab.

5. If there's more than one costume, select the one you want to use. (I'll use orange for my grub.)

6. Change the costume name to *Food1* (in case you want to add different snacks later) and then delete the other costumes.

Randomize food location

The hardest place to get food in a snake game is right near the edge of the screen. If the snake misses the turn, it will touch the edge and end the game. Drag your food sprite to the lower-left corner of the Stage. Then use the X and Y coordinates to set the values for your random movement blocks.

1. Drag the food sprite to the bottom-left edge of the Stage.

2. Click the Scripts tab.

   In the top-right corner is a faded version of the sprite with its current X and Y coordinates beneath it.

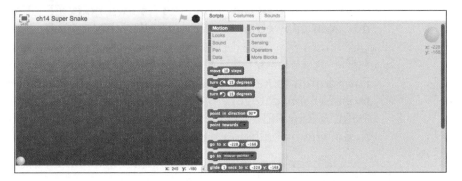

 People are often confused by the X and Y coordinates that appear right below the Stage. Those are not for the sprite; they are the position of the cursor on the Stage. You can test this by moving your cursor across the Stage and seeing how the values change until your cursor is beyond one of the edges.

3. Drag WHEN GREEN FLAG CLICKED and GO TO X Y blocks into the Scripts Area.

4. Drag two PICK RANDOM # blocks into the two GO TO slots.

5. Use the X value and Y values from your food's position on the bottom-left corner for your random range. (Scratch will pick a number between the negative and positive values.)

Click the Green Flag button several times and the food sprite should appear in a different location each time.

The Stage is 480 pixels wide (X) and 360 pixels tall (Y). So the maximum values are X = 240 and Y = 180 (the top-right corner of the Stage), and the lowest values are X = –240 and Y = –180 (the bottom-left corner).

Set Up Game Collisions

In the *Ping-Pong* game, *Sensing* category blocks detect when a ball hits a paddle and the ball bounces when it hits the edge of the Stage. This game will check whether the snake head touches the food, the edge of the screen, or its own body. (That's right. You're not even allowed to touch *yourself* in this game!)

Check for snake and snack collision

For Scratch to keep checking whether a collision has happened, most *Sensing* category blocks must go inside a loop, such as FOREVER or REPEAT. An IF THEN block gives instructions on what to do when a collision happens.

1. Click the *Food* icon beneath the Stage and click the Scripts tab.

2. Shift-click (or right-click) the GO TO X Y block, choose *Duplicate,* and drag the copy off to the side. (You will use the copy to move the food if collision is detected.)

3. Drag and snap these blocks beneath the GO TO X Y block:

4. Click inside the TOUCHING COLOR block and then click one of the snake's eyes.

5. Drag and snap the copied GO TO X Y block into the IF THEN block.

Click the Green Flag button and steer your snake toward the food. Each time the head collides with the food, the food instantly moves to another location.

Make the edge of the Stage deadly

In the *Ping-Pong* game, the ball bounces off the sides of the Stage because of the IF ON EDGE, BOUNCE block. But you don't want the snake to *bounce;* you want it to *die!* So you need a different *Sensing* category block here.

1. Click the snake icon beneath the Stage and click the Scripts tab.

2. Instead of adding another FOREVER block, you can snap the TOUCHING block inside the FOREVER block that's already there beneath MOVE *2* STEPS.

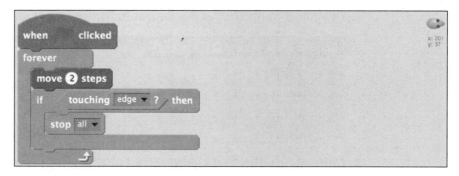

3. Make sure the TOUCHING block's value is *Edge*.

4. Click the Green Flag button to test your code.

When you steer your serpent to the edge of the screen, the game stops. The other event that ends the game is the head running into its tail, as if it is a poisonous snake that bites itself. Stupid snake! (Who am I to talk? One night I was chewing some tough meat and practically *bit my own tongue off!?!*)

Make the snake's body deadly

You must be getting the hang of collisions by now. You can use different *Sensing* category blocks to check whether sprites are touching each other, a specific color, or the edge of the Stage. But how do you check for a collision between the head and the body if they are the same sprite? I said you can give instructions to each clone when it is created (by using a WHEN I START AS A CLONE block). That's how you change the clones to use the *Body* costume. Since that costume does not have any black in it, you can use the same *Sensing* category block you used to detect the food.

1. Click the snake icon beneath the Stage and click the Scripts tab.

2. Drag another WHEN I START AS A CLONE block into the Scripts Area (beside or beneath the other blocks).

3. Drag and snap these remaining blocks beneath it:

Test your code. I bet the snake starts to move and then the entire program stops within one second. Can you figure out why?

Look for the code that creates clones after the Green Flag is clicked. Your program waits .25 second and then creates the first clone. As soon as that clone is created, it checks to see if it is touching anything black. Since the clone is in exactly the same position as the head, *of course* it is touching something black, *the eyes!* You can use another WAIT block before checking to see whether the clone is touching black, but where does *that* block go?

Delay body collision

You need to add a WAIT block to the second WHEN I START AS A CLONE set of blocks. Be careful where you snap it in or you might throw off your head-to-body collision.

Set the value of the WAIT block to *1* SECS and test your game again. Each clone waits just long enough to be behind where the eyes are on the head and your snake slinks around until the head runs back into the tail. You may need to increase the WAIT time, depending on the size of your sprite costumes and the speed the player is moving.

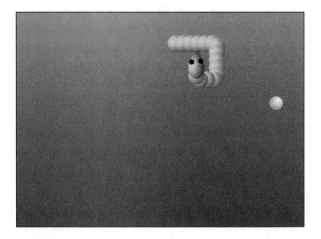

Oops, I spotted a few problems that mess up the head-to-body collision in my game.

Troubleshoot snake collision

If the snake's head is touching the edge of the Stage at the beginning of the game, the game ends right away. And because the eyes are on the side of the head, they may touch the side of a body clone in a tight turn.

An easy fix for the first problem is to set the snake's position at the beginning of the game. Go to the first WHEN GREEN FLAG CLICKED block and add a GO TO X Y block <u>before</u> the FOREVER block that keeps the snake moving.

As for the eyes, you can either move them closer together in the Paint Editor or make the body a bit smaller. I think the second solution is better because my snake still looks a bit too much like a centipede (which is an *entirely* different game). The body size is set to 75%. I'm going to try 50%.

When I click the Green Flag button, the snake begins at the center of the Stage. When I move the snake around, the eye collision is working. Best of all, the smaller body sections make it look more snakelike.

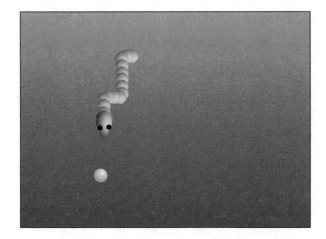

So what's missing to make this a SUPER snake game? You haven't added the code to make the snake grow each time it swallows a snack. The snake growing longer and longer is what makes for a challenging (and fun) game. You know the other missing piece for sure. There's no way to keep score yet!

Code Snake Growth

In your snake scripts, can you find what determines how long the snake is? Look under the first WHEN I START AS A CLONE block. That WAIT block value makes the snake shorter or longer, right? Try changing it to *8* seconds and testing your game. Then try *2* seconds.

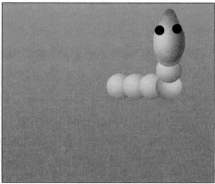

You need to increase that value each time the snake eats. Instead of using a *set value* (a number that doesn't change) inside the WAIT block, you should use a *variable,* which you can increase each time the snake collides with the food.

Variables are vital for programming video games (and just about anything else people use code for) because they allow you to change values while your program is running.

Create the snake's length variable

Scratch offers three options for displaying a variable on the Stage: with-title, without-title, and slider.

The slider allows a player to change a variable during the game by dragging left and right. This could be used to change the speed of a vehicle, the color of a sprite, or even swap costumes.

Here's how to display your snake's length:

1. Beneath the Scripts tab, click the *Data* category.

2. Click the Make a Variable button, type **Length**, choose *For All Sprites,* and click OK.

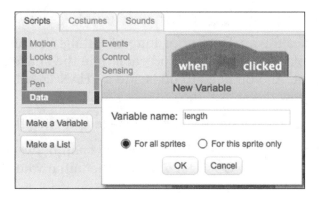

3. Drag and snap a SET TO block beneath the first WHEN GREEN FLAG CLICKED block and make sure the value is *2*. (This begins the game with a short snake.) If you have more than one variable, be sure to choose the variable you want to use.

4. Drag a LENGTH variable into the WAIT block beneath WHEN I START AS A CLONE.

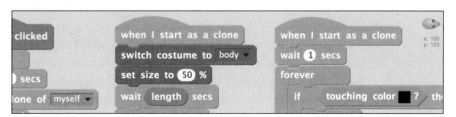

If you click the Green Flag button, your snake begins with a short length. The LENGTH variable also appears on the top-left corner of the Stage. You will eventually want to hide the variable from players, but it can be useful there while completing your scripting.

You can change the look of the LENGTH variable on the Stage by double-clicking it. To see the variable slider in action, change it while your game is running.

Control the snake's length with code

What causes the snake to grow longer? Eating! You already have blocks in place to move the food each time the snake's head collides with it. All you need to do is add a CHANGE LENGTH BY block to grow the snake, too.

1. Click the *Food* icon beneath the Stage and click the Scripts tab.

2. Drag a CHANGE LENGTH BY block to snap between the IF THEN block and GO TO X Y. Leave the initial value of 1 for now.

When you start the game, the snake starts short but grows longer each time it eats a snack. You also can confirm the variable is working by watching the length display on the Stage.

Track Player Score

Unlike the other game projects in this book, in *Super Snake,* the score is based on how long the player survives before hitting the edge or itself. You can use Scratch's built-in timer to increase the score throughout the game. With the snake length working, you can hide that variable to make room for a new score variable.

Hide the length variable

1. Click the snake icon beneath the Stage.

2. On the Scripts tab, click the *Data* category.

3. Uncheck the *Length* variable box to hide it behind the Stage.

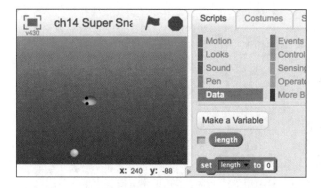

Create the player's score variable

1. Beneath the Scripts tab, click the *Data* category.

2. Click the Make a Variable button, type **Score**, choose *For All Sprites,* and click OK.

3. Drag the Score display into position on the Stage.

4. Drag the following blocks into the snake sprite's Scripts Area:

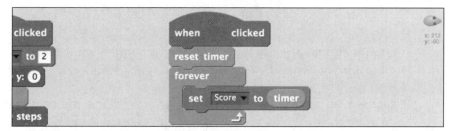

In Scratch, the timer is always running, so you need to be sure you include a RESET TIMER block so the score starts over at the beginning of each game.

It's that time, my Scratch Friend. Click that beautiful Green Flag button and test your COMPLETED SUPER SNAKE GAME!

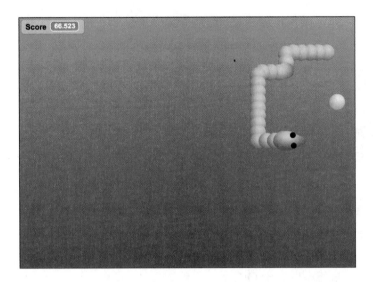

Ways to make *Super Snake*
more challenging

Though it should already be fun to play, you may want to make the game tougher for your friends. Here are some quick solutions.

- **Increase the snake speed:** The faster the snake goes, the harder it becomes to control. (*Note:* You will need to adjust some of your clone settings so the body parts don't get farther apart.)

- **Decrease size of food:** You could do this at the beginning of the game or have the size decrease as the game progresses.

- **Increase the pause between turns:** You used a WAIT block to keep the player from turning around and around You can increase the WAIT value to make turning exactly when a player wants to even more.

- **Add baby snakes:** Once the snake reaches a certain length, or if it eats the wrong snack, you could have a small part split off and become another snake. If the player touches the new snake, it's lights out.

- **Rig the game:** If you want to be really sneaky, you could place the snacks right on the edge of the Stage at set intervals.

A-Maze-ing Game

While *Pong* is the first videogame I ever played, *Pac-Man* is the only game I ever saw my *grandmother* playing! Maybe that explains why it became the highest grossing game in history. (More than ten billion quarters. You do the math!)

Who can say what makes one game wildly popular while another gathers cobwebs in a dark corner of the arcade? As a game designer, you should always strive to create a game that *you* would want to play. For legal reasons, I cannot show you how to create a game *exactly* like *Pac-Man,* but I *can* share what I know about creating a fun maze game in Scratch.

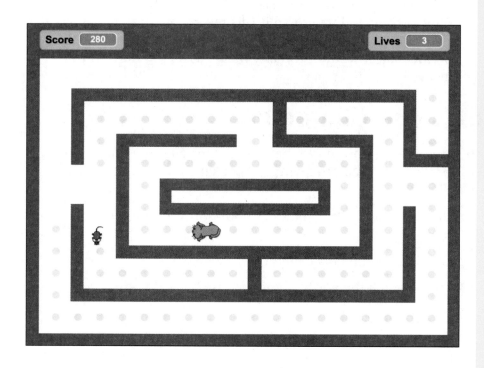

Create a New Project

Before choosing a title, pick out the characters you want to include in your game. After browsing through the Sprite Library, I decided the best ones to use for a maze game are *Mouse1* and *Cat2* because each is drawn in a top-down view the way the maze will be. Because the player will be the mouse, I will call my game *Amazing Mouse*. Okay, not the most creative title, but what does *Pac-Man* even mean?!

1. Go to `scratch.mit.edu` or open the Scratch 2 Offline Editor.

2. If you are online, click Create. If offline, select File⇨New.

3. Rename your project. (If online, select the title and type **Amazing Mouse**. If using the offline version of Scratch, select File⇨Save As and type **Amazing Mouse**.)

4. Delete the cat with the Scissors (or Shift-click the cat and choose *Delete*). I must admit this feels a bit strange because I am about to *choose* a cat for my game. If a mouse saw the Scratch cat it would probably be laughing too hard to run away.

Choose Game Characters

Before drawing your maze, having all your character sprites on the Stage is helpful. Then you can design a maze in which they can fit into.

1. Beneath the Stage, click the Choose Sprite from Library icon.

2. Choose the *Animals* category.

3. Double-click the sprite named *Mouse1*.

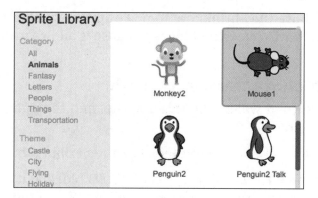

4. Repeat Steps 1–3 but choose the sprite named *Cat2*.

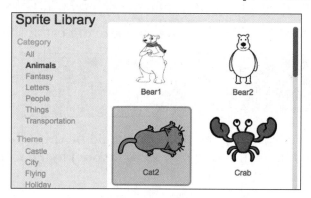

When I click and drag the animals side-by-side onto the Stage, I notice two things. First, the mouse is nearly the same size as the cat. Second, the sprites are way too large to fit inside the maze.

You could use the Shrink tool to make sprites smaller with each click. I prefer to use code blocks because it allows me to be more precise.

Resize characters with code

Because the cat will be the larger sprite, find the right size for that character first.

1. Click the cat sprite and then click the Scripts tab.

2. Drag the WHEN GREEN FLAG CLICKED block and the SET SIZE TO block into the Scripts Area and snap them together.

3. Change the value to *30* inside the SET SIZE TO block.

4. Click the SET SIZE TO block to resize the cat sprite.

I did not know right away that 30% would be the right size for the cat; I had to try a few different sizes before I found the one that looked right.

Copy blocks between sprites

The mouse needs the same blocks you just created. Here's a quick way to copy them over.

1. Drag the WHEN GREEN FLAG CLICKED block from the cat Scripts Area to the mouse sprite.

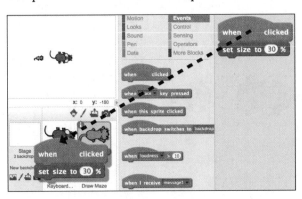

2. Click the mouse sprite and make sure the code copied over.

3. Change the value of SET SIZE TO from *30* to *20*.

4. Click the SET SIZE TO block once to resize the mouse sprite.

If you compare the cat and mouse sizes on the Stage, they should look proportionate now. So onto maze building!

Design Maze Background

A maze backdrop requires a bit more thought and design work than the other game projects in this book.

Create cheese bits

Remember in *Pac-Man* having to eat little dots before getting to the next level? I want to have little bits of cheese for the mouse to munch all the way around the maze.

Lining up all those bits inside your maze could be tricky, though, so what if we place the bits first and then use them as a guide to help draw the maze walls?

1. Beneath the Stage, click the Paint New Sprite icon.

2. Click the Costumes tab.

3. Click the Zoom In button (plus sign) four times to get to 1600%.

4. Click the Brush tool.

5. Drag the Line Width slider to the middle.

6. Click a yellow color swatch.

7. Click the middle of the Paint Editor canvas one time.

8. Shift-click the new sprite, choose *Info,* change the name to *Cheese,* and click the Back button to close the Info window.

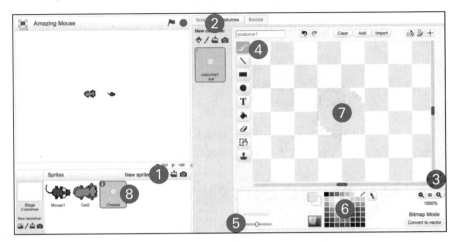

Imagine how long it would take to duplicate hundreds of cheese sprites and drag each one into place. Fortunately, Scratch provides an easier way to precisely place a bunch of identical sprites on the Stage.

Place rows of cheese using clone blocks

Cloning enables you to create up to 300 copies of a sprite. Each clone includes the scripts, costumes, sounds, and properties of the original sprite (which is referred to as the *parent* of the clone or clones).

1. Click the Scripts tab of *Cheese.*

2. Drag the following code blocks into the Scripts Area and change the values to match:

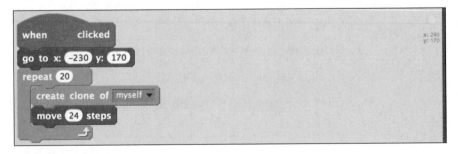

If you click the Green Flag button to test your code, you should see one row of cheese drawn across the top of the Stage. The GO TO X Y block moves the cheese to the starting position, creates a clone, moves 24 steps, and creates another clone. The REPEAT 20 block creates 20 clones, but if you count across, you will find 21 pieces of cheese. Do you have any idea why?

That 21st piece on the right side of the Stage is the original piece, so you have 20 clones and 1 original. Eventually, you will hide the original.

Fill the Stage with cheese bits

Here's how to finish filling the Stage with 15 rows of cheese.

1. Drag and snap a SET X TO block and a CHANGE Y BY block to the bottom of the REPEAT 20 block.

2. Change the SET X TO value to *–230* and the CHANGE Y BY value to *–24*.

3. Drag and snap another REPEAT block between the GO TO X Y and REPEAT 20 blocks.

    Notice how the REPEAT block wraps around the REPEAT 20 and the GO TO and CHANGE Y blocks beneath it.

4. Change the value of the new REPEAT block to *15*.

```
when      clicked
go to x: -230  y: 170
repeat 15
    repeat 20
        create clone of myself ▼
        move 24 steps
    set x to -230
    change y by -24
```

Now, when you click the Green Flag button, the entire Stage should be filled with cheese (every mouse's dream).

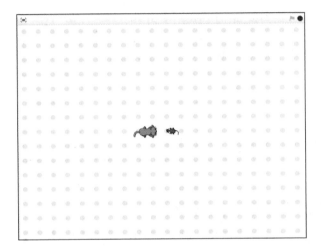

That extra piece of cheese (the parent) is now near the bottom-left corner of the Stage. To hide the original sprite, you can add a HIDE block to the bottom of your code. But, because the clones need to be created each time you run your code, you will need a SHOW block at the beginning of your code. Here's what the final cheese cloning code should look like:

```
when    clicked                              x: -230
                                             y: -180
show
go to x: -230 y: 170
repeat 15
    repeat 20
        create clone of myself
        move 24 steps

    set x to -230
    change y by -24

hide
```

Scratch only allows you to create 300 clones, so I went with 15 rows and 20 columns (15 × 20 = 300).

The cloned cheese sprites will now serve as a grid to help you place the walls of the maze. You will need to click the Green Flag button to place all the clones. DO NOT click the Stop button. (If you click Stop, all the clones disappear.)

Create maze walls

You have many ways to draw a maze in Scratch. I recently stumbled onto this quick and easy way using a series of rectangles in Vector Mode.

1. If the cheesy grid is no longer on the Stage, click the Green Flag button to draw the clones again.

2. Click the Stage button beneath the actual Stage, to the left of your sprites.

3. Click the Backdrops tab.

Convert to vector 4. Click the Convert to Vector button.

 5. Click the Rectangle tool.

6. Click the Outline option button.

7. Drag the Line Width slider all the way to the right for maximum line thickness.

8. Click the color swatch you wish to use for the walls. (I will use a dark blue.)

9. Click the = sign between the Zoom In and Zoom Out buttons to zoom back to 100%.

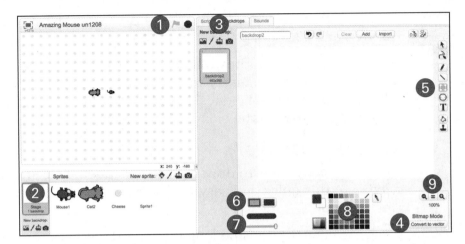

The trick here is to draw a rectangle on the Paint Editor canvas and then resize it (by clicking and dragging the center points) while also looking at the Stage, so you can see where the walls intersect each row of yellow dots. The first rectangle should intersect the left, right, and bottom dots. You will skip the first line of dots to leave room to display the score and lives information for the player.

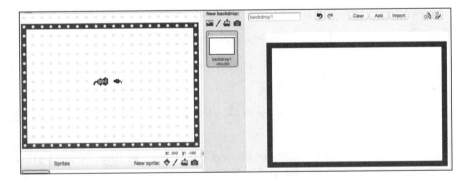

Draw three more rectangles and adjust the sides so each is centered over a row or column of cheesy dots.

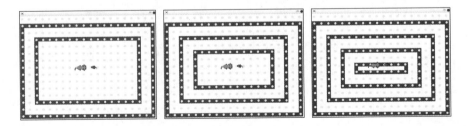

Being careful about where you place your walls is not just about making sure your maze looks good. It's also important to provide enough space between all your walls for your sprites to move and in the corners for them to turn around.

Cut through maze walls

You may be thinking, "Hey Scratch man, that's not a maze. It's just four blue rectangles!" You're right. You could cut holes in the walls using the Reshape tool, but I have an even better solution. Instead of blue rectangles, what if we draw a few solid white rectangles over the blue walls?

1. Click the Rectangle tool.

2. Choose the Solid option and the white color swatch.

3. Click and drag a small rectangle over one of the blue walls.

4. Check the position of the new "hole" on the Stage and adjust the position to fit directly over a yellow dot. (You can nudge the selected rectangle by clicking the Left- or Right-Arrow keys on your keyboard.)

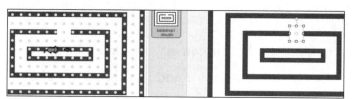

Duplicate wall openings

You can quickly place several wall openings by using the Duplicate tool.

1. Click the Duplicate tool.

2. Hold the Shift key on your keyboard. (This allows you to repeatedly duplicate objects on the Paint Editor canvas.)

3. Click the white rectangle and drag to another location, and another, and another.

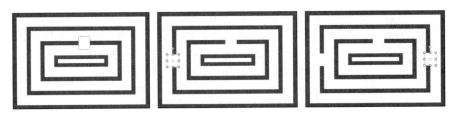

4. Adjust the position of each wall opening on the Paint Editor canvas to line up with yellow dots on the Stage.

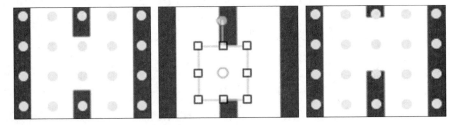

If white rectangles serve as openings, how could you add a few dead ends?

Complicate the maze with dead ends

Instead of the Rectangle tool, use the Line tool to draw a few extra walls.

1. On the Paint Editor canvas, click the Line tool.

2. Choose the same color and line thickness you chose for the rectangles.

3. In a few locations, click and drag from one wall to another to create dead ends. (Hold the Shift key while dragging to keep your line perpendicular to walls.)

4. Check the Stage and adjust the line position to intersect the yellow dots.

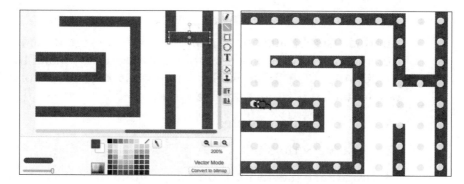

See how easy it is to vary the layout of your maze backdrop?
I usually include two or three dead ends in a maze this size to
keep players on their toes.

It may help to drag your mouse and cat where you want them to
start on the Stage (between walls and not facing dead ends) so
you can make sure you do not accidentally trap them. Be sure all
the cheese bits along the white paths are accessible because the
player will need to eat each bite to finish.

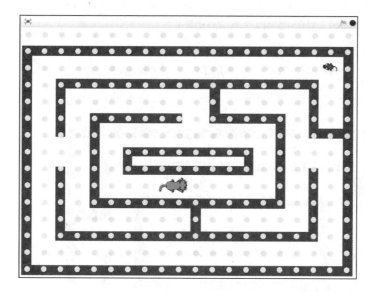

While the cheese dots were handy for placing all your walls, pas-
sageways, and dead ends, all the ones inside the blue lines will be
impossible for the player to reach. Adding a few blocks of code to
the cheese sprite will take care of those in a jiffy!

Remove cheese inside walls

Another useful thing about clones is you can give them instructions to carry out as soon as they are created by using the WHEN I START AS A CLONE block. So, why not instruct each clone to delete itself if it's touching the walls?

1. Click the cheesy sprite.

2. Click the Scripts tab.

3. Drag these blocks into the Scripts Area until they snap together.

4. Click the small color swatch inside the IF TOUCHING COLOR block, move your cursor over to the Stage, and click your wall to select the exact same color.

If you click the Green Flag, the clones will start filling the screen, but now any cheese touching a wall disappears.

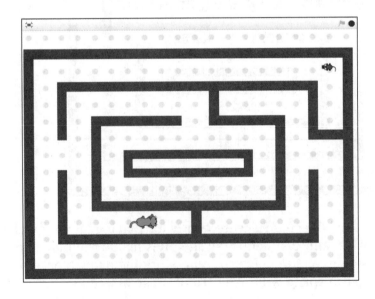

Isn't that cool? If you use the dots to position your walls, Scratch deletes the extra ones as soon as the player starts the game. So what's the easy way to get rid of those dots across the top of the screen? Fill it with a rectangle the same color as your walls!

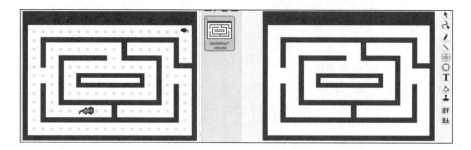

With your maze walls and cheese in place, you are ready to add movement to your game characters.

Add Player Keyboard Controls

I called my game *Amazing Mouse,* so the player will control the mouse by using the arrow keys on the keyboard. I prefer to use the KEY PRESSED? block in the *Sensing* category because it gives smoother movement than the WHEN KEY PRESSED block used in the previous chapter.

1. On the Stage, click the mouse sprite and drag it to a good starting position between walls and not too close to the player.

2. Click the Scripts tab and the *Motion* category.

3. Drag and snap a GO TO X Y block to the bottom of the SET SIZE TO block in the Scripts Area. Because the mouse is the last sprite moved on the Stage, X and Y will be its current position.

4. Drag and snap the rest of these blocks to the bottom of the GO TO X Y block and change the values inside the blocks to match those in the image:

Click the Green Flag button to test your new code. When you click the Right-Arrow key on your keyboard, the player sprite (*Mouse1* in my game) should move smoothly to the right.

Duplicate code blocks

You will need the same blocks to check for the other three arrow keys (left, up, and down). Let's duplicate the blocks to save time.

1. Shift-click the IF THEN block and choose *Duplicate.*

2. Drag the copied blocks down to snap beneath the previous IF THEN block, making sure they are still inside the FOREVER loop.

3. Change KEY PRESSED to *Left Arrow* and POINT IN DIRECTION to *−90.*

4. Repeat Steps 1–3 for *Up Arrow* and *Down Arrow.*

```
forever
    if       key  right arrow ▾  pressed?     then
        point in direction  90▾
        move  2  steps

    if       key  left arrow ▾  pressed?     then
        point in direction  -90▾
        move  2  steps

    if       key  up arrow ▾  pressed?     then
        point in direction  0▾
        move  2  steps

    if       key  down arrow ▾  pressed?     then
        point in direction  180▾
        move  2  steps
```

Click the Green Flag button to test your code, and you will find the arrow keys now move the sprite in all four directions, but it will pass right through walls. How do you program sprites to bounce off walls? It's a bit like deleting extra cheese.

Make walls stop the mouse

The same way you used the wall color to delete unwanted cheese clones, you can check to see whether the mouse is touching walls. You can add the code for each direction or take the easy way: Use another WHEN GREEN FLAG CLICKED block.

1. Drag these blocks into the Scripts Area for the mouse sprite:

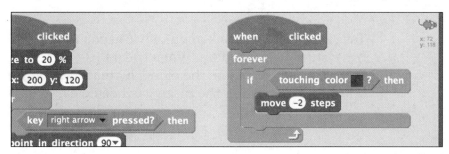

2. Click the color swatch inside the IF TOUCHING COLOR block and then click anywhere on the wall over on the Stage.

3. Set the MOVE block to –2.

4. Click the Green Flag to test your new code.

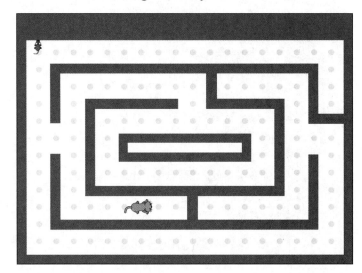

You should be able to control your mouse movement with the arrow keys the same as before, but when it gets to a wall it should stop in place. Why do you need the MOVE –2 STEPS block? When the player moves *into* the wall, it has gone forward two steps, so it needs to go back to *stop* touching the wall.

If you decide to increase or decrease the speed of the player sprite, be sure to update the negative move value in the script that detects whether the mouse is touching a wall.

Now, I think it's time to eat!

The Mouse Eats the Cheese

Take a moment to think about what needs to happen as the player travels through the maze. When the mouse gets to each cheese ball, you need to delete the clone, increase the player's score, and check to see whether the maze has been cleared of cheese.

Delete the cheese on collision

If the mouse and the clone are colliding with each other, which sprite should you put the code on to delete the clone? On the cheese! (Is it just me or does that sound kind of weird?)

1. Click the Cheese sprite beneath the Stage and then click the Scripts tab.

2. Drag and snap a FOREVER block to the bottom of the blocks connected to WHEN I START AS A CLONE.

3. Drag these blocks over to snap into the FOREVER block and change TOUCHING to *Mouse1*.

After clicking the Green Flag button, you should find each cheesy clone disappears as soon as the mouse scurries over it.

Connect score to snacking

You will need to create a variable to keep track of the score and then add code blocks to increase the score with each cheese chomp.

1. Beneath the Scripts tab, click the *Data* category.

2. Click the Make a Variable button and type **Score**, leave *For All Sprites* selected, and then click OK.

3. Drag and snap a SET TO block to the bottom of the WHEN GREEN FLAG CLICKED block in the Scripts Area and make sure the Score value is *0*.

4. Drag and snap a CHANGE SCORE BY block between IF TOUCHING MOUSE1 and DELETE THIS CLONE.

5. Set the CHANGE SCORE BY value to the amount each piece of cheese is worth. (I'll use 10.)

6. On the Stage, you can drag the *Score* display to reposition it.

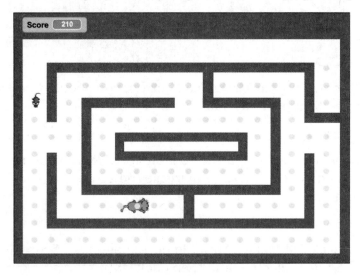

This is one of my favorite moments! When you click the Green Flag and move through the maze, the bits of cheese should disappear and the score should increase.

But, how do you keep track of the number of cheese bits eaten? You could count the number of clones inside the maze, but then any change you make to the walls means you'd need to count again.

Keep track of the cheese left

What if you create another variable, set it to 300 at the beginning, and then subtract one each time a clone is deleted?

1. Create another variable named *Cheese*. (Follow Steps 1–3 in the previous section.)

2. On the Stage, drag the *Cheese* display to the top-right corner. (You will hide it after confirming the cheese counter code works. Try saying that five times in a row!)

3. Drag and snap a SET TO block beneath SET SCORE TO in the Scripts Area. Change the value to 300 and make sure the *Cheese* value is selected.

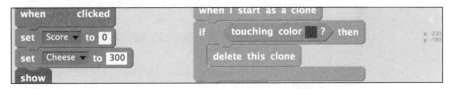

4. Drag and snap a CHANGE BY block to the top of each DELETE THIS CLONE block and set the values to *Cheese* and *–1*.

As soon as a DELETE THIS CLONE block runs, no other code on that code can execute. That's why you must snap the CHANGE CHEESE BY –1 <u>above</u> each of these blocks.

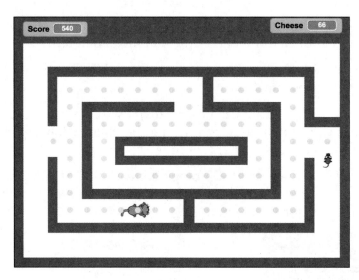

When you click the Green Flag button, the cheese counter should start at 300 but immediately decrease as clones touching the wall are deleted. Now, it's time to bring that cat to life.

Program Enemy Patrol

In modern videogames, enemy movement is generally controlled by artificial intelligence (A.I.). As you learn more about programming, you will be able to create more devious enemies. For now, we just need the cat to wander around the maze and take a life away from the player each time the cat and mouse collide until the player has no lives left. And, you want to prevent the cat from walking through walls, right?

Give the enemy marching orders

1. On the Stage, drag the enemy sprite (the cat in my game) into a good starting position (between walls and not too close to the player).

2. Click the Scripts tab and then the *Motion* category.

3. Drag and snap a GO TO X Y block to the bottom of SET SIZE TO in the Scripts Area.

   Because the cat is the last sprite moved on the Stage, the X and Y values will be current x and y positions of the cat.

4. Drag and snap the rest of these blocks to the bottom of the GO TO X Y block and change the values inside the blocks to match those in the image. (Don't forget to select the wall color inside the TOUCHING COLOR block.)

Clicking the Green Flag button sets the size and position and the FOREVER loop starts the cat roving. For now, the cat just moves back and forth through one horizontal section of the maze.

You can make the enemy patrol more territory by turning 90 degrees each time it reaches a wall instead of 180 degrees.

If you find your enemy sprite just spinning around in place, there are several possible fixes. The easiest may be to adjust the sprite's starting position or make it a bit smaller. If you do not want to decrease the size of your enemy sprite further, you can either adjust the length or change the center of rotation.

Adjust the sprite length

I don't know about your enemy, but in some corners my cat gets stuck. It appears the tail is getting caught in the wall. You can avoid such problems by adjusting the length of your sprite. I need to tuck the tail in to make my cat shorter.

1. Click the Costumes tab.

 2. Click the Select tool.

3. Click the tail and drag it against the body.

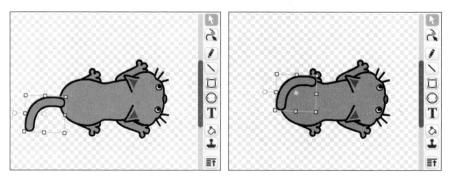

Click the Green Flag button to test the new shape. After tweaking the tail, my cat has an easier time navigating corners.

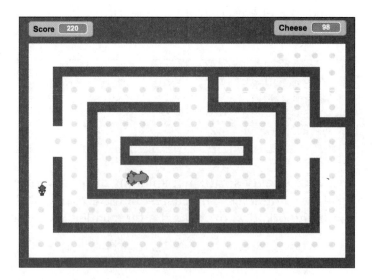

If you have a different sprite that gets stuck in maze corners, you may need to adjust the sprite's *costume center* (the point around which the sprite rotates).

Change the center of rotation

If the costume center is off, when the sprite gets to a corner of your maze, it will hit a wall, turn 90 degrees, and then may still be touching a wall, so it turns again and again and again.

Here's how you can fix it:

1. Click the sprite you wish to edit and then click the Costumes tab.

 2. Click the Set Costume Center button.

3. Click and drag to adjust the center of the black crosshairs over the part of your sprite that should be the center.

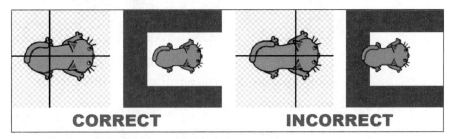

CORRECT   INCORRECT

 The costume center is the precise point Scratch uses to determine the position of each sprite on the Stage. Keep this in mind when you use any of the *Motion* category blocks (such as GO TO X Y).

Track Player Lives

By now, you should be a sprite collision master, but don't forget a new variable must be created if you want to give your player more than one life.

1. Go to the Scripts tab for the player sprite. (That's *Mouse1* for me.)

2. Click Data and then click the Make a Variable button. Name the new variable *Lives* and click OK.

3. Uncheck the box next to the *Cheese* variable (as you no longer need to display this on the Stage).

4. Drag and snap a SET TO block between WHEN GREEN FLAG CLICKED and FOREVER, then change the values to match (*Lives* and *3*).

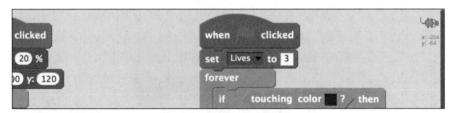

5. Beneath IF TOUCHING COLOR and MOVE –2 steps, add the blocks pictured here (another IF THEN block):

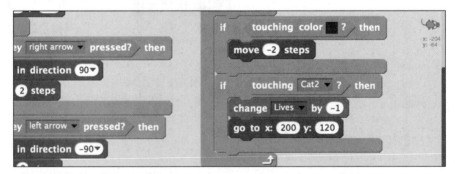

6. Change the values in the GO TO X Y block to the player's starting X and Y values.

7. To end the game when the player has no more lives left, add these blocks between CHANGE LIVES BY and GO TO X Y:

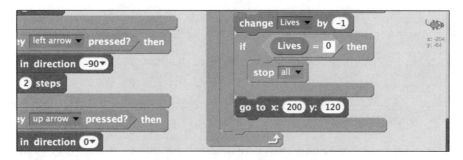

8. On the Stage, drag the Lives indicator to the top-right corner.

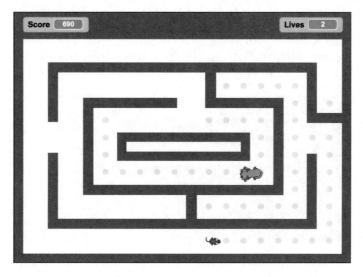

Click the Green Flag button and run right into the enemy to make sure a life is subtracted. If you touch the enemy three times, the game should end.

Give Player a Chance to Win

You created a variable to keep track of the number of cheese bits left in the maze, but what if the player clears the maze of all the cheese? After all that scurrying about and avoiding the enemy, the player deserves SOMETHING, right?

To trigger some sort of victory sound or message once the maze is cleared, use another IF THEN block.

1. Click the enemy icon (*Cat2* for me) and then click the Sounds tab.

2. Click the Choose Sound from Library button and pick a suitable tune. (I like the one named *Triumph*.)

   You can preview sounds by clicking the Play button beside each one.

3. Double-click a sound to load it into your sprite.

4. Click the Scripts tab and then drag and snap an IF THEN block along with the other blocks shown into the FOREVER block above the MOVE block:

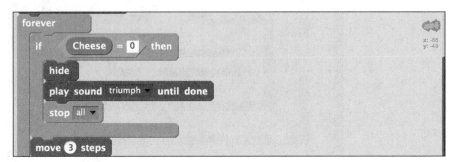

5. Whenever you add a HIDE block, it's a good idea to put a SHOW block near the beginning of your code or the enemy will not appear in the next game or level.

   I chose a PLAY SOUND UNTIL DONE block for the final sound, so the *Triumph* music can finish playing before the STOP block ends all scripts.

Having only a victory sound seems kinda lame to me. Why not add sounds to these events in the game:

🖚 Munching each cheese bit. (Add to the *Cheese* scripts.)

🖚 Being caught by the cat. (Add to the *Mouse1* scripts.)

🖚 Losing your last life. (Add to the *Mouse1* scripts.)

Of course you don't have to use the same sounds I've chosen from the Sound Library. You can choose other sounds, upload sounds, or record your own! (See Chapter 9 for tips on recording and editing sounds in Scratch.)

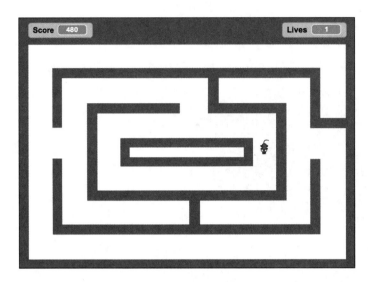

Enhance your game

Here are some other ways you might improve your maze game.

- **Add more enemies:** Try duplicating your enemy sprite, starting in a different location and having it turn –90 degrees instead of 90 degrees.

- **Add additional levels:** When cheese = 0, you could to switch to another maze backdrop and repopulate the maze with cheesy clones.

- **Change enemy speed:** You could have the enemy get faster as there are fewer cheese bits left or allow the player to choose a difficulty level that speeds up the enemy, slows down the player, or both.

- **Add power-ups:** Remember in *Pac-Man* how the ghosts would turn blue for a few seconds after chomping one of those fat dots? You could transform the player into a dog for a few seconds to give the cat a run for its money.

Attacking the Clones

While *Pong* was the first videogame I ever played, my videogame addiction really began with *Space Invaders.* The stand-up arcade version appeared in 1978, just a year after the first *Star Wars* movie (*Episode IV,* that is, which I saw in the theater — *THAT'S* how old I am).

I could not imagine designing a game like this in earlier versions of Scratch, which did not provide a way to clone sprites. While the cheese clones in Chapter 13 just sit in place waiting to be eaten, these clones march across the screen and fire deadly watermelon bombs! Fortunately, you can fire back with your own laser clones!

Create a New Project

As always, you can name your project any way you like. I'm going to avoid the title *Space Invaders* because I *have* to (by law) and because my game is going to look much cooler!

1. Go to scratch.mit.edu or open the Scratch 2 Offline Editor.

2. If you are online, click Create. If offline, select File⇨New.

3. Name your project. (If online, select the title and type **Space Attack**. If using the offline version of Scratch, select File⇨Save As and type **Space Attack**.)

4. Blast that cat out of existence with the Scissors (or Shift-click the cat and choose *Delete*).

Choose a Game Background

Although you can import a drawing or photograph or design your own backdrop on the Paint Editor canvas, let's take the easy route for a quick start: choosing one from the Backdrop Library.

1. On the Backdrops tab, click the Choose Backdrop from Library icon.

2. Scroll to the backdrop you wish to use (I will use the one named *Space*) and double-click it.

If you would like some guidance for drawing your own backdrop, check out Chapter 8, which covers several techniques for designing vivid backgrounds.

Create Player and Enemy Sprites

I will take inspiration from the original *Space Invaders* game, which had a single. . . . Actually, I don't know what the player image from the old game was supposed to be! You will begin with a spaceship that moves back and forth across the bottom of the screen.

1. Beneath the Stage, click the Choose Sprite from Library icon.

2. Click the *Transportation* category.

3. Double-click the sprite named *Spaceship*.

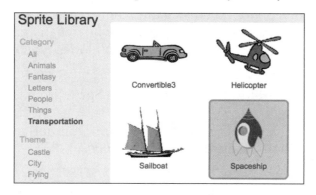

Resize and position the spaceship

The spaceship sprite is far too large. To resize it precisely, you will use a bit of code (rather than just using the Shrink tool). This is also a good time to set the starting position near the bottom of the screen.

1. Click the Scripts tab.

2. Click, drag, and snap these blocks into the Scripts Area:

3. Try these values: Size = *30*, X = *0*, and Y = *−140*.

4. Click the Green Flag button to test your code.

Your spaceship should now appear about a third of the size it was and be positioned in the bottom center of the Stage. The only value I knew for sure was X = *0* for the center of the Stage; I had to try a few different values for the Y position and size before it looked right to me.

 While choosing the correct sizes for your game sprites, be sure to alternate between standard view and full screen view (using the button above the top-left corner of the Stage). You can't be sure which one players will use, so you want to make sure your game looks good at both sizes.

In the original *Space Invaders* game, there were 55 aliens per screen (5 rows, 11 columns). No matter how many enemies you want to include in your game, thanks to clones, you only need one sprite!

1. Beneath the Stage, click the Choose Sprite from Library icon.

2. Click the *Animals* category.

3. Double-click the sprite named *Ladybug2*.

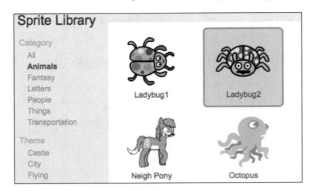

That's right. I'm going with killer ladybugs from outer space! *(Cue the terrifying space theme music.)*

I could leave the cute little bugger alone, but I think I'll make a few tweaks on the Paint Editor canvas to make it a bit more alien-looking.

Modify a sprite from the Sprite Library

I won't get into too much detail on this process because you can refer back to Chapter 4 or Chapter 7; each shows you how to design your own characters using the Vector painting tools.

1. On the Costumes tab, click the Select tool.

 2. Click the Zoom In button to get a closer look.

3. Click the ladybug on the Paint Editor canvas to select it.

 4. Use the Color a Shape tool to change colors.

 5. Use the Reshape tool to sculpt individual shapes (like the eyes).

 6. Use the Select tool to select, resize, and move shapes.

Clone a Bunch of Aliens

In the olden days (before 2013), if you wanted 20 or 30 aliens, you needed to duplicate your alien 20 or 30 times. Eventually, you ended up with dozens of sprites. This wasn't such a bad thing until you wanted (or needed) to change the look of the sprite or make changes to the code. Then you had to make the same changes to all your sprites, one at a time, or delete all but the first sprite, make the changes, and then make all your duplicates again! TOTALLY LAME!

Instead of duplicating, you can now use a single code block to clone as many aliens as you want when the game begins. Can you see why this is so much better? You only have to make changes to that first alien and all the clones will have those changes, too. (This is called *inheriting*.)

Evenly position alien clones

In case you skipped over the cloning section in Chapter 12, here's the pattern for making clones: Move the original ladybugalien (called the *parent*) to a specific position and make a clone; move the parent to the next position and make another clone; move the parent to a third position and make a clone. . . . You get the idea.

I'm getting sick of typing *ladybugalien,* so why don't you change the name of the sprite to *Alien* before adding the CREATE CLONE block.

1. Shift-click the ladybug sprite (beneath the Stage), choose *Info,* and then change the name to *Alien.*

2. Click the white triangle button to exit *Info.*

3. Click the Scripts tab.

4. Drag the following blocks into the Scripts Area and change the values to match (you will find the CREATE CLONE block in the Control category):

```
when    clicked
set size to 50 %
go to x: -200 y: 100
create clone of myself ▼
```

If you followed the above instructions correctly, when you click the Green Flag button the alien will shrink by 50%, jump to a new position, and then . . . nothing?!?

Reducing the size of the alien to 50% will allow you to fit more of them on the screen. But why can't you see the alien clone? Because the original alien and the clone are in exactly the same position!

Add a CHANGE X block, change the value to *90*, click the Green Flag button, and see what happens.

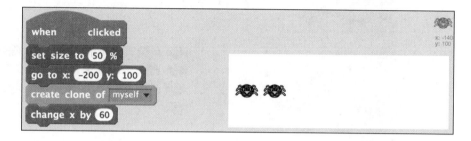

Now the original sprite (the *parent*) makes a clone of itself then moves 60 pixels to the right so you can see the two aliens side-by-side.

How do you create an entire row of aliens? Drag a REPEAT block over to surround CREATE CLONE and CHANGE X BY. Set the REPEAT value to *7* to fit the maximum number of aliens across the Stage.

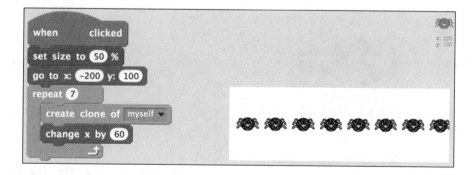

If you need to change the X value by 60 to place alien clones side-by-side, what do you need to change to create additional *rows* of aliens? The Y value!

You can add another REPEAT block, but you also need to set the X value back to -200 so the parent sprite starts each row in the same location (along the left side of the Stage).

Once you have all your clones lined up on the Stage (3 rows, 7 aliens across), you need to hide your parent sprite. Add a HIDE block at the end of your alien cloning code, then add a SHOW block at the beginning of the code, so each time you click the Green Flag button the original alien sprite will appear, create all the clones, and then hide during the game.

Now that you have all those aliens on the screen, how about telling them to do something?

Give clones their marching orders

The WHEN I START AS A CLONE block enables you to give instructions to all clones as soon as they appear onscreen. To make all your aliens march to the right at the beginning of the game, drag the following blocks to the right of the other alien code blocks and change the values to match:

When you click the Green Flag button, the aliens move to the right until there is an alien traffic jam along the side of the Stage.

Click the Stop button to clear the Stage traffic.

In the original game, when any alien reaches one side, all the aliens change direction at the same time (and drop a bit closer to the player). How can one clone send instructions to other clones?

Broadcast message to turn

In videogame design, there are many times when you'll want to send a message to several sprites (or clones) at once. In Scratch, this is called *broadcasting*.

You need your alien clones to do two things: broadcast a message if they reach the edge of the Stage (if X position is greater than 210) and change direction if they receive a broadcast (TURN 180 DEGREES). You will find the BROADCAST blocks in the *Events* category.

```
when        clicked                    when I start as a clone          x: -200
                                                                        y: -20
show                                   forever

set size to 50 %                         move 1 steps

go to x: -200 y: 100                     if      x position  > 210  then

repeat 3                                   broadcast message1

  repeat 7

    create clone of myself
                                         ↺
    move 60 steps
                                       when I receive message1
  ↺
                                       turn ↻ 180 degrees
  set x to -200

  change y by 40
```

When you click the Green Flag button, the aliens should change direction at the same time. But they are no longer lined up in neat columns, and as soon as they change direction they all flip upside down!?!

Change a sprite's rotation style

If you want a sprite to point only left or right (and not look like a legs-up-dead bug), you can change the rotation from *All Around* (360 degrees) to *Left-Right* (90 degrees or –90 degrees). You also should set an initial direction so the aliens always start facing right.

1. On the alien sprite's Scripts tab, drag and snap the following blocks between WHEN GREEN FLAG CLICKED and SHOW:

```
when       clicked
set rotation style  left–right ▼
point in direction  90▼
show
```

2. Inside the SET ROTATION STYLE block, choose *Left-Right*.

3. Inside the POINT IN DIRECTION block, choose the direction you want the alien invaders to move first (I keep *90* or *Right*).

4. Click the Green Flag button to test the new code.

When your marching aliens reach the right side, they should now change direction without flipping upside-down. Cool! But then they get jammed up on the *left* side of the Stage. NOT cool!

Add the following code and change the values to broadcast a message and change direction when any alien clone reaches the *left* side of the Stage (when the X position is *less than* –210).

```
when       clicked
set rotation style  left–right ▼
point in direction  90▼
show
set size to  50 %
go to x:  -200  y:  100
repeat  3
    repeat  7
        create clone of  myself ▼
        change x by  60

when I start as a clone
forever
    move  1  steps
    if       x position  >  210   then
        broadcast  message1 ▼

    if       x position  <  -210   then
        broadcast  message1 ▼
```

If you click the Green Flag button, those alien clones march back and forth across the Stage.

But what happened to our nice, neat columns?

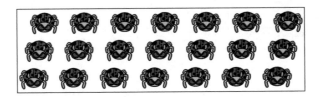

I'll give you a hint. Think about the *precise moment* each alien begins to move.

Straighten alien clone columns

As soon as the first alien is cloned, the code blocks under WHEN I START AS A CLONE make it move (*before* the parent is finished making all the clones). Why not have the clones wait until the last one is created by having the parent sprite send a *Start Marching* broadcast?

Before adding another broadcast message, give the first broadcast message a more descriptive name.

1. On the enemy's Scripts tab, go to the first BROADCAST block, click *Message1,* and select *New Message*.

2. Type *Change Direction* and then click OK.

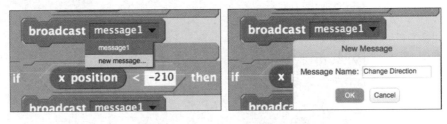

3. In the second BROADCAST block, select *Change Direction.*

4. Change the WHEN I RECEIVE block to *Change Direction.*

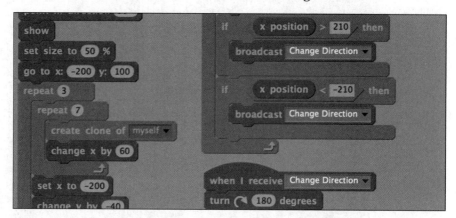

Now you can add a BROADCAST *Start Marching* block beneath the REPEAT blocks that create all the clones. Then replace the WHEN I START AS A CLONE block with WHEN I RECEIVE *Start Marching.*

1. Drag and snap a new BROADCAST MESSAGE block between the REPEAT blocks and the HIDE block in the Scripts Area.

2. In BROADCAST MESSAGE, select *New Message* and type **Start Marching.**

3. Drag another WHEN I RECEIVE block to the right of the WHEN I START AS A CLONE block.

4. Click and drag the FOREVER block from beneath the WHEN I START AS A CLONE block and snap it under WHEN I RECEIVE.

5. Drag the WHEN I START AS A CLONE block to the left, outside the Scripts Area to delete it.

6. Change the WHEN I RECEIVE message to *Start Marching.*

7. Click the Green Flag button to test your code.

```
when [] clicked
set rotation style left-right ▾
point in direction 90 ▾
show
set size to 50 %
go to x: -200 y: 100
repeat 3
    repeat 7
        create clone of myself ▾
        move 60 steps
    set x to -200
    change y by -40
broadcast Start Marching ▾
hide

when I receive Start Marching ▾
forever
    move 1 steps
    if x position > 210 then
        broadcast Change Direction ▾
    if x position < -210 then
        broadcast Change Direction ▾

when I receive Change Direction ▾
turn ↻ 180 degrees
change y by -20
```

The clones wait patiently until the final clone appears on the Stage, and then the clones should begin marching in nice, straight columns!

Make aliens move down, too

Each time the aliens reach one side, they also should move down the Stage, getting closer and closer to the player. So what do you need to add?

You don't need another broadcast message; just add a CHANGE Y block after the TURN 180 DEGREES BLOCK to make clones turn *and* drop closer to the player each time the *Change Direction* broadcast message is received.

1. Add a CHANGE Y BY block beneath the TURN 180 DEGREES block.

2. Set CHANGE Y BY to the amount you want enemies to get closer to the player on each turn. (I'll start with *–20*.)

3. Click the Green Flag button to test the code.

Your alien invaders should all change direction at the same time and drop down closer to the player each time they reach a side of the Stage.

Whaddya say we give the spaceship an upgrade to defend it against all these advancing alien clones?

Add Laser Blaster to Spaceship

Cloning isn't just for aliens, my friends. You also can use clones to shoot them out of the sky!

Create a laser sprite

1. Beneath the Stage, click the Choose Sprite from Library icon.

2. Click the *Things* category and then double-click the sprite named *Button2.*

3. Shift-click the Button2 icon (beneath the Stage) and choose *Info.*

4. Change the name to *Laser.*

5. Click the Back button (white triangle in blue circle) to close the Info window.

6. Click the Costumes tab, then change the name of the first costume to *Blue* and the name of the second costume to *Orange*.

7. Click one of them to choose a starting costume. (I'll use *Orange;* I may use *Blue* later as a bonus weapon, perhaps a freeze ray!)

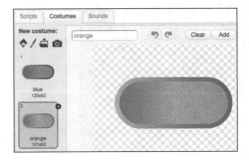

8. Take a moment to think about how you might transform the button to look more like a laser blast. You could modify it with the Paint tools, but I'm going to show you a shortcut.

9. Click the Scripts tab.

10. Drag these blocks into the Scripts Area and change the values to match:

11. Click the SET SIZE TO block one time.

Clicking any block will run that block and any blocks snapped beneath it. These blocks should have made the button sprite much smaller and rotated it 90 degrees, with its nose pointed upward, to look more like a laser. Don't worry about where it is on the screen; you're about to fix that!

Fire the laser with the spacebar

You can have the spaceship sprite clone the laser so it will appear to be shooting at the aliens.

1. Click the spaceship sprite's icon beneath the Stage and then click the Scripts tab.

2. You should have the first set of blocks already there to set the scale and position when the Green Flag button is clicked. Now, add a second set of blocks for when the player clicks the spacebar:

```
when    clicked          when space ▼ key pressed
set size to (30) %        create clone of Laser ▼
go to x: (0) y: (-140)    wait (1) secs
                                                 x: 0
                                                 y: -140
```

3. In the CREATE CLONE OF block, change *Myself* to *Laser*.

Each time you press the spacebar, a clone of *Laser* will be created. But, why did I put that WAIT 1 SECS block in there? Without that delay, a player could fire hundreds of lasers and easily beat the game. You can increase or decrease the time value to change the difficulty of the game.

One of the most important decisions you will make as a game designer is how hard your game should be. If your game is too hard, players will get frustrated and quit. And, if it's too easy, players will quickly become bored. A term that professional game developers use is *hard fun:* Your game should be hard enough to be challenging but still fun to play.

Before you can fire, you will need to add a bit of code to the laser sprite, too.

Create laser clones

1. Click the laser sprite's icon beneath the Stage and then click the Scripts tab.

2. Click, drag, and snap a HIDE block to the bottom of the POINT IN DIRECTION block.

3. Drag a WHEN I START AS A CLONE block into the Scripts Area and add the blocks shown here:

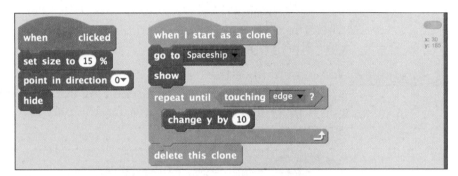

4. In the GO TO block, change *Mouse Pointer* to *Spaceship,* and set the CHANGE Y BY block's value to 10.

5. Click the Green Flag button.

When you press the spacebar, a laser clone should appear, move from the spaceship to the top of the screen, and disappear when it touches the top edge of the Stage. (I'll switch back to a white backdrop for now to make spotting the laser easier.)

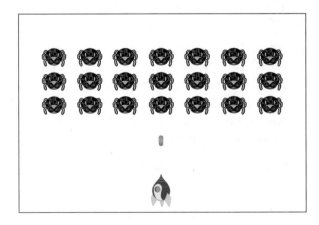

Enable Spaceship Movement

The programming technique I showed for the *Ping-Pong* paddles in Chapter 11 works fine when you are just chasing after a single ball, but with all those aliens coming after you, it's time for a coding upgrade.

1. Click the spaceship's icon beneath the Stage and then click the Scripts tab.

2. Drag and snap a FOREVER block to the bottom of the GO TO X Y block, drag the remaining blocks below into the FOREVER block, and change the values to match:

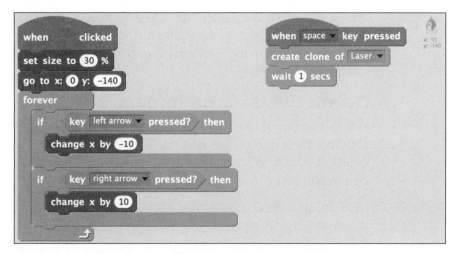

3. Click the Green Flag button to test your code.

When you press the Left- and Right-Arrow keys on your keyboard, the spaceship should move smoothly left and right. You can adjust the player movement speed by increasing or decreasing the CHANGE X BY value.

Use Collision to Destroy Aliens

Instead of the laser passing right through the aliens as if they were ladybug-shaped clouds, you want to destroy them, right?

1. Click the alien sprite and then click the Scripts tab.

2. Drag the highlighted blocks into the FOREVER block.

3. Click inside the IF TOUCHING block and choose *Laser*.

4. Click the Green Flag button to test your game.

When you click the spacebar, a laser should shoot out of your spaceship and destroy any aliens it hits. Can you figure out why the laser goes through an entire column of enemies instead of destroying just one?

Delete the laser on impact

When a clone of the laser is created, it will move up until it touches the edge of the screen. You can use an OR block to check whether it is touching the edge *or* touching an alien, and then delete the laser in either case.

1. Click the laser sprite and locate the REPEAT UNTIL block under the stack with the WHEN I START AS A CLONE block.

2. Drag an OR block into the laser sprite's Scripts Area. (The OR block resides in the *Operators* category.)

3. Drag a new TOUCHING block into the first OR slot and change the value to *Alien*.

4. Drag a TOUCHING block into the second OR slot and make sure the value is *Edge*.

5. Drag the OR block into the REPEAT UNTIL block, replacing the previous contents.

```
when I start as a clone                                    x: 100
                                                            y: -88
go to Spaceship ▾

show

repeat until  touching Alien ▾ ?  or  touching edge ▾ ?

    change y by 10
                                                       ↻
delete this clone
```

If you were to test your game now, the laser would still appear to pass right through the aliens because of a double collision effect: Each alien clone disappears before the laser has time to detect it has collided. The easy way to fix this is to add a slight time delay between when a laser hits an alien and when the alien clone is deleted.

1. Go to the alien sprite's Scripts tab.

2. Drag and snap a WAIT block to the top of the DELETE THIS CLONE block.

3. Change the WAIT value to *.01*.

4. Click the Green Flag button to test your updated laser blasting.

At last! Each laser should now destroy just one alien or disappear when it reaches the top edge of the Stage.

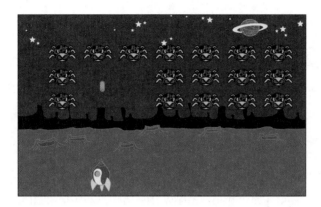

 Increasing the value inside a MOVE block will make a sprite move faster. But, the MOVE block works a bit like kids leapfrogging. If your laser moves too far on each move, it might not collide with the enemy. So, if lasers are still passing right through aliens, try lowering the MOVE value. (A value of *20* was too much for my game, but *10* worked well.)

The game will be a *lot* more challenging if the aliens can fight back. Since they are bug-shaped, I think we should give them some exploding egg bombs!

Program Enemies to Drop Bombs

You can use the same cloning technique to have aliens attack the player, but it will require a bit more programming to have different enemies attack at random.

Create an enemy bomb sprite

I found the *perfect* sprite for our alien bug bombs!

1. Beneath the Stage, click the Choose Sprite from Library icon.

2. Click the *Things* category and then double-click the *Watermelon* sprite.

3. Shift-click the *Watermelon* sprite and choose *Info*.

4. Change the name to *Bomb*.

5. Click the Back button to close the Info window.

6. Click the Scripts tab and drag the following blocks into the Scripts Area and change the values to match:

```
when      clicked                                          x: 86
point in direction (180▼)                                  y: 11
set size to (25) %
```

If you click the POINT IN DIRECTION block to test the new code, the sprite should transform from a big, fat watermelon into an alien bomb ready to drop onto the player. But, how do you tell just one enemy to attack at a time?

Randomize enemy attacks

In the *Operators* category of blocks, you will find the PICK RANDOM block, which chooses a random number between any two numbers. Can you figure out how this might help randomize when a clone drops a bomb?

What if you combine a PICK RANDOM block with a WAIT block?

1. Click the alien sprite and then click the Scripts tab.

2. Drag an additional WHEN I RECEIVE block to the right of WHEN I RECEIVE *Start Marching* and choose *Start Marching* for this additional block, too.

3. Drag the other blocks pictured to the bottom of the new WHEN I RECEIVE block and change the values to match.

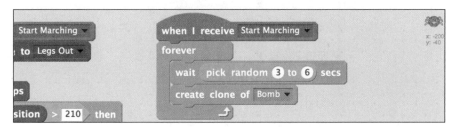

So every three to six seconds, each alien will clone a bomb. Now you need to add code to the bombs to enable them to drop toward the bottom of the Stage.

1. Click the *Bomb* sprite and click the Scripts tab.

2. Drag a WHEN I START AS A CLONE block to the right of the WHEN GREEN FLAG CLICKED block in the Scripts Area.

3. Snap the blocks pictured to the bottom of the WHEN I START AS A CLONE block and change the values to match.

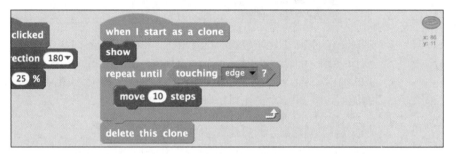

If you click the Green Flag button to test your game, bombs will drop at random times, but from the same place instead of different enemies. You need to instruct the bombs *where* to fall *from*. You can have each alien clone tell the bomb where it is by using variables.

1. On the Scripts tab, click the *Data* category.

2. Click the Make a Variable button.

3. Change the variable name to *bomb x* (for the x position) and then click OK.

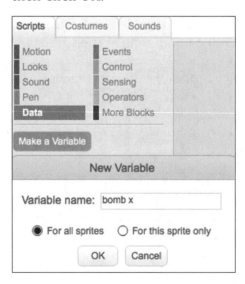

4. Make another variable named *Bomb y* (for the y position).

5. On the alien sprite's Scripts tab, add the following blocks under CREATE CLONE OF BOMB:

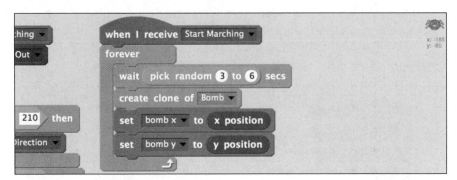

6. On the bomb sprite's Scripts tab, add a GO TO block under WHEN I START AS A CLONE and drag BOMB X and BOMB Y blocks from the *Data* category into the X and Y slots:

Go ahead and click the Green Flag button to test your game. The bomb drops from random enemies. If your code works, GREAT JOB, because that's some tricky Scratching! If the bombs are not working for you, don't be discouraged. Double-check the preceding images to make sure you have all the blocks *and* have the correct values or settings for each block.

Hide variables on the Stage

I assume you do not want to have your *Bomb x* and *Bomb y* variables showing on the Stage during your game. I sure don't! To hide them, pull two HIDE VARIABLE blocks over to the bomb's Scripts tab, choose *Bomb x* in the first and *Bomb y* in the second block.

```
when      clicked
point in direction 180▾
set size to 25 %
hide
hide variable bomb y ▾
hide variable bomb x ▾
```
x: 86
y: 11

If you don't want to wait until your next Green Flag button click, you can click directly on the two blocks to hide them right away.

Add Sound to Your Game

Have you ever played a videogame with the sound turned off? NO THANK YOU! Sound effects are a vital part of the gaming experience, and Scratch makes adding them to your project simple. Although you can import custom sounds or record them inside Scratch (covered in Chapter 9), I'll stick to sounds you can find in the Sound Library.

Make lasers a blast

You need only one block to play a sound in your Scratch project. If you want players to hear a sound each time they fire a laser at the aliens, where should that sound block go?

1. Click the spaceship sprite beneath the Stage and click the Sounds tab.

2. Click the Choose Sound from Library button.

3. Click the *Electronic* category and then double-click *Laser1* (or choose your favorite laser blaster sound).

4. Click the Scripts tab.

5. Drag and snap the PLAY SOUND block to the bottom of the CREATE CLONE OF Laser block.

6. Press the spacebar on your keyboard.

As soon as you hit the spacebar, you should hear your laser blast. What sound should we add next? How about a little explosion each time you hit one of the alien invaders?

Play sound when an alien is hit

1. Click the alien sprite beneath the Stage and click the Sounds tab.

2. Click the Choose Sound from Library button.

3. Click the Electronic category and then double-click *Screech*.

4. Click the Scripts tab.

5. Drag and snap the PLAY SOUND block to the bottom of the IF TOUCHING *Laser* THEN block.

6. Click the Green Flag button to test your game.

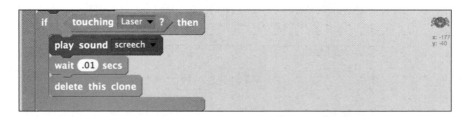

You should now hear the sound effect you chose (or the freaky screech I went with). See what a difference a few sound effects can make?

Now, let's give the remaining aliens a bit of satisfaction by allowing them to destroy the player!

Give the Player Three Lives

Although the average cat may get nine lives, the original *Space Invaders* only gave me three! For your game, you can grant the player as many lives as you want. Anything more than one life requires another variable to track and show the number of lives a player has left.

Create a variable to track player lives

1. On the Scripts tab, click the *Data* category.

2. Click the Make a Variable button.

3. Change the variable name to *Lives*.

4. On the spaceship sprite's Scripts tab, add another WHEN GREEN FLAG CLICKED along with the other pictured blocks and change the values to match:

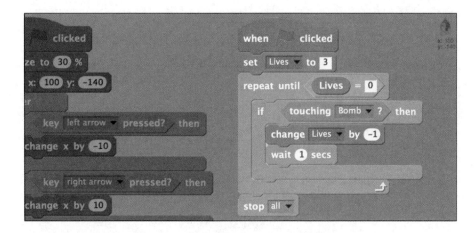

At this point, the player starts with three lives and each time an enemy bomb collides with the spaceship, the player loses one life. The blocks inside REPEAT UNTIL will keep running until *Lives = 0* and then the STOP block will cease all scripts on all sprites, ending the game.

Now how about some explosions to liven things up?

Destroy a Player on Impact

If you play the game now, a bomb hitting the player will subtract a life, but you do not see or hear anything when that happens. Choose an appropriate sound effect and then design a new costume that looks like a puff of smoke.

Play sound when the player is hit

1. Click the spaceship sprite beneath the Stage and click the Sounds tab.

2. Click the Choose Sound from Library button.

3. Click the *Percussion* category and then double-click *Cymbal*.

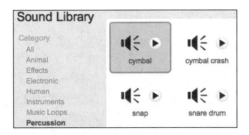

4. Click the Scripts tab.

5. Drag and snap the PLAY SOUND block to the bottom of the IF TOUCHING BOMB THEN block.

When any bomb collides with a spaceship, you should hear the explosion sound. Next you will add the visual to go along with it.

Animate the player explosion

A quick way to create an explosion is to paint a new costume for the spaceship that looks like a puff of smoke.

1. Click the spaceship's Costumes tab.

2. Shift-click the first costume, choose *Duplicate,* and name the new costume *Explode.*

3. Click the Ellipse tool, choose the Solid option, and then click a medium gray color swatch.

4. Click and drag to draw several circles over the spaceship image.

5. Click the Select tool, click the spaceship, and then click the Delete key on your keyboard.

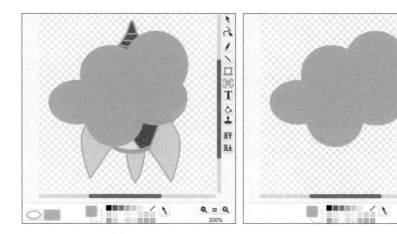

6. Click the Scripts tab.

7. Drag the following highlighted blocks into place and change the values to match:

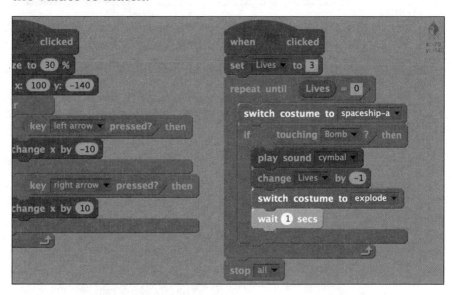

If you click the Green Flag button, whenever the player is hit by a bomb, the costume should switch to the smoke cloud for 1 second and then switch back to the spaceship costume.

Once you have explosions working, you should be ready to add a bit more code and a new variable to keep score.

Keeping Score

This is a one-player game, so keeping score is even easier than it was for the *Ping-Pong* game. First, you must add code to the Spaceship to set the Score to 0 at the beginning of each game.

1. Choose the *Data* category on the spaceship's Scripts tab.

2. Click the Make a Variable button, name it *Score,* and then click OK.

3. Drag and snap a SET SCORE TO block beneath SET LIVES and keep the default value of *0.*

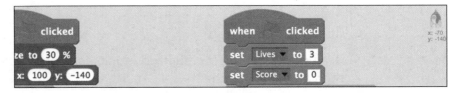

Since the score will increase each time an enemy is destroyed, you will set the code to increase the score on the alien sprite.

1. Go to the Scripts tab for the alien sprite.

2. Drag and snap a CHANGE SCORE BY block between the IF TOUCHING LASER THEN block and the PLAY SOUND SCREECH block.

3. Set the CHANGE SCORE BY value to *100* (or whatever value you want to assign to each destroyed enemy).

4. Click the Green Flag button to test your game.

The score should appear on the Stage and increase each time the player hits an enemy with a laser blast. The only thing I don't like is the position of the *Score* and *Lives* counters on the Stage.

Fortunately, you can drag a variable to any place you want. I prefer my game variables along the top of the screen.

1. On the Stage, click and drag the *Lives* display to the top-right side.

2. Click and drag the *Score* display to the top-left side.

Time to invite your friends to try out your game. If it's too easy, you can speed up the aliens or slow the spaceship. Too hard? Allow players to fire their lasers more quickly!

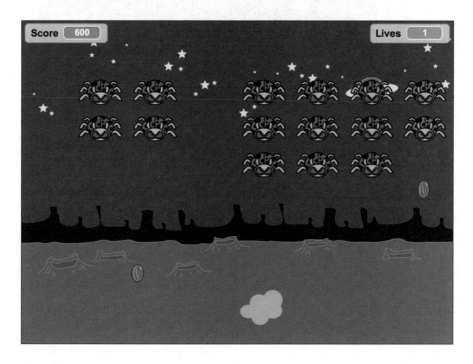

You can use the techniques in this chapter to design just about any shooter game you can imagine. You also could invert the gameplay by making a game in which the player has to catch objects falling from the sky or in which the player has the role of the aliens instead of the spaceship. Or you could design a game like my pal Jonah's, where the sprites try to stay away from you rather than attack.

So many possibilities when YOU are in control of the game-making! Now close this book and go make a TOTALLY NEW kind of game!!!

Enhance your game

Here are some ways you might improve your space blaster game.

- **Animate enemies:** In addition to moving left and right, you could switch between costumes to make the legs move.

- **Add additional levels:** You could create a new variable named *Enemies* that tracks the number of enemies left on the screen. When *Enemies = 0*, you could use a BROADCAST block to create another set of enemies, perhaps changing their appearance or movement.

- **Gradually change enemy speed:** Like the original arcade game, you could increase the enemy's speed as the number of enemies onscreen decreases.

- **Add more sound effects:** You could have a marching effect that plays faster as the enemies speed up. Having an end-of-game sound (try *Spiral*) could be fun, too.

- **Time delay fuse:** You could have the bombs land on the ground and wait a second or two before exploding.

- **Add power-ups:** Occasionally, you could have a special enemy bomb with a different costume fall; catching this bomb could add a life or give the player a more powerful laser for a short time.

Game Not Over!

I wish I had more pages and more time to fill them, but I am running out of both, and driving my editors CRAZY with the pages I keep REwriting AND the images I keep REplacing AND changing my mind about whether *Attacking the Clones* should come before *A-Maze-ing Game* OR whether the collage chapter should be shorter OR the *Flappy* chapter longer. There is SO MUCH I STILL HAVEN'T SHARED! Honestly, I've only *scratched* the surface of the programming power in those colorful blocks.

If I could fit in another chapter, maybe it would cover the *Pen* blocks, which enable you to program Scratch to draw and paint anything from a simple square to a complex repeating pattern. And I REALLY wanted to have a chapter about the *Sound* blocks, which enable you to program and produce your own music. I haven't even shown you how you can create your OWN Scratch blocks!

Fortunately, this is the 21st century, where books do not have to end on the last page. Guess who is building the website to go along with this book? Sensei Derek Breen! You will not only find all the projects in this book there, you will also find bonus chapters, new projects, and a TON of other freebies. So if you loved some of the chapters in this book, visit www.scratch4kids.com for more of 'em. If you HATED this book, then you can tell me all about the stuff that didn't work for you by clicking the CONTACT button there.

Now, instead of filling the last few pages with (more) goofy pictures or a last-minute tutorial, I've designed some special SCRATCH PAGES that you can use to plan your next project or start writing your own *Scratch For Kids* chapter.

So what are you waiting for? Scratch-ON!

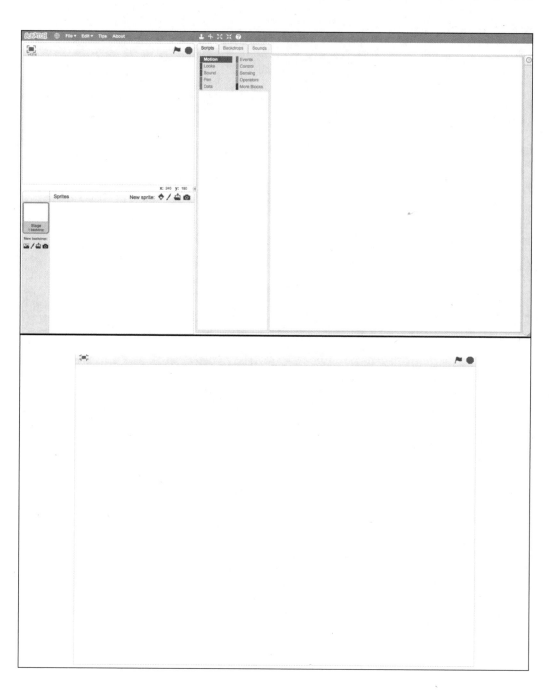

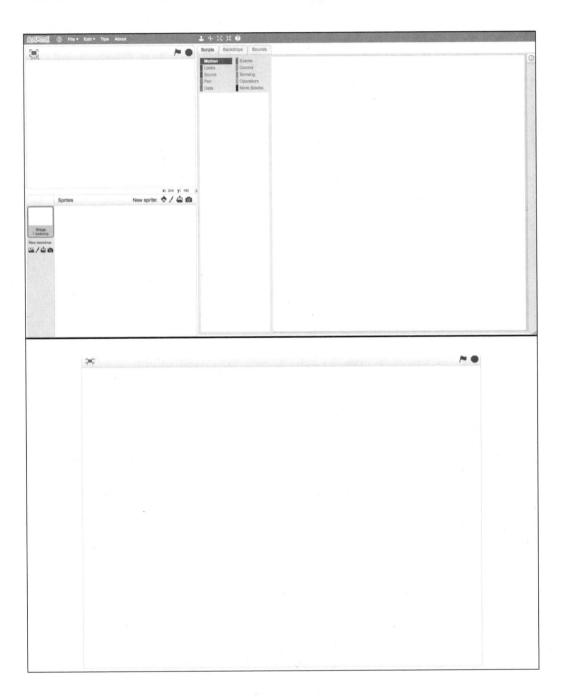

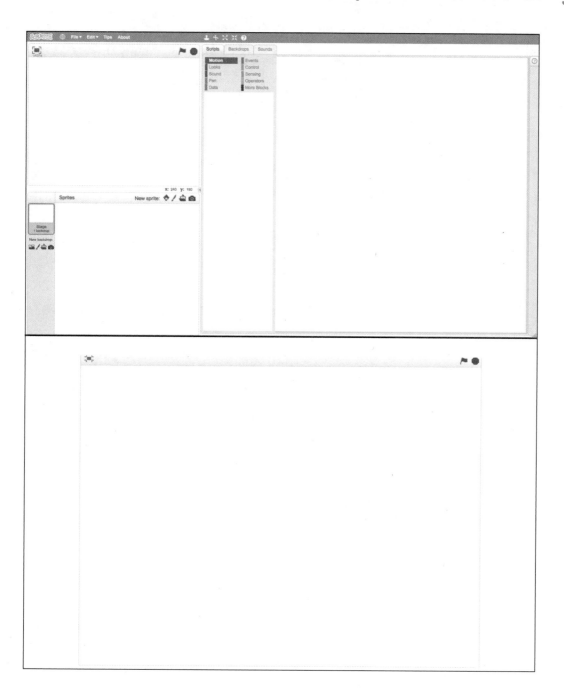

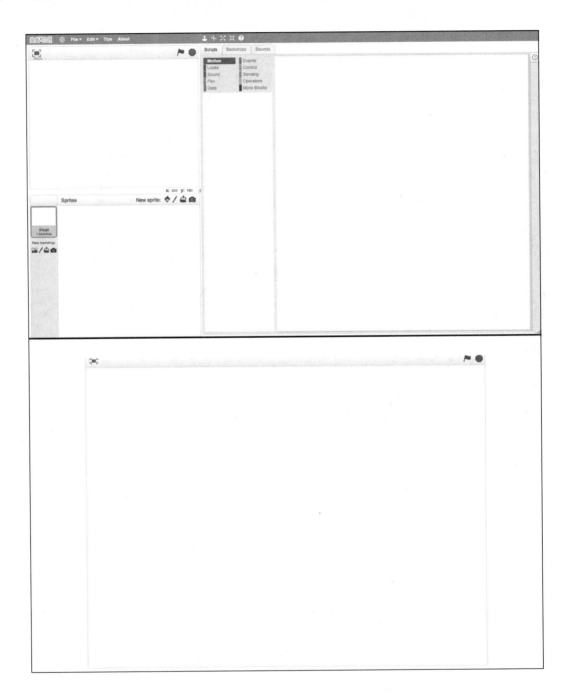

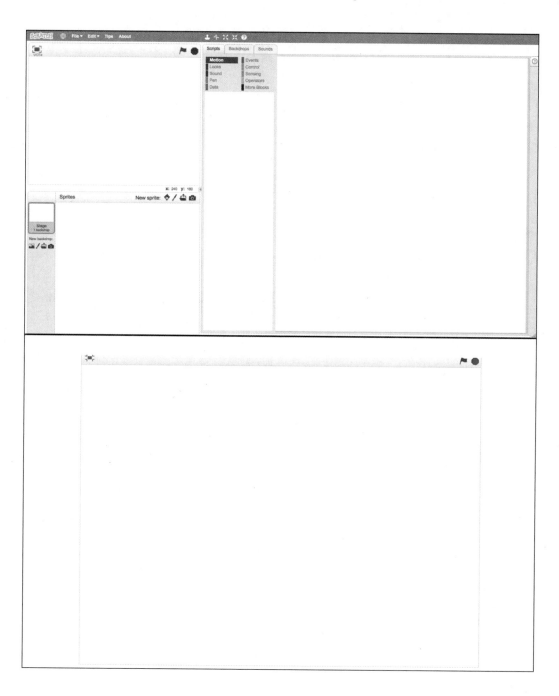

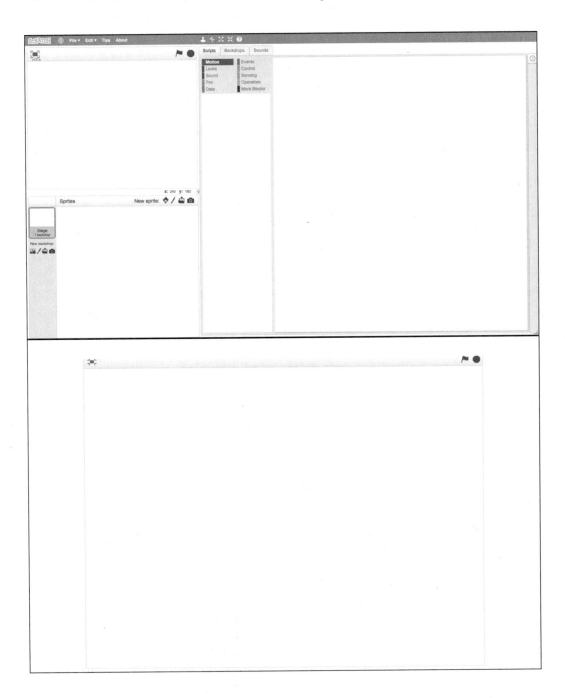

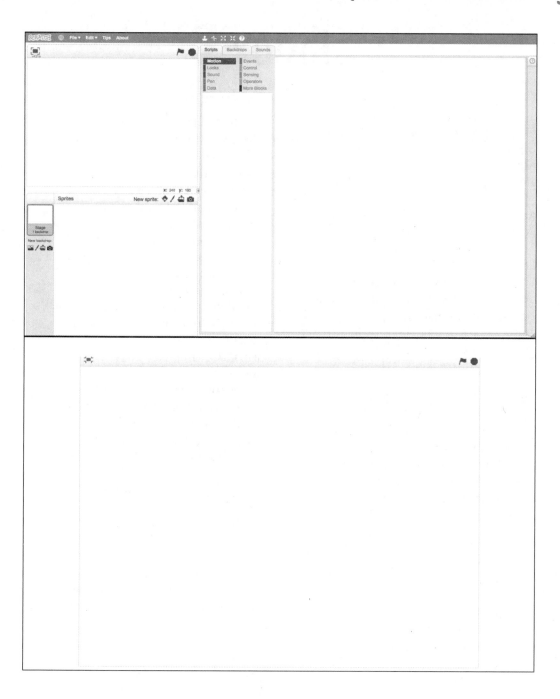

Index

A

Advanced Color Palette, 171
alien game. *See* Space Attack sample
  game
Amazing Mouse sample game
  cat sprites, adjusting size of, 314–315
  cat sprites, controlling, 312–314
  centers of rotation, changing, 315
  character sprites, choosing, 292–293
  character sprites, resizing, 294–295
  cheese bits, creating, 295–296
  cheese bits, filling Stage with, 297–299
  cheese bits, removing, 304–305
  cheese left, tracking, 311–312
  collisions, adding, 309
  dead ends, creating, 302–303
  enhancements, tips for, 320
  keyboard controls, adding, 305–308
  maze walls, creating, 299–301
  maze walls, cutting through, 301
  new projects, creating, 292
  player lives, tracking, 315–317
  player speed, increasing/decreasing,
    308
  rows of cheese, cloning, 296–297
  scores, tracking, 309–311
  sounds, adding, 317–319
  wall opening, duplicating, 301–302
animals. *See* hippogriff sample project;
  turtle sample project
animation. *See also* audio; characters;
  scenes, animation; stick-figure
  animation

  audience focus, controlling, 226
  broadcast messages, creating,
    234–237
  coding, tips for, 140
  costume size, increasing, 226–228
  fade-in and fade-out, 225
  Flappy Bat game, adding to, 19–26
  new projects, creating, 219–220
  night scenes, creating, 221–225
  robot, adding to, 95
  skills, expanding, 240–241
  speech bubbles, adding, 148–150
  of sprite entering scene, 232–234
  turtle, adding to, 67–69
arms, drawing, 160–161
audio
  allowing to record, 202–203
  in Amazing Mouse sample game,
    317–319
  beginning, trimming, 205–207
  code blocks for sound, 207–208
  custom phoneme costumes, 214–216
  dragging between sprites, 209
  editing clips, 204–205
  in hippogriff sample project, 75–76
  lip-synching, 209–214
  mistakes, editing, 206
  recording, 200–203
  in robot sample project, 95–96
  for separate character, recording, 202
  in Space Attack sample game,
    346–348
  tips for, 217
  writing dialogue, 199–200

B

Back a Layer button, 89
Back button, 16
Backdrop Library, 38–39, 76
backdrops
  blocking, 46
  choosing from library, 38–39
  for collages, 102–103
  for comics, 38–39
  as costumes, 183
  gradients, using, 269–270
  hippogriff sample project, 76
  immersive, making, 182
  movement, scrolling, 234
  pixelation in, 97
  robot sample project, 96
  scene design, in, 178, 180–182
  similar colors in, 189
  Space Attack sample game, 322
  sprites, contrasting against, 189
  sprites, making from, 183
bat game. *See* Flappy Bat game
bitmap graphics
  identifying, 72
  modifying with, 39, 105
  versus vector graphics, 81–82, 97
  vector graphics, converting to,
    113–116
bitmap painting tools
  characters, modifying with, 39
  in Paint Editor, locating, 72
body parts
  details, adding, 64–65
  drawing, 130–131, 159–162
  duplicating, 91–92
  rotating, 167
boy sample character
  facial features, changing, 172–173
  posing, 173
  reshaping, 170, 172
  zombie character, creating from, 170

BROADCAST block, 240
broadcast messages, 234–237
broadcasting, defined, 329
Brush tool
  hippogriff, modifying, 73
  Line tool, comparison, 42
  sample turtle, creating, 64
  sprites, modifying, 40–41

C

cat sprite
  deleting, 14–15
  vector graphic, example of, 80
Categories, code block, 20
centers of rotation, 167, 315
characters. *See also* animation;
    dialogue; *specific sample characters*;
    sprites; stick-figure animation
  arms, 160–161
  audio for separate, recording, 202
  back views, creating, 228–230
  bitmap painting tools, modifying
    with, 39
  bodies, drawing, 159
  cloning, 163–164, 170
  for comics, choosing, 36–37
  for comics, zooming in on, 39–40
  details, adding, 162
  hair, drawing, 156–158
  improving, 174–176
  legs, drawing, 160
  mouths, creating, 158
  new projects, creating, 155
  noses, creating, 158–159
  perspective, scaling for, 195–196
  posing, 167, 173, 176
  scaling, 195–196
  side views, creating, 230–232
  simple, creating, 153–154
  skin color, 171
  sprites, painting, 155–156

circles, 48–49
CLEAR GRAPHIC EFFECTS block, 121, 222
clones
　body cloning loops, creating, 275
　characters, creating from, 163–164, 170
　costumes, changing, 276–278
　Scratch limits for, 299
code blocks. *See also specific games or projects*
　animating with, 137–140
　categories, 20
　dragging, 29, 119
　locating, 67
　playing sound, 207–208
　shapes, meaning of, 23
　sound blocks, 208
　variables, 286
coding. *See specific games or projects*
Coding Connections icon, explained, 4
collages
　advanced, designing, 107–108
　backdrops, choosing, 102–103
　bitmap and vector graphics, converting, 113–116
　bitmap graphics, erasing shapes from, 113–117
　composition, starting, 101–102
　elements, adding, 104
　final sample layout, 123–124
　images, erasing parts of, 117
　images, importing, 109–110
　images, uploading, 110
　jagged edges, erasing, 112–113
　new projects, creating, 100–101
　photographs, erasing parts of, 110–111
　sprite brightness, adjusting, 119–120
　sprite color, adjusting, 120–121
　sprites, choosing, 100–101
　sprites, dragging, 104

　sprites, duplicating, 103–104
　sprites, hiding and showing, 111
　sprites, making transparent, 117–119
　sprites, transforming, 105
　techniques, usefulness of, 125
　text, troubleshooting, 107
　text for titles, adding, 121–123
　themes, choosing, 100
　vector graphics, adding, 106–107
collisions
　in Amazing Mouse sample game, 309
　blocks, copying, 28–29
　detecting, 27–28
　in Flappy Bat sample project, 25–26
　in Space Attack sample game, 339–342
comics
　areas, filling with color, 44–46
　backdrops, choosing, 38–39
　bitmap painting tools, using, 39
　characters, choosing, 36–37
　characters, zooming in on, 39–40
　costumes, outlining, 46–48
　description boxes, adding, 50–51
　description boxes, adding text to, 51–52
　description boxes, trimming, 52–53
　masks, painting, 40–41
　new projects, creating, 36
　ovals and circles, drawing, 48–49
　speech and thought bubbles, adding, 54–57
　sprites, adding new, 58–59
　sprites, erasing parts of, 41–42
　straight lines, drawing, 42–44
composition, defined, 101
costume centers, defined, 315
costumes
　backdrops as, 183
　centers of rotation, changing, 167, 315
　Costumes tab, picking from, 39–40
　Duplicate tool, modifying with, 47

outlining, 46–48
phoneme, 214–216
size, increasing, 226–228
Costumes tab, 39–40
curves
    adding to rectangles, 85
    Reshape tool, modifying with, 84–85

D

DELETE THIS CLONE block, 312
description boxes
    adding, 50–51
    text, adding, 51–52
    trimming, 52–53
dialogue. *See also* audio
    animating, overview, 208–209
    custom phoneme costumes, 214–216
    lip-synching, 209–214
    recording, 200–203
    SAY block for, 199
    for separate character, recording, 202
    tips for, 217
    writing, 199–200
drawing, tips for, 78. *See also* images;
        specific projects
Duplicate tool
    alternative to using, 187
    poses, re-creating with, 167
    sample turtle, creating, 65
    several changes, making with, 47

E

editing. *See specific projects*
elements, defined, 101
Ellipse tool
    circles, dragging, 48
    ovals and circles, drawing, 48–49

sample turtle, creating, 61–62, 65
Erase tool
    sample hippogriff, modifying, 72–73
    sprites, modifying, 41–42

F

Fill with Color tool
    areas, filling with, 44–46
    sample turtle, creating, 62–64
Flappy Bat game
    additional pipes, creating, 31–32
    bat size, adjusting, 31
    collisions, adding, 26–29
    enhancements, tips for, 34
    flapping speed, adjusting, 21–22
    flapping wings, adding, 20–21
    gravity, adding, 24–25
    ground sprites, painting, 16–17
    keyboard controls, adding, 22–23
    new projects, creating, 13–15
    pipe, moving, 25–26
    pipe location, adjusting, 29–30
    pipe size, adjusting, 30–31
    pipe sprites, painting, 17–18
    player sprites, choosing, 15–16
    sky gradients, painting, 18–19
FOREVER block, 27
Forward a Layer button, 89
Full-screen Stage mode, 24
furniture, drawing, 186–188

G

games. *See specific games*
geometry, 66–67
GO BACK LAYERS block, 57
GO TO FRONT block, 57
GO TO FRONT LAYERS block, 57

gradients
  colors, using, 92–93
  defined, 18
  game design, using in, 269–270
  scene design, using in, 190–192, 197
  sky, painting, 18–19
graphics. *See* bitmap graphics; images;
    vector graphics
gravity, in Flappy Bat sample project,
    24–25
grayscale, 121
Green Flag button, 21
Group tool, 90
Grow tool, 64

H

hair, drawing, 156–158
hard fun, defined, 337
hippogriff sample project
  backdrops, adding, 76
  beak and claws, adding, 74
  bitmap graphic, converting to, 72
  code for sounds, adding, 75–76
  new projects, creating, 71
  new tail, adding, 73–74
  sprites, choosing, 71–72
  unicorn features, erasing, 72–73
  wings and eyes, adding, 75
horizon lines, 192–193

I

icons, explained, 4–5
IF THEN block, 27
images
  collages, adding custom to,
    113–117
  free sources for, 108–109
  importing, 58–59, 78, 109–110

Info button, 16
uploading, 110
inheriting, defined, 325

K

keyboard controls
  in Amazing Mouse sample game,
    305–308
  in Flappy Bat sample project, 22–23
keyframes, defined, 212

L

layers
  locating, 89
  positions, changing, 57, 104
  vector graphics, moving between,
    88–89, 162
legs, drawing, 64, 160
LENGTH variables, 287
Line tool
  sample robot, adding details to, 93–94
  straight lines, drawing with, 42–44
Line Width slider, 94
lip-synching
  custom phoneme costumes, 214–216
  defined, 209
  easy, 210–211
  overview, 209–210
  realistic, 212–214
locations. *See* scenes, animation

M

masks
  painting for comics, 40–41
  vector graphics as, 117
math, 66–67

Math Connections icon, explained, 5
maze game. *See* Amazing Mouse
    sample game
mouse, computer
  drawing accurately, tips for, 78
  right-clicking tips, 15
mouths
  creating, 158
  lip-synching, 209–211
MOVE blocks, 342

N

night scenes, creating, 221–225
noses, creating, 158–159

O

online projects, 5
online resources
  animation skills, expanding, 240–241
  audio-editing applications, 217
  bonus projects, 356
  public domain images, 108–109
ovals, 48–49

P

Paint editor canvas, 64, 86
Paint Editor, 72
parallel, defined, 66
Pencil tool, 157
perspective
  characters, scaling, 195–196
  defined, 191
  objects, spacing equally, 194–195
  in scenes, 191–195
phonemes
  costumes, switching to match, 215–216
  custom costumes, creating, 214–215

defined, 212
example use, 213–214
photos. *See* images
Ping-Pong sample game
  background colors, changing, 247
  ball sprites, bouncing, 256–257
  ball sprites, creating, 247–248
  ball sprites, moving, 248–252
  end-of-game code, creating, 265–266
  end-of-game sprite, creating, 264–265
  improving, 267
  new projects, creating, 246
  paddle sprites, adding, 253
  paddle sprites, moving, 254–256
  player scores, tracking, 260–264
  second players, adding, 257–260
  sound effects, adding, 266–267
piracy, image, 108
pixelated, defined, 39
pixels
  bitmap versus vector graphics,
      81–82, 97
  problems with, 39
posing characters, 167, 173, 176
projects. *See also specific projects*
  new, creating, 13–15
  online, 5
  saving, 49
props, defined, 186
public domain images, 108–109

R

Record button, 201–203
recording audio, 200–203
rectangles
  curves, adding to, 85
  description boxes, making, 51–52
  repositioning, 51
  Reshape tool, sculpting with, 82–84
  trimming, 52–53

Reshape tool
  curves, adding to rectangles, 85
  curves, on ellipse, 84–85
  filling shapes before using, 85
  points, adding and removing, 83–84
  stick figures, sculpting, 131–132
  straight edges, using on, 83
  vector shapes, combining, 85–86
robot sample project
  backdrops, adding, 96
  body parts, duplicating, 91–92
  code for animation, adding, 95
  code for sounds, adding, 95–96
  curves, reshaping, 84–85
  design, starting, 86–88
  gradient colors, adding, 92–93
  line tool, adding details, 93–94
  new projects, creating, 80
  personalizing, 98
  points, adding and removing, 83–84
  rectangles, adding curves to, 85
  Reshape tool, sculpting with, 85
  shadows, adding, 94
  shapes, creating, 82–83
  shapes, grouping, 89–91
  Stage layers, moving between, 88–89
  straight edges, reshaping, 83
  vector shapes, combining, 85–86

S

saving projects, 49
SAY block, 148–149, 199
scene descriptions in comics, 51–52
scenes, animation. *See also* animation
  backdrops, changing into sprites, 183
  exterior, designing, 189–191
  furniture, drawing, 186–188
  horizon lines, tips for, 192–193

immersive, overview, 182
improvements for, 197
interior, designing, 178, 180–182
interior and exterior, combining, 189
new projects, creating, 178
perspective in, 191–196
similar colors in, 189
switching between, 237–240
windows, designing, 183–186
Scratch. *See also specific games and
    projects*
  book overview, 3–4, 6–7
  Cheat Sheet, 5
  online/offline use, 12–13
  overview, 1–3
  resource pages, 356–363
  software compatibility, 12
  updates, 6
  Web Extras, 5
Select tool
  rotating with, 145
  sample hippogriff, modifying, 72
  text, editing, 107
  trimming with, 52–53
SET BRIGHTNESS EFFECT TO block,
    120
SET EFFECT TO block, 120
set value, defined, 286
shading, 175
shadows, 94, 197
Shift button
  rectangles, repositioning, 51
  straight lines, drawing, 44
Shrink tool, 64
SIZE blocks, 64
skin color, 171
sound
  allowing to record, 202–203
  in Amazing Mouse sample game,
    317–319

beginning, trimming, 205–207
code blocks for sound, 207–208
custom phoneme costumes, 214–216
dragging between sprites, 209
editing clips, 204–205
in hippogriff sample project, 75–76
lip-synching, 209–214
mistakes, editing, 206
recording, 200–203
in robot sample project, 95–96
for separate character, recording, 202
in Space Attack sample game, 346–348
tips for, 217
writing dialogue, 199–200
Sound Editor effects, 206–207
sound effects
  defined, 206
  Ping-Pong sample game, 266–267
sound waves, 204
Sounds Library, 75–76
Space Attack sample game
  alien columns, straightening, 332–334
  alien rotation style, changing, 330–332
  aliens, marching, 329
  aliens, moving down, 334–335
  aliens, positioning, 326–328
  aliens, turning, 329–330
  backdrops, choosing, 322
  bombs, creating, 342–346
  collisions, adding, 339–342
  enhancements, tips for, 354–355
  laser blasters, adding, 335–338
  new projects, creating, 322
  player and enemy sprites, creating,
    323–325
  player lives, tracking, 348–349
  players, destroying, 349–351
  scores, keeping, 352–353
  sounds, adding, 346–348
  spaceship, moving, 339

speech blocks, 54–55
speech bubbles
  creating, 54–55
  positioning, 55–57
  for stick-figure animation, 148–150
Sprite Library, 36, 71–72, 100–101
sprites. See also animation; characters;
    specific games or projects
  backdrops, changing into, 183
  brightness, adjusting, 119–120
  color, adjusting, 120–121
  contrasting against backdrop, 189
  defined, 15
  directions, changing, 252
  dragging sound between, 209
  images, importing, 109–110
  images, uploading, 110
  layer positions, changing, 57
  multiple, working between, 225
  personalized, adding, 58–59
  sharing between projects, 179
Stage
  defined, 15
  Full-screen Stage mode, 24
  layer positions, changing, 57
  X and Y coordinates, finding, 255
  X and Y maximum values, 280
stick-figure animation
  animation basics, 133–137
  body parts, drawing, 130–131
  with code blocks, 137–140
  example of, 144–148
  humor, adding to, 140–143
  improving, 151
  line thickness, adjusting, 132
  new characters, creating, 141–142
  new projects, creating, 130
  Reshape tool, sculpting with, 131–132
  speech bubbles, adding, 148–150
Stop button, 21

Super Snake sample game
  challenge, adding, 290
  collisions, adding, 280–285
  gradient backgrounds, creating, 269–270
  movement, controlling, 274
  new projects, creating, 269
  player scores, tracking, 288–289
  snake food, adding, 278–280
  snake growth, coding for, 285–288
  snake sprites, adding body to, 274–278
  snake sprites, constructing, 270–273
  snake sprites, moving, 273–274
synchronization, defined, 209

T

Technical Stuff icon, explained, 4
text
  changing or correcting, 52
  collages, adding to, 106–107
  collages, editing in, 107
  description boxes, adding to, 51–52
  vector graphics, 106–107, 121–123
texture, 175
thought blocks, 54–55
thought bubbles, 54–57
Tip icon, explained, 4
trackpads
  drawing accurately, tips for, 78
  drawing and erasing with, 73
  right-clicking tips, 15
turtle sample project
  body details, adding, 64–65
  code for crawling, adding, 67
  crawl, slowing down, 67–68
  crawl, speeding up, 68–69
  head, legs, and tail, adding, 64

legs, animating, 69–70
shell, filling with color, 62–63
shell details, adding, 65–66
shell outline, drawing, 61–62
shell segments, drawing, 63–64
starting out, 61

V

variables
  length, 286–287
  score, 289
  video games, using in, 286
vector graphics. *See also* robot sample project
  advantages of, 81–82
  versus bitmap graphics, 81–82, 97
  bitmap graphics, converting to, 72, 113–116
  curves, reshaping, 84–85
  defined, 72
  examples of, 80–81
  identifying, 72
  layers, moving objects between, 88–89
  as masks, 117
  modifying, 82, 86
  new projects, creating, 80–81
  points, adding and removing, 83–84
  rectangle, creating, 82–83
  rectangles, adding curves to, 85
  Reshape tool, 83–86
  shadows, adding, 94
  text as, 106–107, 121–123
  vector shapes, combining, 85–86
Vector mode. *See also* robot sample project; vector graphics
  advantages of, 81–82
  identifying, 72, 80–81
  layers, moving objects between, 88–89

line width, adjusting, 94
modifying sprites in, 82, 86
text, handling, 106–107
Vector Text tool, 121
video games. *See specific games*

W

Warning icon, explained, 5
webcam
    new images, adding, 110
    new sprites, adding, 59
werewolf sample character
    details, adding, 167–169
    fangs, creating, 165–166
    posing, 167
    reshaping, 166
    zombie character, creating from,
        163–164
WHEN GREEN FLAG CLICKED block, 23
WHEN I RECEIVE button, 236

WHEN KEY PRESSED block, 23
windows, 183–186

X

X coordinates, 255, 280

Y

Y coordinates, 255, 280

Z

zombie sample character
    bodies, drawing, 159–162
    details, adding, 162
    hair, drawing, 156–158
    mouths and noses, creating, 158–159
    sprites, painting, 155–156

Notes

About the Author/Designer

Derek Breen began his first job, a daily paper route, back in 1980 with the intention of saving up enough money to buy his first computer. He purchased a Commodore 64 computer toward the end of sixth grade and spent most of the summer before starting junior high designing sprites, learning the Basic programming language, and coding rudimentary games.

Derek was introduced to Scratch while working as a summer instructor for ID Tech Camp at MIT in 2011. He appreciated how the software enabled younger children to quickly produce animation and simple games, but the pixelated graphics and programming limitations kept him from using it in the high school computer science classes he was teaching that fall.

Then Scratch 2.0 came along and his mind was blown by all the possibilities. The addition of vector graphics, cloning, and cloud-based variables added enough power to make it a complete multimedia-authoring platform; basically, Adobe Flash for kids.

Derek is a founding member of the Instructional Design and Interactive Education Media Association (IDIEM) and is an active member of the Scratch Educator (ScratchEd) community. Most recently, he worked as a graphic designer for the StarLogo Nova project at MIT, as a teaching fellow in Instructional Design at Harvard Extension school, and as a curriculum developer for i2 Camp.

Previously, Derek worked as a computer science teacher and educational technology specialist at Prospect Hills Academy in Cambridge, Massachusetts, was the owner and operator of Mod, a cybercafé and digital learning center in Charlottesville, Virginia, and served as a new media producer for KCAL9-TV in Los Angeles, California.

Author's Acknowledgments

This book began with a LinkedIn request from Amy Fandrei, who trusted a first-time author with an eagerly anticipated *For Kids For Dummies* title. She let me hire my IDIEM ally Sam Rausa as my right-hand man and technical editor. But my Wiley hero is Brian Walls, the project manager who kept me writing (and laughing) through a long, cold, winter.

I am grateful to Daniel Wendel, Wendy Huang, and Josh Sheldon for showing me the true power of blocks-based programming and Eric Klopfer for hiring me into the StarLogo family. Check out `www.slnova.org`.

I am eternally indebted to Karen Brennan and Michelle Chueng for fostering the ever-growing Scratch Educator network.

I am continually inspired by educational technology colleagues in Massachusetts, New York, and beyond, especially Cindy Gao, Sean Stern, Sharon Thompson, Keledy Kenkel, Ingrid Gustafson, Barbara Mikolajczak, and Steve Gordon.

I am humbled by the vibrant folks in IDIEM (Instructional Design and Interactive Education Media Association) who keep pressuring me to schedule a book-release party.

I would have been ill-equipped to take on such a herculean instructional design challenge without the fabulous ED103 and ED113 courses at Harvard Extension School, under the masterful direction of Stacie Cassat Green and Denise Snyder.

I am in serious trouble with Ethan Berman and Vicky Vlantis at i2 Camp. Thank you for understanding deadlines are tricky when racing toward publication.

There would have been far fewer tips and tricks throughout the book were it not for the invaluable Scratch Wiki (`wiki.scratch.mit.edu`) and Scratch Discussion Forums (`scratch.mit.edu/discuss`).

Without the pioneering work of the Lifelong Kindergarden Group at the MIT Media Lab, I would just be scratching my head (and wishing for something like Scratch to fill my head with tinkering ideas). Thank you Mitchel, and Natalie, and so many other team members who have made time for my questions and dealt gracefully with my potentially overwhelming enthusiasm for blocks-based programming over the past three years.

Then there are the Onoratos. . . the Breens. . . the Dowdens. . . the Nangeronis and the Tupelo-Schnecks for ALWAYS being there!

And a very special note of gratitude for Mr. Forge and Ms. Carter, my junior high and high school computer science teachers. I recently learned Mr. Forge is still teaching at Pierce Middle School, more than 30 years after he gave me my first professional job teaching Logo there in 8th grade. He taught me almost as much about mentorship as he did about programming the TRS-80 and also sent me off to my first computer classes at MIT.

Now it's your turn. Go write a book about something you are passionate about. Surely, you have something you can teach me!

Publisher's Acknowledgments

Acquisitions Editor: Amy Fandrei

Project Editor: Brian H. Walls

Technical Editor: Sam Rausa

Production Assistant: Miguel Melendez

Editorial Assistant: Anne Sullivan

Sr. Editorial Assistant: Cherie Case

Cover Image: Courtesy of Mitchel Resnick, Lifelong Kindergarten Group, MIT Media Lab

Chapter figures, illustrations, and Scratch projects: © Derek Breen

Additional figures and illustrations: Katelyn Dowden, Ryan Dowden, Gwendolyn Tupelo, and Jonah Tupelo.